GOD, HUMAN NATURE AND EDUCATION FOR PEACE

What prevents the human species from finally learning the lessons of social justice and global peace in an unreconciled world? Are Christians better off?

Presenting new challenges to moral and religious education, this book clarifies the true image of the biblical God around the topics of justice and reconciliation. Rejuvenating interpretations of the most outstanding traditions of the Old and New Testament, Karl Ernst Nipkow's approach of 'elementarization' – well known in German-speaking countries – is introduced for the first time in the English language.

Theological perspectives are confronted with data from evolutionary ethics and social psychology, through practice-based examples of the roots of aggression, violence, xenophobia and ethno-centrism. The analysis ends with peace and spirituality in the light of different faiths.

This book presents a striking blend of theology, education and the social sciences, to explore central issues in moral and religious education.

Explorations in Practical, Pastoral and Empirical Theology

Series Editors: Leslie J. Francis, University of Wales, Bangor, UK
and Jeff Astley, University of Durham and Director of the North of England
Institute for Christian Education, UK

Theological reflection on the church's practice is now recognized as a significant element in theological studies in the academy and seminary. Ashgate's new series in practical, pastoral and empirical theology seeks to foster this resurgence of interest and encourage new developments in practical and applied aspects of theology worldwide. This timely series draws together a wide range of disciplinary approaches and empirical studies to embrace contemporary developments including: the expansion of research in empirical theology, psychological theology, ministry studies, public theology, Christian education and faith development; key issues of contemporary society such as health, ethics and the environment; and more traditional areas of concern such as pastoral care and counselling.

God, Human Nature and Education for Peace

New Approaches to Moral and Religious Maturity

KARL ERNST NIPKOW

ASHGATE

Published by
Ashgate Publishing Limited
Gower House, Croft Road
Aldershot, Hants
GU11 3HR
England

Ashgate Publishing Company
Suite 420
101 Cherry Street
Burlington, VT 05401-4405
USA

Ashgate website: http://www.ashgate.com

British Library Cataloguing in Publication Data
Nipkow, Karl Ernst
God, human nature and education for peace : new approaches to moral and religious maturity. - (Explorations in practical, pastoral and empirical theology)
1. Christian ethics 2. Maturation (Psychology) - Religious aspects - Christianity
3. Judgment (Ethics)
I. Title
241

Library of Congress Cataloging-in-Publication Data
Nipkow, Karl Ernst.
God, human nature, and education for peace : new approaches to moral and religious maturity / Karl Ernst Nipkow.
p. cm. — (Explorations in practical, pastoral, and empirical theology)
Includes bibliographical references and index.
ISBN 0-7546-0863-8 (alk. paper) — ISBN 0-7546-0872-7 (pbk. : alk. paper)
1. Peace—Religious aspects—Christianity. I. Title. II. Series.

BT736.4.N56 2004
261.8'73—dc21

2003044387

ISBN 0 7546 0863 8 (Hbk)
ISBN 0 7546 0872 7 (Pbk)

Typeset in Times by J. L. and G. A. Wheatley Design, Aldershot, Hampshire
Printed and bound in Great Britain by MPG Books Ltd, Bodmin, Cornwall

Contents

Preface

The idea for this book was born at the end of July 2000 at the 12th Conference of the International Seminar on Religious Education and Values (ISREV) in Kiryat Anavim near Jerusalem. The conference topic was 'Education for Peace', and I had been asked by John M. Hull of the University of Birmingham, the chairperson of ISREV, and the convenor Yaacov J. Katz, Bar-Ilan University, Jerusalem, to present the keynote paper for the opening session. My rather sceptical analysis focused on the tension 'Between Self-interest and Altruism' in an attempt to explore the chances for and difficulties of peace education against the background of hypotheses and data of evolutionary research, in particular 'evolutionary ethics'.

All too soon, sad facts were to corroborate the analysis. At the very same time the Camp David negotiations between Prime Minister Jehud Barak of Israel and President Yassir Arafat of Palestine failed; shortly after that the Al-Aksa Intifada broke out, and as yet there is no end to it in sight. Meanwhile, in my own country of Germany violence against foreigners has been spreading; despite much will to prevent it, there has been little success. In a time of breath-taking new technologies prompting everyone to accelerate lifelong learning, human beings are in contrast very slow to learn the old lesson of how to overcome our species' propensity to xenophobia, aggression and war. In the meantime, since 11 September 2001 the civilized world has been confronted anew with the bitter knowledge of what human beings are capable of doing. War and peace have been propelled to the very top of the list of burning issues.

In the same year, two months earlier in May 2000, I was Visiting Lecturer in the Faculty of Theology and Religious Studies in Riga, Latvia, taking as my theme, according to an appointment with my own theological faculty, 'The Righteousness of God and the Justification of the Sinner'. I traced the topic back to the Book of Genesis, starting with the story of Cain and Abel. In the Hebrew (Jewish) Bible, or the Old Testament (I use the terms interchangeably without intending any theological implication), human violence begins with a fratricide, in the context of worship, moreover. But might the murder have been avoided if the brothers had shared their offerings? The issue of peace is of prime concern for interfaith dialogue and multi-religious education, and perhaps now is the time to explore what the spiritual traditions of the different religions can offer to a panic-stricken world.

Spiritual renewal in the church and religious education in schools, in state as well as church schools, have to keep abreast of the serious situation and the international debate on values. A spirituality that is drifting apart, becoming superficial and losing sight of substantial topics, will not do. For Jews, Christians and Muslims God is the centre of their faith and hope for the future. For many years I have been concentrating my studies, including empirical ones, on the issue of God. Surveys about the religious quest among young people support the paramount role of this subject in the curriculum.

Much in this book has been written with a view to 'children's right of religion' (Friedrich Schweitzer), looking at our problem through their eyes.

However, from the very beginning, in the first chapter, the focus could not be as narrow as the confines within which much literature concerning religious education is restricted. The most daunting question is the anthropological one of how it can be that human nature is as it is. Thus, my prime intention is to focus on the harsh confrontation between a religious vision of life apparently contradicted by reality. Biblical promises have to face analyses from the social sciences, knowledge about God has to face knowledge about human nature.

I see an alliance of realistic approaches to human nature between the disillusioning stories of the Book of Genesis and the hypotheses and sober data of evolutionary research, a field I have been observing for the last seven years. In current literature in practical theology, pastoral theology and even empirical theology, the field of evolutionary psychology and ethics is completely neglected, it is simply absent. This study is a first attempt to link these areas. In doing so, we will proceed on a journey through different landscapes. The methodology is a blend of social analysis, hermeneutical interpretation of the Bible, empirical testing, philosophical-anthropological reflections, and the practical educational consequences, covering several topical sub-fields and with the main thrust on the issues of justice and peace. Tracing God's promises and actions and highlighting the current meaning of the concept of justification makes the book a theological one; exploring effective integrated ways towards peace, justice and tolerance makes it an ethical and spiritual one; the advocacy for the sake of still unborn generations makes it an educational one, in accordance with my work over decades in two faculties, those of Protestant theology and the social sciences (Department of Education).

I am grateful to have been invited to contribute to the Ashgate interdisciplinary perspective series with a volume of this kind. I owe very special thanks to Leslie J. Francis and Jeff Astley, the encouraging and helpful editors of the series. The first reader of the book was John Shepherd of St Martin's College, Lancaster, who carefully perused the manuscript and corrected my English. For his help in reading and improving the text I am most grateful.

I thank the staff of Ashgate, and in particular Sarah Lloyd, for having accepted and accompanied my project with professional expertise.

The book is dedicated to my friends and colleagues in the International Seminar on Religious Education and Values, who meet regularly in considerable numbers from numerous different countries. They have been urging me for some time to publish in the English language in order to reach a larger audience and trigger a broader exchange of ideas. But this incentive did not seduce me to forget readability; I have tried to stick to my 'elementarizing' approach, developed years ago for the benefit of teachers and young people, so why not for experts as well?

Karl Ernst Nipkow
Tübingen, Germany

Chapter 1

Global Challenges and the Role of Religion

Global Human Progress?

Where is the world society with its globalized economy going? Why has education obtained a paramount role in this process? What expectations are pursued by the market, the state and individuals? The educational boom responds to the requirements of economic production and labour market reproduction, much less to the demands of global humanization, although individual managers may personally also have this idea in mind.

The sceptical questions above are aimed at the dominant economic structures, which are highly competitive and often ruthless. School systems are supposed to prepare the younger generation to cope with them. The qualifications needed concentrate on instrumental knowledge and on abilities like flexibility, team spirit and lifelong-learning, which are to fit the accelerating technological, economic and scientific developments. The overall purposes are national and international efficiency.

The global market cannot by itself deliver moral and spiritual human goals that transcend the economic instruments. It is ruled by the law of supply and demand which states that economic stability can only be reached if those two factors are in approximate balance. The pressures on global economic survival help enforce a rigid discipline of working and a harsh spirit of achievement with repercussions felt in families and in children's lives from an early age.

Can global progress preserve a human face without a vision of humanity? Can Christians help to overcome a childhood of 'spiritual void' (International Catholic Child Bureau 1984)? The questions address the present adult generation and their view of the future. In a memorandum on Christian adult education the Protestant Church in Germany criticized progress as 'an empty space'.

> The imperative of progress is called renewal, but renewal is only in a formal way defined by 'the new'. Progress is an empty space, no goal that might be reached in any concrete terms. Nobody knows where the journey leads. However, all are forced to display their intensive and continuous efforts in order to arrive more quickly. But where?
>
> (Evangelische Kirche in Deutschland 1997: 15)

Voices from the field of evolutionary research are even more sceptical. In their eyes politicians ought to be aware of the moral implications of national and international decision-making instead of becoming more and more dependent on influential economic interests. In economics, ethical and political criteria are replaced by quasi-naturalistic principles with problematic consequences.

> In nature the genetic code dominates as the impact of selection and eradication, and in these processes nature does not know anything about a morality similar to our moral feelings . . . In

contrast, some of our managers take nature as their ideal. They are thinking in short-term categories and forgetting that, from the perspective of long-term categories, they are applying a high-risk strategy, for social deprivation on the part of the losers will endanger social peace and therefore also those who are successful.

(Eibl-Eibesfeldt 1999: 103)

The situation of the human species has radically changed. From the perspective of a theory of culture Peter Sloterdijk describes the transformations involved using metaphors drawn from seafaring to highlight the growing difficulties of political navigation.

The first period of humankind which covers 95 per cent of the whole of history could be represented by the symbol of rafts with small groups of human beings on them drifting through gigantic spaces of time. The second era can be depicted by the world age of coastal navigation with state-galleys and manorial-frigates, heading for risky and far remote destinations, following a vision of grandeur which was psychologically anchored in the Holy Order of males. The third and present period of human history can be imagined as the era of super-ferries which, hardly capable of being steered because of their gigantic dimensions, pass through a sea with people drowning on either side.

(Sloterdijk 1995: 13–14)

A Global Civil Society

To put the imagery aside, that loss of national control will weaken the foundations of national democracies is obvious and is broadly discussed in the debate on who the effective agents in international politics are and how complex international steering mechanisms have become.

The exercise of state sovereignty is undermined by processes of internationalization and globalization, most notably in the economic and ecological realms.

(Bienen *et al.* 1998: 288)

The UN21 project has initiated research on non-governmental actors. In particular, attention is given to transnational (business) corporations as the central actors on the world market sphere. Operating legally across borders, the principal aim of these 'market forces' is legitimate (legal) profit-making. Research also focuses on another set of non-governmental actors, constituting what is frequently termed an emerging 'global civil society'.

(Rittberger *et al.* 1999: 111)

In political discussion a distinction is drawn between the *state* on the one hand, the *economy* or the market on the other hand and *civil society* as a third factor in between. According to Michael Walzer (1995: 7), 'the words "civil society" name the space of uncoerced human associations and also the set of relational networks – formed for the sake of family, faith, interest and ideology – that fill this space.' Following this definition:

- Civil society's first characteristic is *uncoerciveness*, the protection of the social sphere from 'governmental encroachment' and 'the possession of a degree of independence for autonomous action' (Rittberger *et al.* 1999: 111).

- Its second feature is 'the notion of *shared basic values and identity*' (p. 112; my emphasis). Civil society operates outside state institutions within a 'public sphere' where individual rights and welfare, human values and the search for a common identity are supposed to develop more freely and to receive more weight.
- '*Human associations*' point to the third feature, the way of socially organizing *the common commitment* by group-building, interaction and networking.

If they want to shape a future with a human face in peace and justice, our national communities and international agencies need more than just the logic of the global market. In continuing the above distinctions, we can conclude that against the *logic* of economy the *reason* of politics has to be mobilized together with the humanizing *spirit* of a civil society. A new-style globalized market needs a stronger new-style democracy which is less vulnerable to external economic and financial pressures and can become a civil society capable of internally catalysing ideas on 'good governance' for the sake of humanity.

A major factor in this context is a new-style 'educational society' (*Bildungsgesellschaft*) following the concept of critical education as the core of the German idea of *Bildung* (discussed in the next section). Last but not least, according to Walzer's definition, democracies as civil societies provide room for religious life and spiritual growth towards personal maturity.

Self-alienation and Education

Education as understood in the German tradition of a philosophy of 'Bildung' is more than training and learning and also different from mere socialization and enculturation, although never without them. Its structural centre is reflective and personal, not manipulative and collective. In the eighteenth century the purpose of education was changed and directed towards autonomous self-formation in rejection of an oppressive shaping from outside.

The semantic history of the term 'education' shows a remarkable shift of meaning, among others introduced by Anthony Shaftesbury (the 3rd Earl of Sh., 1671–1713) who in *The Moralists* (1709) pleaded that 'form' – his keyword – was to embrace nature, art, human mind and the soul in a process of mutual development. Education has to promote this development in liberal ways by stimulating and carefully regulating the natural 'appetites' and 'inclinations', not by stifling them (Works 1773, II: 293, 313, as quoted in Schaarschmidt 1965: 48–9). The process of forming mind and body was no longer to follow the ideal of imitation or copying a given form, but to display the (Platonic) 'inward form' (I: 207; III: 34).

Consequently, traditional educational methods were harshly criticized, in particular the narrow-minded catechetical approach and the humiliating and indoctrinating practices of Christian nurture (cf. also John Locke, Jean-Jacques Rousseau).

For German philosophers, poets and educators of the following years, the issue was more broadly contextualized, reaching beyond the realm of aesthetics. The 'alienating' pressures on the individual were felt more and more, and they also grew, and so resistance to them grew correspondingly.

Wilhelm von Humboldt was one of the first to use the term 'alienation' in the context of self-loss (1793: 237) which, in his view, was caused by ecclesiastical and political restrictions. Political reflections prompted him to demand a liberal, self-limiting state.

The new economic and scientific structures were another source of deep concern. The growth of the division of labour and the expanding 'mechanical' thought patterns in science, technology, psychology and medicine made the individual a victim of anatomizing objectivizations, a development which Friedrich Schiller paradigmatically accused in his famous *Letters on Aesthetic Education of Man* (1795/1982, 6th letter). Against this background '*Selbstbildung*' (self-formation) became a critical label to ensure the integrity of the self, individual freedom and spiritual growth. The point of departure of the new approach was the feeling of having reached a crossroads in history. 'Humanity' was at stake.

However, the new vision of an autonomous subject developing individually and holistically in harmony with 'inward form' and in the medium of 'free sociability' (*Geselligkeit*) (Friedrich Schleiermacher) was soon blocked. The restoration period after 1815 in Europe revived the authoritarian spirit of the past. Ideas on liberal politics and education were rejected by the state as well as by the church. The reform of the schools by William of Humboldt failed too. Under the influence of the new 'scholastic' pattern (Friedrich Schweitzer) of the school system of the nineteenth century, 'Bildung' ironically became a source of a new alienation.

The Swiss educator Johann Heinrich Pestalozzi had voted for a holistic education of the 'mind', the 'heart' and the 'hand' as an equal opportunity for all human beings, in particular for disadvantaged rural people and lower class industrial workers. In fact, the situation of both, including that of children and young people, deteriorated. The European proletariat (starting in Great Britain) was to suffer from the greatest social and spiritual misery.

As the original idea of education as Bildung was based upon a philosophy of *humanity*, and as to this day inhumanity throws its dark shadows upon humankind's supposed progress, the concept of critical education (*kritische Bildung*) as an education resisting self-alienation has preserved its poignant present importance for all education, including the shaping of religious education.

The Topical Approach in Religious Education

In the last three decades of the twentieth century, religious education in Germany, in state schools as well as church schools, successfully underwent a remarkable paradigm shift in curriculum development. In view of the depersonalizing forces of our times and on theological as well as educational grounds, religious education in Christian perspectives was linked to an agenda of burning issues which was labelled as a 'thematic' ('topical') or 'problem-oriented approach'. Among the most salient issues were, and still are, the following:

- education in respect for the dignity of each human being and in concern for a life to be lived in the fullness of individual humanity (see already the historical point of departure in the preceding section)

- education for a life of responsibility for others on a global scale
- education for the preservation of nature, in view of collective ecological self-destruction
- education for social justice and global solidarity with the poor
- education for peace in combatting violence, xenophobia and racism.

The last issue is the focal point of this study, together with a specific, crucial, overarching religious focus. It is the issue of God in biblical perspectives that guides all the anthropological and educational reflections and empirical analyses to be found in the following chapters. In the debate on religious education such a concentration is rare; in the discussion on moral development it is absent. We will try to show why it is indeed necessary. But can religious dimensions and spiritual traditions successfully intervene and influence the public course of affairs? Or, to be more precise, can faith experiences contribute, without major public controversies, to a human future?

Secular Moral Consciousness and Religion

From the point of view of a radically secular understanding of humanity, the relevance of religions for the solution of global issues is questionable. Modern moral consciousness has largely become independent of any religious foundation. In European history, the period of the Enlightenment led to a separation between religion and morality, with the latter regarding itself as autonomous. Immanuel Kant looked at each individual as being gifted with an intrinsic moral compass which – in principle – rules the moral mind by a cogent interior 'law' telling what alone is truly 'good' and to be obeyed as a necessary inner obligation. Religion was either replaced completely or reduced to the function of an additional source of motivation and hope: God became a useful postulate.

From then on, it was the independent secular forum of the modern mind that judged religious doctrine and behaviour on behalf of independent human moral criteria, the roots of which are seen in ethical foundations of their own, in one's own 'good will' or 'moral feelings'.

While on the one hand, for good reasons, the moral basis of secular law, as well as philosophical ethics or practical philosophy as a whole, regard themselves as independent from any ties to religious belief systems, it is, on the other hand, not appropriate to conclude that religion can easily and simply be replaced by a self-sufficient morality. Religion is not just similar to ethics and a functional equivalent to morality which gradually can be left aside; it is something different from morality because it can be restricted neither to the sphere of values that underly our moral attitudes nor to moral rules regulating our moral actions. Like modern moral consciousness, religion too has a foundation of its own by representing a specific area of human culture and individual spirituality (Schleiermacher 1799). Religion is an irreducible, relatively independent feature of the *conditio humana*.

All religions include, of course, values and moral obligation; even mystical experiences will generate behavioural consequences of moral relevance. But in its very nature religion is broader since it refers to the whole of reality. A religious world view encompasses humans and animals, the organic and the inorganic, space and time, the microcosm and the macrocosm, the beginning and the end. To a greater or lesser extent, and in one way or another, religions display a comprehensive interpretive view of, and emotional attitude towards, the universe. It is only within this wide context that religion gives meaning also to the realm of morality.

As the renowned American moral philosopher Lawrence Kohlberg recognized, the questions 'Why be moral?' and 'Why be just, in a universe which is largely unjust?' cannot be answered within the field of morality itself; they need, so to speak, a transmoral level of reflection. On the highest level of personal human development, human life

> entails the question 'Why live?' and the parallel question, 'How face death?' Thus, ultimate moral maturity requires a mature solution to the question of the meaning of life. This, in turn, we argue is hardly a moral question *per se*, it is an ontological or a religious one. Not only is the question not a moral one, but it is also not a question resolvable on purely logical or rational grounds.
>
> (Kohlberg 1977: 250; cf Kohlberg 1981: 345)

In other words, religious experiences and interpretations of reality transcending moral issues can enrich and fulfil life by leading it into its depth and fullness. A person who does not ask and pursue the two questions 'Why live?' and 'How face death?' reduces the spectrum of spiritual human potentialities on the way to moral maturity.

Education becomes poor without religious education. Religious education includes moral education in ways of its own without devaluing the dignity of an independent moral consciousness. Religion and morality are simultaneously distinct and overlapping entities. Because of its relative independence, modern ethics has obtained a new position which religions have to acknowledge. In return, modern ethics has to acknowledge the independence and specificity of religion.

Religions – Problem-solving or Problem-generating?

However balanced the preceding section on religion and morality may be, the answer we are after is not yet in sight. We have to avoid too positive and too quick a commentary on the value of religion in our world. There is a huge error, which may take some time to rectify, in assuming that in our secularized modern societies citizens believe in religion as *the* reliable solution to our global problems. For many contemporaries, religions themselves are a grave cause of trouble, at least as far as some of their characteristic conflict-laden features are concerned. Far from delivering ready-made answers to the problems, religions are themselves a part of them. This is true from several perspectives.

1 First of all is the long-range memory of human beings. The crimes of the churches that have been committed against the dignity of man are deeply rooted in our historical consciousness. Sins (as we would say today) such as the persecution of religious minorities, of non-believers and heretics, the cruel or unfair treatment of people who did not obey the dominant belief-system, the resistance of the Christian churches to modern liberties like religious freedom, freedom of thought, of the press and so forth are constantly recollected right up to today. Against this

background, knowledge of Christians' positive contributions to humanity and human rights often fades.

2   Autobiographies reflect the harmful psychological effects of a rigid Christian education in moral terms and of a narrow-minded confessional instruction in intellectual terms. Mostly the wounds inflicted on the soul are more painful than those that afflict the body.

3   Representatives of religions all over the world proclaim the moral relevance of religion. But which values precisely are meant? The term 'value' is an overworked word which can conveniently cover many different options. Still today, the enormity of the churches' moral failures, both generally and biographically (see above), renders the growth of new confidence in them rather difficult. This ambiguity of religious values makes it unlikely that today's moral consciousness in the western world will readily applaud self-righteous religious offers to contribute to public education.

4   The religions can hardly become the key to greater peace as long as they themselves nourish religious violence. On the one hand, declarations of church leaders or of representatives of non-Christian religions on the topics of peace and justice are impressive, on the other hand the reality of hate and hostility between believers of different religious traditions fills the news.

5   Hopes placed in religions also encounter pragmatic difficulties. Not being economic factors in the global economy, religions do not count in the strategies of the so-called 'global players'.

6   Religions are used to addressing the individual. But moral proclamations will lose their addressees if in the global economy managers and politicians are more or less forced to react to anonymous pressures rather than respond with individual responsibility (Sennett 1998).

7   Although the demands of global understanding in a plural world have grown greatly, the religions are mostly absorbed by their internal problems of coherence, personal and organizational planning and so forth. Hence there is not much time, energy or courage left for inter-religious cooperation and education. Denominational egoisms prevail where the Christian faith represents one faith among others in a double-sided pluralism, an internal and an external one.

In 1948, the World Council of Churches was founded in Amsterdam. In a solidarity of shame and guilt, but also in the spirit of forgiveness, the churches set up a new agenda of mutual learning, at first primarily to cope with their own worldwide Christian pluralism and denominational barriers. In the meantime they have been overtaken by the heritage of colonialism and international migration. In Germany there are 3.2 million second or third generation Muslims, among them 750 000 Muslim pupils within the state school system. The Christian churches have to come to grips with a new 'interfaith dialogue' for which they are unprepared. In England and Wales a remarkable 'multi-faith approach' has emerged. In Germany efforts in this new field have prompted a wide-ranging analysis of the issue of moral and religious education in a world marked by religious diversity (Nipkow 1998). Thus there are two facts that have to be considered:

> It is a matter of concern that in numerous countries there has been a renewed occurrence of xenophobia, racism and religious intolerance . . . Religion often reinforces, or is used to reinforce, international, social and national minority conflicts . . .

In each of the three main monotheistic religions a basis can be found for tolerance and
mutual respect towards people with different beliefs or towards non-believers.
                                              (The Council of Europe 1993, in Schreiner *et al.* 1995: 36)

In Search of a General Climate of Reconciliation

What is in the public interest is a religiously tolerant world, but educational programmes
alone will not be able to promote that effectively. To be successful such programmes
need political backing and a general cultural climate of reconciliation which in many
parts of the world does not exist. Sometimes fundamentalist religious fanatics form
the primary peace-preventing factor, but mostly they are not the only component.
Deeply rooted ethnic and racial prejudices in the population at large nourish open
violence. And religious differences are not alone in contributing to aggressive
confrontations. Analyses reveal the intricate nature of the struggles and show the
widespread linkage of religious and social factors. A blend of religious, ethnic, social
and cultural factors form a complex syndrome. Last but not least nationalism and
fascism are sources of hostility to outsiders.

The simplistic theory of Samuel Huntington (1993) of an unavoidable 'clash of
civilizations' is poorly informed if it reduces the causal factors to one single cause by
launching the dangerous idea of 'The West against the Rest' (Müller 1998: 29).

Research on the causes of wars (for example Luard 1987; Howard 1984) has failed
to isolate one dominant factor as the background of violence. Second, it is not the
broader cultural differences, but more often the nearer and smaller ethnic ones that
breed open conflicts. Third, the type of war that can be observed most often is civil
war, chiefly in relatively homogeneous regions, and it is, as a fourth point, in particular
the 'Third World' countries which are waging wars amongst themselves.

Moreover, as a major continuing background to ethnic or national hostilities, it is
again economic and political discrimination that plays a prominent role (Gurr and
Harff 1994). The issue of peace is closely connected to the issue of social justice. The
political renaissance of religions has its roots in socio-economic disparities.

As already mentioned, a sign of hope is the emergence of a 'global civil society' as
the extension of the idea of democracy as a civil society with international non-
governmental organizations (INGOs) gaining more and more influence. Thus,
although it is evident that 'national loyalties are not being superseded by global or
regional loyalties' (Peterson 1992: 379), something like a 'global consciousness' is
developing. People identify with and lend principled support to global issues and
global conceptions of citizenship (Rittberger *et al.* 1999: 113).

The international and national efforts for peace and social justice depend on
progress in democratization, primarily on the national but also on the international
level. The first is already occuring; the requirement of more democracy in international
agencies (UNO, NGOs etc.) remains an open question on the agenda of the future.

Openness to the Wisdom of Religious Traditions

Where are we going? What future lies ahead for the world population? Can progress be given a substantial name? At the beginning of this chapter critical remarks about the lack of moral substance could not be suppressed. But our time is not without knowledge of what is good and bad. We can draw on a long history of accumulated moral knowledge as a resource for the future. Knowledge accumulated over a long time is called wisdom, which is experiential, not speculative, knowledge. On the one hand, it has grown out of the pain of people suffering from oppression and exploitation, on the other hand, it reflects the many good lessons learnt about how life might flourish and enemies become friends – a hopeful vision of a better world.

Another fact which makes us look for wisdom is very simple, but all the more shocking, and specific to today. Because of the huge accumulation of technological power, in particular nuclear power, connected with a growing deterioration of the world climate – a situation that is historically unique – the future survival of the whole species lies in the hands of humanity, faced with a burden of moral responsibility weightier than any ever known before in history.

In his famous speech in the McEwan Hall in Edinburgh in September 2000, given at the invitation of the Royal Society, the great scientist Stephen Hawking, sometimes labelled the second Albert Einstein, warned the world in no uncertain terms. He demanded that we learn from the side-effects of limitless emissions and the still pending danger of a nuclear catastrophe. Hawking fears that the human species will not survive the next thousand years.

The more the power of humans grows, the less they can excuse themselves on the grounds of ignorance. As beings with memory they ought to be able to learn from the past. However, if memory is blotted out, the task of shaping the future can easily lose its bearings. The fatal result will be a species with hands full of technological and economical power, but empty and weak in respect of moral goals and purposes.

> Whether we have reached the end of time is not sure; that is not yet settled. What is settled, however, is that we are living in the time of the end, and that is definite . . . 'In the time of the end' means: in that epoch in which we can daily bring forth its end. – And 'definitely' means that, whatever is left to us as an amount of time, it will remain 'time of the end', since it cannot be replaced by another time, but only by the end. The reason why it cannot be replaced by another time is the fact that we are unable not to do tomorrow or at any other time what we can do today, namely to make an end to each of us.
>
> (the writer Günther Anders in Krellmann 1989: 143–4)

Despite 'the time of the end' a human future of social justice and peace remains a meaningful and absolutely necessary vision and goal of our efforts – it is the focus of this book.

In the context of radical value pluralism and religious plurality, the contribution of the biblical faith is surely only one among others. Christians have to be modest, but what they may reasonably expect of a democratic public is 'a pluralism open to voices of tradition' (Placher 1989: 105), and thus open also to Christianity, even in a minority position. As in each society educational responsibility lies upon the shoulders of all groups, Christian responsibility in education is as 'a shared (co-)responsibility with others' (Nipkow 1990).

Humanity and Memory

In the following chapters, memory will mean a specific one, the biblical memories, the treasures of memory of Jews and Christians in their encounters with the God of the Bible. For the Jews they are grounded in the Exodus and related to Sinai, the departure of the Israelites from Egypt under the guidance of Moses and the gift of God's law. These events were followed by a long sequence of further experiences of God, in particular manifested through the prophets, but also apparent in everyday life as we will see in the Book of Psalms and the Wisdom literature.

Gradually the historical, moral and religious experiences developed a *narrative memory* (cf. Ouaknin 1995), mostly shaped as a myth (see the myth of creation with Adam and Eve). This narrative memory was transferred to the next generations in two ways, after a longer period of oral memories by a written report, the *textual memory*, and by rituals as the *gestical memory*.

Tradition usually takes many paths, producing variants in an ongoing process. The critical question 'Has the event taken place in the form in which it is recorded?' or 'Has it taken place at all?' is a silly question, for the myth is not the narrative of a true event in a positivistic sense, but the true narrative of an event. Whatever might have happened, those experiences, which because of their overwhelming convincing power were felt true, were expressed in a concentrated form in a specific story which hereby became the medium of *paradigmatic memories* (see Chaper 3 on Cain and Abel).

Biblical memory serves education and spiritual growth to moral and religious maturity in an interrelated threefold way, by interrelating the past, the present and the future:

*   Education in a biblical perspective helps people to remember the *past* by urging them to learn the lessons that ought to be taken from the past: education as memory, most of all remembering the victims.
*   Second, education proceeds to clarify the true existing situation of humankind beyond romantic illusions, promoting a realistic, clear, courageous and responsible awareness of the *present*, most of all in careful respect for strangers.
*   As the biblical God was and still is being experienced in history, and his spirit wanders together with his people so that his *future* is their future, education in this spirit also fills with hope for the future, on behalf of children and unborn generations.

God is with the victims, the strangers and the children, for he is on the side of the weak. In remembering the past, Jews and Christians remind modern societies of what they should keep holy in God's eyes in the present for the sake of God's creatures in the future.

However, each attempt to propose specific traditions as religious sources for peace and justice (Parts II and III) also requires a test of the religions, for each of them usually thinks itself to be not only unique, but also exclusive. Are they able to enter a faith dialogue in the spirit of tolerance and mutual learning? How can religious education join and contribute to such a dialogue without false compromises and without glossing over what remains theologically different? Do religions contain resources for reconciliation? And, even if they do, how can 'neighbours' love' become 'love of strangers', let alone 'love of enemies', on a broader scale ? How do majorities learn? In sum: how does the global effectiveness of educational and spiritual ways towards peace stand against the background of our empirical knowledge about human nature (Parts IV and V)? In all parts of the book methods and research data in the social sciences (in particular we will draw on evolutionary research) are necessary for our assumptions and for our trust in the importance of memory to be realistically assessed.

The book chiefly draws on biblical memory. But technology, economy and sciences neither need memory nor engage in its cultivation; nor do they care for religious memory in particular. However, peace and justice do need memory and we have to cultivate it; human affairs cannot do without it. Memory keeps people together in the present, in listening to the voices of the past, on behalf of the life of future generations.

The knowledge of this will create traditions of commemorations of the victims, as is the case in the Yad Vashem Memorial in Jerusalem in memory of the millions of victims of the Holocaust. Each year another commemoration is celebrated in Hiroshima. Some other cases with the character of a sacrifice of the innocent have not yet found adequate collective commemorations, such as the catastrophe of Chernobyl where in 1986, apart from those who were killed during attempted repair work, seven million people suffered from the nuclear fallout (the effect of the catastophe was two hundred times bigger than the two bombs of Hiroshima and Nagasaki together).

For technological innovation the older inventions are forever past; for peace on earth memory is never obsolete. For Jews and Christians the biblical traditions about encounters with God are the sources of a human future and are ever present. With God behind them and God's coming before their eyes believers can breathe freely and live boldly with God in their hearts in the present.

The elder tree is an old and holy tree. It is modest and grows anywhere. Its wood is tough and hard to destroy, as Peter Beier, the late head of the Protestant Church in the Rhineland, remarked in the year of his premature death (Beier 1997: 100), when commenting on the poem Holunderblüte by the German poet Johannes Bobrowski, which ends with the words

> Leute, es möchte der Holunder
> sterben
> an eurer Vergesslichkeit.
>
> People, the elder might
> die
> of your forgetfulness.

'Youth might die, even shortly after birth, of your forgetfulness', Peter Beier adds, remembering the forgetfulness of his own adult generation. Forgetfulness is the death of human relationships.

I
GOD'S HUMANITY

Chapter 2

Human Images of God and God's Humanity

Who Defines Whom?

Whoever draws on religious traditions with the intention of proving their relevance for contemporary education, social life and spiritual growth must expect the question of whether he or she wants to impose supernatural knowledge on others. Is not 'revelation' exclusive in terms of epistemology, that is in the rational dimension, and does it not therefore exclude non-believers in the social dimension? However, to oppose the 'natural' and the 'supernatural' in this way and to assume dogmatic exclusiveness is misleading and falsified by historical consciousness. The very terminology of 'natural' and 'supernatural' is inappropriate because there is no other place for perceiving divine relevation than the world of human life and experience, in short, of human nature.

The relation to experience strongly bears upon the issue of religious truth claims and their communicability in our times. If truth *claims* are rooted in faith *experiences*, they are open to mutual exchange and argumentation – provided they have not made us become fanatics. Normally we are used to sharing our experiences with others. Like all experiences, faith experiences too become a part of our common language. We are asked what we mean by our faith. Hence, religious talk in human conversation implies questions and doubts as well as new insights which we feel prompted to pass on to others. When faith experiences are handed down to coming generations it is mostly through generalized faith knowledge (*Glaubenswissen*). Faith is linked to reasonable arguments – and all of this happens, too, in *human* terms.

However, the experiential faith perspective, although being integrated into our daily life and language, leaves open the question of how exactly we can discern and identify the 'divine' manifestation – as something truly divine, that is, coming from God – in the context of 'human' experience. Consequently, when speaking of 'the human image of God', hereby indicating the relevance of God's 'humanity' in shaping a human future (Chapter 1), we have to ask *who defines whom*? Does the experience of human beings define God or does God throw a new, unexpected light on human beings and their experiences?

From Dogmatic Doctrines about God to Experience-related Images of God

Today the majority of theologians and religious educators regard experience as a proper means of access to God. 'Revelation' and 'experience' are considered as complementary processes in which revelation is seen as a process of 'disclosure' (Herms 1992: 242, 259, 282, following Ian T. Ramsey).

The idea is not new. Martin Luther understood himself explicitly as a theologian through 'experientia'. For Reformation theology the Holy Scriptures are the foundation of any dogma, but not without having understood the biblical texts in their truth through one's own inner experience. For the renowned Protestant theologian Gerhard Ebeling texts documenting acts of relevation and experiences form a hermeneutical circle. 'Scriptures and experience . . . are not sources independent of each other.' Hermeneutical reflections show that the two movements of God 'speaking' his 'word', which generates the 'text' and our listening to, or reading of, the 'text' and 'hearing' 'God's word' will reach a human being only 'if the word does not pass our life by, but enters life, that is, if it has to do with experience in the full range of human experience' (Ebeling 1979: 42).

Thus, 'the sources of dogmatics' which are based in the Holy Scriptures as the original witness of Christian faith can, surprisingly enough, 'be summed up in one word: experience' (p. 41). The term 'experience' covers, first, the whole of the biblical and later historical experiences of Christian faith within church history. Second, it also embraces the experiences of our own biography, including the enrichment we owe to encounters with other religions and cultural phenomena. Third, it means the scientific world experience (pp. 41–2). Against this hermeneutical background we can understand 'faith as *an experience* which we have, and have to have, *with our experience*' in life, as Eberhard Jüngel has put it in accordance with G. Ebeling (Jüngel 1972: 8; my emphasis). In other words, faith is a new experience in the context of, related to and transforming our old experiences.

It follows from this that whatever is said about God is shaped by human experience. In this perspective the classical dogmatic theological doctrines with their abstract and metaphysical descriptions of God's divine attributes in supranatural terms such as eternity, omnipotence and Last Judgement have lost their convincing power and communicability. In modern theology they have been replaced by anthropological descriptions – talking about what God feels, thinks, suffers and does – with corresponding God-images. For Christians Jesus Christ is *'the* image of God' (Jüngel 1977), not in separation, though, from the experiences with God in the Hebrew Bible, the Old Testament, as we will see.

Images of God in Religious Education

The relevance of experience has been elaborated also for religious education, in a way even more extensively than for systematic theology (for summing up of the German discussion see Ritter 1989, for the British see Robinson 1977; M. Grimmitt). Recent research emphasizes the aesthetic qualities of images and, in addition, the relation between religion and imagination (Ritter 2000). The access to faith experiences takes its way through the senses as a matter of 'perception' in the 'life-world' (Heimbrock 1998; Lotz 2001, in drawing on E. Husserl's philosophical concept of 'phenomenology' and M. Merleau-Ponty). This is a new development from the 1930s to the 1960s. During the peak of the 'Word of God-Theology' in the 1950s, 'listening' to the 'word' was the leading practical theological perspective, but now the intuitive, meditative recognition of the meaning of religious 'imagery' is being highlighted. For the Eastern Orthodox churches the crucial religious role of icons was never given up. Some German practical theologians such as Hans-Günter Heimbrock and Peter Biehl even favour a complete paradigm shift to a 'perceptional approach' in practical theology as a whole.

As is well known, all children use anthropocentric images of God which are shaped under the influence of identification with real parents (and other adults) and imagined or hoped for parents, in a mixture of male and female, paternal and maternal characteristics (Schweitzer 1994). In childhood images of God can already vary between positive and negative associations, though usually they bear kind traits; amongst teenagers in the western world images of God usually change considerably (Ziebertz 1994). When young people have to cope with severe crises of belief, the God of their childhood is mostly dropped, provided of course that in highly secularized societies Christian faith has had the chance to develop at all.

The overwhelming creativity in imagining God which we meet with in childhood has also gathered great attention in empirical research (Heller 1986; Coles 1990, chap. 1 and 2), in personal observations of one's own children (Hull 1991) and, last but not least, in collections of texts and pictures of children which display the spectacular richness of their religious world. We will come back to this later.

To speak of God appropriately is a very old challenge. The more we take God seriously as the living God in our life, instead of talking about him from a distance, we become aware of the risk of any form of human expression. Nevertheless there are three roads in history along which religious language in private prayer, in liturgy and in theological descriptions has mainly travelled:

- First, the *via negativa*, when God is described by negating the language which is commonly applied to human beings (the Infinite God vs. finite human beings).
- Second, the *via eminentia*, when statements are used which surpass human attributes (the Almighty God vs. mighty people).
- Third, a way that could be called the *via analogica* when in a symbolical, metaphorical form images of human language point approximately in the direction of God's divine mystery.

In the following chapters we will have to deal more or less with all three ways, mostly the last. We shall try to avoid abstract God-talk. The best remedy against it is the language of the Bible itself: the imaginative power of biblical narratives (Chapter 3), the prophetic language and the language of prayer in the Psalms (Chapter 4), the language of parables told by Jesus (Chapters 5 and 6), the story of Jesus on the cross (Chapter 7), and Paul's life story told by himself and by Luke as the basis of his theology and an example of biographical speech (Chapter 8). However, before entering these fascinating territories of human experience and God experience the preliminary epistemological and hermeneutical question already mentioned of how to distinguish between the 'human' and the 'divine' needs further clarification.

Misinterpretations and Misuse

From the very beginning of our analysis the idea of progress revealed its deep ambiguity. The optimistic assumption of a continuous growth of morality had to be questioned. If we review the crimes committed by human beings against other human beings, the twentieth century could not have been worse. Inhumanity, not humanity, was triumphant. Humanitarian progress has been paralysed by moral retrogression. The general deterioration in human affairs has been sharpened by the unintended side-effects of technological and economic developments. In drawing on a remark of John Amos Comenius (1592–1670) we can say: 'At first we suffered from diseases, then from the remedies, now from both' ('Ita prius morbis laboratum est, post remediis, nunc utroque', *Consultatio catholica*, *Panegersia*, cap. VII). Against this background it is understandable that a new longing for (at least) a 'human God' emerged. In the last decades of the century we also observed a growing emphasis on speaking of the 'human image' of God in academic theology (paradigmatically Ziebertz *et al.* 2001). Why?

The human predicament necessitates theologians competing and aligning with secular humanitarians to cope with a development that can hardly be controlled. When in November 1962 nuclear missiles were installed in Cuba, the Third World War as an impending disastrous nuclear war beyond any imagination came very close to being a reality, and it was 'sheer luck' (McNamara) that it did not break out. Nuclear weapons still exist; something similar can still happen. Does God any longer control the 'good' course of the world ? Or is what happened in the twentieth century to be interpreted as God's punishment? In the past, ambiguous images of God unfortunately contributed to the latter view – and it was accepted by the pious! Today God seems to be either weak or inhuman. Therefore, the 'conscience of the world' has gradually dropped religious guidance and emigrated to non-religious moral standpoints. Philosophers have developed various types of secular philosophical ethics (I. Kant, J. Rawls). Along the same lines secular law has been installed, based on a separation of church and state. What are the factors in our ecclesiastical inheritance that still inhibit an effective contribution on the part of the churches today?

1   Throughout its history the church has taught an image of God which presented him to church members at large primarily as a stern judge who, through his son sitting at his right hand, will execute the Last Judgement 'on all flesh'. Still today it is not easy, even for theologians, to reinterpret this doctrine in a new way, as we will attempt to do below by focusing on an appropiate understanding of God's 'justice' or, better, 'righteousness' (Chapters 4 and 5).
2   Even the Reformation movement was to bring forth similar ambiguous fruits. The much misinterpreted Lutheran 'doctrine of the two realms' prolonged some of the fatal effects of the late medieval doctrine of God – and in particular also of Jesus Christ – as judge. By establishing a separation of spheres (instead of only a necessary distinction), between the 'law' here and the 'gospel' there, the image of God was split in two.
3   Furthermore, the 'law' was regarded as the necessary sombre, oppressing entrance door to the 'gospel'. This temporal sequential pattern became important in Christian education, for education has to do with growing up. Education was one-sidedly focused on the 'law' and bound to contribute mainly to a Christian nurture under the 'law'; in Germany this view dominated until the 1950s.

In all these respects the term 'law' was seen from three perspectives:

- The first was the political meaning of the 'law', the inculcation of the God-given laws of the political order understood as the order of the ruling authorities ('politicus usus legis', 'the political use of the law').
- The second meaning of the 'law' aimed at the confrontation of the sinners with their sins in order to prepare them in their hearts for the reception of the gospel as the message of God's grace ('theologicus usus legis', 'the theological use of the law').
- Whereas the first two 'ways' of God's usage of the law are shared by both the Lutheran and the Calvinist wings of Reformation theology, the third meaning is a specific feature of the Calvinist tradition only: it is the (self) education of the Christian who is summoned to it and supported by the congregation. After having received grace, the Christian has to strive for a pious moral behaviour according to a 'new' law: 'Christ's law' ('tertius usus legis', 'the third use of the law').

Thus in educational practice, in congregational and daily life, and in society, the individual was, as it were, completely surrounded by manifestations of the 'law', with each of them being authorized by God as the highest authority. The dialectic relationship of 'law' and 'gospel' was broken, the 'Good News' often wholly absent.

The negative effects of this theological tradition can be observed in the sometimes almost panic-stricken responses of adolescents today when they are asked to describe their image of God. Data of an empirical study (Nipkow 1988) show that the young people (N = 1236; region Württemberg in Germany; aged 16–24) want to be accompanied by a God (if they are interested in him at all) who will not impose on them any dogmatic and harsh moral obligations.

God is rejected if he still appears as one who 'punishes', let alone as one who will render his 'judgement' on them for their 'sins', sin being a term the adolescents do not like to use at all. If God is allowed to play a role in their life, they want him to become associated with 'nice feelings' only, as one 17-year-old girl put it. This new God of 'nice feelings' is another one-sided image. In the last two or three decades the one extreme idea of God is understandably generating an opposite extreme idea; the image of a God of judgement and punishment is replaced by the image of a therapeutic God of sheer benevolence.

One of the last nationwide German surveys on young people and value change (Deutsche Shell 2000) shows that the values of obedience and discipline, which fitted the stern countenance of previous patterns of Christian nurture, have been swept away and widely replaced by the ideals of a morally permissive society in which, besides economic and monetary ideals, 'fun' is a paramount goal. Although among German youngsters several value milieus exist side by side, the values of 'autonomy', 'self-management', 'attractiveness', 'modernity' and 'authenticity' are becoming dominant (1: 98–116). In this new context God, if he plays a role at all, is expected to be mainly an amiable friend and companion who will no longer require people to fulfil any duties. He is supposed to accept individuals in unconditional love and on their terms of bargaining, not on his.

The search for a kind, human God is understandable on several grounds, historical and biographical. Today it is the autonomous individual who sets the moral standards and dares to assess God's humanity by ideals of our time. This attitude seems to need no justification. On the contrary, the image of God is subjected to a massive process of streamlining to contemporary needs and desires. This process is structurally quite similar to the process of assimilation of earlier times, when God's image was shaped and domesticated according to interests in political loyalty, subordination and obedience. The new expectations are framed by new compulsions which direct life to the pursuit of private well-being and self-fulfilment. Religion is no longer looked to in order to find redemption from sin, but to help cope with the hectic stresses of daily life and the unsolvable contingencies of reality.

Obviously images of, and relations to, God depend on historical and biographical factors. They change as times change. As long as human beings exist, the perception of God's 'divine' reality will necessarily be affected by our perception of 'human' reality. Hence the images of God differ and so will the adjectives attached to him and the notion of what is truly human.

The Semantics of 'Human' and 'Humane' – Compatible and Incompatible Relations

Can a semantic analysis provide safer ground? I do not intend to investigate the 'human images' of God in terms of anthropomorphic and non-anthropomorphic, iconic and non-iconic representations (Pieper and van der Ven 1998). These aspects are useful to describe to what extent (young) people imagine God in resemblance to human form or shape, an approach which is relevant to religious education (and theology in general), for example as a means of exploring the 'inexpressibility' of God (Pieper and van der Ven 1998: 76–7). In this chapter we rather ask for the meanings and connotations of the terms 'human' and 'humane' as a matter of content, envisaging their suggestive emotional content as well as their anthropological and ethical significance.

One can identify the following ways in which the two terms 'human' and 'humane' are commonly used:

1   In a neutral, value-free definition, 'human' means pertaining or relating to people, as in the phrases the 'human race', the 'human body' or 'human history'.
2   In an evaluative sense, 'humane' means someone (or something) characterized by kindness, thoughtfulness and compassion: 'He is one of the most humane people I have ever worked with' or 'Animals must be killed humanely'. In some contexts the term 'human', too, can acquire this meaning, for example if we want to say that a person acts in a caring, empathetic way: 'In helping the sick he showed his human face'.
3   Sometimes the expression 'human' is used to suggest weakness – understandable weakness. The phrase 'It is only human' means that the behaviour of human beings should not be too harshly judged because it is in our nature to be fallible. P.D. James uses the word in this sense when she writes: 'It is good for us to be reminded from time to time that our system of law is human and, therefore, fallible and that the most we can hope to achieve is a certain justice' (1998: 481) Or when she speaks of 'the fascinating evidence of human depravity' (p. 344).
4   The term 'human' refers to both sides, to the positive side of human nature and to its ambiguous and negative sides, on the one hand to 'human weakness and wickedness' (James 1998: 386), on the other hand to possible human 'perfection':

'death would have been seen as a rounding-off, something achieved, something distinctively human, a perfection of loving which left no regrets, no hopes unfulfilled, no unfinished business' (p. 229).

5   Summing up the observations above, one can say that the main semantic content of the emphatic use of the word 'human' (which is different from the neutral denotation, see 1) relates ontologically to what is known as the *conditio humana*, or 'human nature', whereas the terms 'humane' and 'humaneness' refer more specifically to the ethical realm of moral behaviour. This is also true of one of the derivatives of human/humane, the word 'humanitarian', describing a person who works to improve the welfare of humankind and to end suffering and pain.

Against this background, what can be said about the term 'human' in the phrase 'the human image of God'? In its first, neutral descriptive meaning, the word 'human' would describe an image that bears a resemblance to the general human form and shape. As already suggested, it could, second, also be used to emphasize the kind, compassionate side of God by analogy with human beings who appear to us as kind and compassionate persons. Third, and more recently, the word 'human' is sometimes also used in a specific theological way, in order to say that God participates in the weakness of his creatures. Some theologians speak of the suffering God as the 'crucified God' (Jürgen Moltmann and others), as the Almighty who descended into our human weakness in the suffering and death of the powerless Jesus of Nazareth.

In sum, taking the term 'human' in the connotations of ordinary language as identified above, it is, on the one hand, adequate to apply some connotations to God; it is impossible, on the other hand, to stretch the term 'human' in its application to God in all denotations. In particular it is inadequate to apply, except for (human) weakness as God's own choice, human 'wickedness' to God too. In short, as to its semantic content the theological application of the adjective 'human' remains ambiguous.

The Emergence of God's Different 'Humanity'

The topic of this book is justice and peace and its destructive opposites. We cannot deal with the positive without the negative, without looking at illegitimate aggression and violence as expressions of human wickedness. On the one hand, the history of humankind shows continuous efforts to resist or at least to tame evil. In this perspective one can outline a human image of God, God as an ally of the best human intentions. We are allowed to picture God's nature in accordance with these 'humanitarian' efforts of ours to master destructive human powers.

On the other hand, these efforts are impeded by constant human failure and culpability. In reviewing history it seems as though the atrocities committed by human beings against other people (and in the present time also against nature) have grown worse. The sinister balance shows two world wars, the Holocaust, genocides, unending bloody conflicts between neighbouring nations, the misery of refugees, the death of millions through starvation and poverty, emissions that destabilize the climate, and so forth – altogether a sad story of humankind's inhumanity. It is in the face of these phenomena that we have to pose the question of how to approach God's self-relevation in the Bible and to compare him with human affairs.

In the Old Testament God manifests himself not in a temporary and limited humanitarian way, but with his everlasting faithfulness to and unlimited love of Israel in spite of Israel's continuing disloyalty and wickedness, which are compared with an 'incurable' disease: 'Your hurt is incurable, your wound is grievous,' God says to Israel. 'There is no one to uphold your cause, no medicine for your wound, no healing for you' (Jer. 30: 12–14). And yet, as God tells the prophet Jeremiah, 'I have loved you with an everlasting love, therefore I have continued my faithfulness to you. Again I will build you, and you shall be built, O virgin Israel!' (Jer. 31: 3–4).

For Christian faith Jesus is *the* image of God. In Jesus and through him God's paradoxical love in its encompassing intention towards all people is universally and unequivocally manifested. A central concern of this love is the paradoxical way in which violence is refused and reconciliation and peace are demanded, definitely and succinctly expressed in Jesus' injunctions to his followers:

> You have heard that it was said, 'An eye for an eye and a tooth for a tooth.' But I say to you, Do not resist an evildoer. But if anyone strikes you on the right cheek, turn the other also.
>
> (Matt. 5: 38–9)

> And again: You have heard that it was said, 'You shall love your neighbour and hate your enemy.' But I say to you, Love your enemies and pray for those who persecute you.
>
> (Matt. 5: 43–4)

In the following chapters we shall see step by step that the human image of God in Jesus is not merely an extension of what we are accustomed to thinking of as 'human' nature, even if we would take the grand total of our positive human capacities as a criterion. The encounters with God in both the Old and New Testaments reveal that God's humanity is at the same time comparable and incommensurable with our human images of him, although we cannot but use our human language to express the radical difference. The term 'human' remains dependent on the ontological structure of human beings as finite and fallible creatures with a language that participates in the ambiguous ontological structures of our species. Human language unites people and separates them; it speaks truthfully and it cheats, it heals wounds and it causes harm.

The Bible itself teaches us this dialectic in using our language by tentatively comparing God and human beings (*via analogica*), and at the same time by breaking up our speech semantically through the use of negations (*via negativa*) and exaggerations (*via eminentia*). The last is achieved by the use of what Paul Ricoeur has called 'extravagant' language. It consists mainly of antithetical statements (as in the Sermon on the Mount), surprising imagery (like that used in Jesus' parables) and paradoxical wording (which we also find in doctrinal, dogmatic language). All these forms of language lead to a 'broken' hermeneutics.

To give an example of antithetical exaggerations: in Genesis 4 we read, 'Whoever kills Cain will suffer a sevenfold vengeance' (Gen. 4: 15). Some lines later Lamech declares, 'If Cain is avenged sevenfold, truly Lamech seventy-sevenfold' (v. 24) – an expression of an evil spirit exaggerated semantically to the extreme. In Matt. 18 we read as Jesus' answer to Peter's question, 'How often should I forgive? As many as seven times?' 'Not seven times, but, I tell you, seventy times seven' (v. 21) – an expression of God's quite different goodness to human beings' goodness (God's nature and coming rule are meant since Jesus with this statement introduces a parable of God's Kingdom), and again being exaggerated semantically to the extreme, that is to a limitless perspective, put antithetically against our thoughts of justified retaliation, and even against a form of forgiving which we might view with a particular moral pride.

To give an example of paradoxical wording we draw on very famous doctrinal phrases. Speaking of Jesus as being simultaneously 'human' and 'divine', 'true man' and 'true God', is the appropriate paradoxical doctrinal expression of our faith in Jesus as the 'Christ', the appearance of God himself. By God's appearance in Jesus as a human being the original true human nature is restored, as a promise of the restoration of all humanity. This is the basic eschatological perspective of Jesus' teaching as well as of Paul's proclamation (1 Cor. 15: 20–28). The restoration is not a moral transformation; it is an ontological process, for it is the ontological state of human affairs that is fundamentally inadequate and can only be put right by God's ontological creativity as 'creator', whose 'righteousness' (justice) is bestowed on his 'creatures' by grace only (justification).

Human life is under the rule of guilt and death. Consequently, 'the last enemy to be destroyed is death' (1 Cor. 15: 26), a divine destruction that includes guilt and sin in a process that has already started. To use traditional theological language once more: when Jesus died on the cross God's love overwhelmed death and guilt. Thus, the true 'human' image of God is that of the crucified Jesus as the revelation of abundant 'divine' love. Strictly speaking, it is something unbelievable because it is so paradoxical. The story of God's paradoxical love, of his 'saving justice' as the response to human wickedness and self-justification, begins in history very early (see the next chapter).

Educational Consequences

We would fail to deal properly and completely with the reality of life and with the nature of God if we tried to establish a false harmony. This would happen in two ways, first by denying the facts about the true state of human nature, second by downplaying or even forgetting the basic difference between God and humans.

Some approaches in religious education tend to gloss over this difference. On the one hand, the experience-oriented approach (see above), is based on the valid hermeneutical principle that 'faith means having experiences with our experiences'. Thus the approach takes seriously the notion that God relates himself to human life since he himself has entered life and is a friend of life. On the other hand, the approach becomes reductive if it adapts and assimilates God's entry into life (or, seen from the point of view of the subject, the new healing experiences with God against the background of our old shaming experiences with ourselves) in a way that lets God's radical creative action disappear.

One of today's trend is towards a society that avoids self-questioning and self-reproach, even though honesty would demand this. The general mood tends towards a culture of individual ease. We are 'at ease' if we feel comfortable and secure; the opposite we call being 'ill at ease', that is, to feel anxious and worried. Many seem to be no longer able to stand the troublesome reality of life as it is. They are tired and exhausted by the problems of the world and shrink away from becoming aware that they themselves have caused them.

A specific allergic resistance is being developed against facts which bear negatively upon one's own good conscience, thereby generating feelings of guilt. To speak of failure and even more of guilt in connection with God is inconvenient and annoying. We have also already indicated above the historical reasons for some characteristic shifts in the image of God which result from the sad legacy of Christian education that was often fixed upon nothing else but producing a bad conscience because of sinful behaviour. But the solution cannot be religious escapism either.

Christian education and spiritual growth to moral and religious maturity have to avoid the traps at either end, and to follow a clear-sighted path with a realistic anthropology. The sources for it are the anthropology of the Bible (see Parts II and III) and the history of evolution (see Part IV).

Our task also requires a fresh view of biblical language because the doctrinal language game of the churches is another legacy that prevents children and young people from an understanding of what it is all about when parents or teachers, ministers or Christian youth workers speak of God and of his peace and justice.

The crucial educational response will be given by a pluralizing hermeneutics and a corresponding plural methodology for religious education. In this context one approach will be discussed in particular because it integrates several dimensions which seem to me important for religious and moral education: the approach of 'elementarization'.

In the concluding part (Part V) we consider what it means that our global situation is characterized by a diversity of many different religions, all of them confronted with the issue of mutual understanding as a factor of global peace.

II
PEACE THROUGH JUSTICE

Chapter 3

God, Cain, War and Evil in Children's Eyes

The First Murder in the Bible – Homicide in the Context of Worshipping

Can worshipping become the death of human relationships? The first murder reported in the Bible takes place in a liturgical context. Cain and Abel are brothers at that; they have very much in common, but their religious cults differ. Would the homicide not have happened if they had worshipped together?

> Abel was a keeper of sheep, and Cain a tiller of the ground. In the course of time Cain brought to the Lord an offering of the fruit of the ground, and Abel for his part brought of the firstlings of his flock, their fat portions.
>
> (Gen. 4: 2–4)

Hostility can spring from religious plurality (see Chapter 1): Differences in cult weigh heavily because of their 'hot' emotional purposes. They have to do with the correct ritual instruments in addressing the transcendent powers or gods. The very essence of life depends on their benevolence. Envy 'is lurking at the door' like a crouching demon, if another person benefits more than oneself from their grace. Cain, a young man, was filled with envy and anger when he saw that God was not with him, but with his brother, denigrating his offer: 'And the Lord had regard for Abel and his offering, but for Cain and his offering he had no regard. So Cain was very angry and his countenance fell' (Gen. 4: 4–5). God asks him why and calmly tries to appeal to his self-control: 'If you do not well, sin is lurking at the door; its desire is for you, but you must master it' (v. 7).

In early history, religious correctness in offerings, on the one hand, and prosperity, on the other hand, were seen as being in close interrelationship. In the Hebrew Bible, old age, numerous offspring and overflowing richness were the recurrent content of divine promises. They represented the visible fruits of the truth of the divine promises, the undeniable expression of the reality of God's blessings. Those who differed in religious rituals ran a risk of disturbing others in their religious security and of failing themselves with deadly outcomes. In this study we are looking for causal factors which generate human violence and prevent peaceful community. Obviously religious competition between different rituals belongs to the negative factors, since it can give offence to other believers. There is much historical data by way of illustration.

In the disciplines of archaeology and history of literature many investigations have proved the social meaning of offerings. To give a first example, the irrational hatred of the Jews, which had already started in the first millennium before Christ, can perhaps at least partly be explained by Gunnar Heinsohn's hypothesis (see Brumlik 1991: 359–60) that during their Babylonian captivity the Jews had found out good reasons why the habit of offering to many gods was futile. The people in their surroundings believed in the demonic influence of the stars, in particular of the planet Venus, which was made responsible for originating disastrous earthquakes and floodings. By becoming more familiar with an empirical astronomy the Jews dropped that explanation and shaped their monotheism. It had, of course, other roots, too. But anyway, their religion became a religion of a very new type. It practised and propagated a denial of plural offerings and robbed the advocates of offerings in their neighbourhood of their religious security. It seems to be a plausible hypothesis that the emotions of their neighbours, which were generally nourished by deep religious anxieties and had usually found an outlet in the bloody cults, were now diverted and directed against the Jews.

Heinsohn's explanatory model presents a 'coherent' thesis for the development of ancient Judeophobia. However, whether it is apt, with its rather strong psychoanalytical assumptions, 'to explain the Holocaust, Islamic hostility against the state of Israel and anti-Zionism in Western metropolises today, is questionable' (Brumlik 1991: 360). Nevertheless, still today for many believers a change in patterns of ritual correctness touches the very roots of their convictions. They refuse to give up the ritual they are used to, because it is the very core of their 'cultural capital' (Pierre Bourdieu) as holy practice that now comes to the surface (for the general positive role of rituals as 'memory' see pp. 10–11).

Today the phenomena of religious fundamentalism furnish further examples of the topic. The ultra-orthodox Jews are highly irritable keepers of ritual correctness who do not shrink away from murder, neither do their Palestinian fundamentalist opponents. The great tragedy of the conflict in the Middle East has many roots. In particular it is nourished by religious fanaticism and is focused on the Temple Mount, the place of worship.

As for Protestantism, in the early days of the Reformation the famous controversy between Martin Luther and Ulrich Zwingli about the correct way of celebrating the Holy Supper – does the bread only 'mean' the body of Jesus Christ (Zwingli) or 'is' it his body (Luther)? – split the Protestant camp for hundreds of years. The sharing of the Holy Communion became impossible, and separated members of the different Protestant denominations in many other respects. Only in recent decades have things changed for the better. Again it was ritual that had offended religious feelings, impeding religious and social peace. Religious rituals are the most intimate form in which the truth of one's own faith is lived out.

The lack of sacramental community between the Protestant churches and the Roman Catholic Church is also derived mainly from a different liturgical understanding, concerning the controversy surrounding the Holy Mass in its traditional Catholic interpretation as a sacrifice (linked to the doctrine of priesthood). From Reformation times onwards Catholic doctrine spoke of the 'unbloody repetition' of the sacrifice of Jesus Christ at Golgotha. This view was sharply rejected by Luther because Christ's sacrifice needs no repetition by us. Although in the meantime the Catholic liturgical formula has been modified, the separation of the churches continues. At the central point of the believers' living faith, in the Eucharist, Christians do not share community in Christ, although it is He who invites.

The story of Cain and Abel can serve as an eye-opener to religious rivalries and anxieties as disastrous factors of religion-based hatred, with violence as the most extreme eventuality. Cain didn't care for God's warnings. Do the churches care now?

Cain said to his brother Abel, '"Let us go out to the field." And when they were in the field, Cain rose up against his brother Abel, and killed him' (Gen. 4: 8).

Homicide as Fratricide

As they are saturated with experience, the stories of the Old Testament are also brimful of experienced-based truth. For the purposes of religious education this fact is very important for it forbids dealing with the texts in an abstract dogmatic way and urges us to choose an experiential approach (see Chapter 2). The story of Cain and Abel highlights the embarrassing possibility of a deadly struggle between people related by blood, members of the same family. How can it be explained? (As to general factors, in particular taken from evolutionary research, see Chapter 9.)

Behind our story there might have been another story, the story of the relationships of the Israelites to the Kenites. They also adored Jahweh and joined the Israelites in their conquest of the land of the Canaanites. 'The descendants of Hobab the Kenite, Moses' father-in-law, went up with the people of Judah from the city of palms into the wilderness of Judah which lies in the Negeb near Arad' (Judg. 1: 16). But they did not settle in the same fertile and cultivated land around Hebron and the region north of it on the hills between Jerusalem and Hebron as the dominant tribe of Judah did. Instead they seem to have stayed in the more desert region south of Hebron where they settled and lived, probably mostly as nomads (Herrmann 1973: 105, 144). The Kenites had connections to the Rechabites, who are reported to have been ascetic and passionate adorers of Jahweh who maintained the ideals of nomadism (Jer. 35) (Herrmann 1973: 105). Later on in history we hear that David had made the Kenites and other minor tribes become his allies with whom he shared his spoil, sending it to 'the towns of the Kenites' (1 Sam. 30: 29). In the list of places which finally belong to Judah those of the Kenites are included (Josh. 15: 57), the first town being called 'Cain'!

Why do we mention the historical data about the Kenites? They are called after Cain: 'The Kenite Eponym Cain is behind the legend of Gen 4: 1–16' (Donner 1984: 132). But what sort of experiences might have been the true background? Most probably those of a certain subtle religious difference with social consequences, a dialectical relation of identity and non-identity: here the members of our tribe who belong to us, there those who do not, although being nearer to us than most of the others. Here we ourselves as truthful believers, there those who boast of being more ardent believers. While the tribes were related by blood, they were not exactly identical by cult. It is the questioning of one's own cultural and religious identity by the otherness of others which seems to be the ethno-religious material from which tensions spring up. In a tentative assumption, we dare say that the ambivalence between the two 'brother'-tribes (Judah and the Kenites being 'associates of the community', Donner 1984: 132) might explain at least to some part the paradigmatic core of our story.

Brothers (and siblings in general) are not exempt from feelings of envy and even hatred towards each other. Homicide as fratricide is an abominable crime, in theological language a mortal sin. Criminal statistics show that in many cases of capital crime the victim and the offender knew each other. Later in this study we will see that usually it is the family and the social ties between near relatives that nourish the feelings of caring behaviour that make up the affiliative ties between human beings and create community. The stronger these affiliations, the more atrocious the violation of them. Murder can happen despite the closest genetic relationship between the murderer and the victim. However, it can also be assumed that the more disgusting the violation, the greater the desire to find a way of reconciliation.

In the story this ambivalence shows up in the following elements. Two pieces of information have been handed down: Cain is cursed and driven 'away from the soil' to become 'a fugitive and a wanderer on the earth' (a nomad, see the [early] locations of the Kenites) (Gen. 4: 14). But some lines later another text says that he again 'settled' (v. 16) and – much more astonishing – became the ancestor not only of 'those who live in tents and have livestock', but also of 'those who play the lyre and pipe' (vv. 20–21) and 'made all kinds of bronze and iron tools' (vv. 21–2). The professions of craftsman and artist are typical of life in towns. This tradition tells that Cain became the ancestor of the founders of urban civilization, of builders of a city. The background of the story probably mirrors also the difference of urban and non-urban patterns of life.

Sin – Its Passive and Active Structure

Is sin an animal hovering cunningly in the dark behind the door waiting for its moment to attack? Our story describes sin in this way: 'If you do not do well, sin is lurking at the door. Its desire is for you' (Gen. 4: 7). Human beings are described as the prey of sin, comparable with smaller or weaker animals that become the prey of predators. Sin is seen as a power that overwhelms us from outside, thereby laying open our weakness; it makes us passive victims. The pride of humans when comparing themselves with the world of animals is a self-deception. It is dangerous to trust too much in one's own free will. Although God had cautioned him, Cain succumbed to sin, he was not able to control himself any longer. The Lord's warnings had been in vain.

Nevertheless, despite this dependence, human beings are regarded as being able to deliberately make up their minds: 'Cain said to his brother Abel, "Let us go out to the field"'(v. 8). Looking for a suitable location for murdering his brother is more or less a matter of deliberate choice; the open field provided a site for killing out of reach of observers, 'a good opportunity': 'And when they were in the field, Cain rose up against his brother Abel, and killed him' (v. 8).

Thus, human wickedness has two aspects, a passive and an active one: our fallibility in being liable, first, to temptation at any moment – therefore, Jesus asks us to pray each day 'Lead us not into temptation' (Matt. 6: 13, ecumenical version) – second, to our active bad intentions. This second fact calls upon the individual to be strong and resist evil in an act of self-mastering: 'you must master it' (v. 7).

Today people experience both human fallibility and guilt in new dimensions. They are pressed by anonymous social forces that exert massive powers of temptation. 'Since everyone does it, I can't help doing the same', is the low-spirited excuse. Sin has gained a structural character; it appears widely as a systemic imprisonment fostered by a general climate of permissiveness and temptation.

Why did God not Prevent the Murder? The Risky Freedom of Human Beings

The murder has happened, the crime is committed: 'Then the Lᴏʀᴅ said to Cain, "Where is your brother Abel?" He said, "I do not know, am I my brother's keeper?"' (Gen. 4: 9).

Any act of aggression and violence is more or less destructive of life; killing is more, it is a final end to life. There is no going back. The Lord did not prevent the murder. Why not? Some may ask more sharply and indignantly, as many commentators, among them Jews, have done before: did he not indirectly provoke Abel's death by acknowledging his offering and not Cain's? Why did he not act on fair and equal terms? A contemporary Jewish observer makes a similar point: 'In this story, God behaves like the most inept of parents' (Armstrong 1996: 36; as quoted in Dershowitz 2000: 52). Is God's free will that of an arbitrary despot? Children will surely ask this for they want fair treatment at home and school from their parents and teachers. Do they have to learn that 'the good God' is less than just? Such an idea could lay the ground for a growing scepticism. What does the Bible say? 'I will be gracious to whom I will be gracious, and will show mercy on whom I will show mercy' (Exod. 33: 19).

'Here it is', we are inclined to exclaim, 'what a proof of pure arbitrariness!' In the past, sentences like this have served to produce an incoherent, divided and psychologically disastrous image of God. And fatally so, the result being a dualism between an arbitrary God of vengeance governing under the rule of the 'law' in the Old Testament – the God of the Jews – and the loving, redeeming God of the 'gospel' in the New Testament, the God of the Christians. This mistaken and dangerous separation has relentlessly contributed to an anti-Judaism that continues today. The second misunderstanding concerns the meaning of God as free and almighty: in parts of Reformation theology, as in Calvinism, it has led to the doctrine of predestination. The first concept of a dualistic distortion of God's nature will be discussed and refuted later in this chapter and in the following one. The second distortion concerning the understanding of the Almighty God and the freedom of human beings is rooted in three highly problematic interpretations of the term 'almighty':

- The first equates God's power ('Almighty') with an overall pseudo-naturalistic determinism that regards God's actions as if they were processes governed by a sort of natural law.
- A second misinterpretation fails to grasp God's faithfulness to his creation as the basis of even those of his actions that seem to be arbitrary.
- The third theological misunderstanding concerns the very nature of creation. In creating the world, two acts are interrelated. God gave the created universe its own laws of finiteness such as expansion and concentration, life and death, a limited freedom of choice to human beings (different from animals) and, complementarily and voluntarily, he restricted his own divine almighty power. Creation implies, logically, a basic difference between creation and creator. In the Middle Ages Jewish mystics reflected on the implications of this difference as an expression of divine 'love'. The idea of 'self-restriction', of 'zimzum' (Scholem 1962/1973: 72–82), was taken up in the present first by Jürgen Moltmann (1981). Consequently, what happens on earth cannot be any longer

directly and in detail attributed to God in strict causality. God's presence in his creation, as the biblical faith sees it, becomes a matter of mysterious concealment. If God were plainly to be a rational reality that neatly fitted our categories, would he still be God, is a question already asked by the philosopher in the Book of Ecclesiastes. Martin Luther spoke of the 'hidden God', faith becoming a 'confidentia sub contrario', 'confidence in spite of contradicting facts'. These distinctions cast a light upon our story.

Cain knew what he did or at least became aware of it soon after. He realized that he had done something so terrible that he was afraid of simply confessing it. 'Am I my brother's keeper?' Notwithstanding the temptation 'lurking at the door', Cain had been free to choose. His temptation and his fallibility resulted from the finite condition of the fallen created world. To say God should have created a better world is silly. His original creation, that is the 'world' with God, was 'good'. But the two chapters on creation make it clear that now it was up to human beings, in this case Cain, to exercise human responsibility and to decide how to 'respond' to the Creator. The general fallibility of creation results from the condition of the finite character of the world, but does not exclude personal responsibility: on the contrary, it demands it. God did not stop Cain, that is true, for it was Cain who had to prove his human quality. Cain or anybody else is not permitted to say that he did not know about right and wrong. The Lord had kindly reminded and warned him. He did not govern him as a puppeteer, God respected Cain's freedom. Cain had no excuse. 'The LORD has told you, O mortal, what is good; and what does the LORD require of you, but to do justice, and to love kindness, and to walk humbly with your God?' (Mic. 6: 8).

The crime was a felony by any standard, a 'malum in se', something 'wrong in itself', inherently wrong and committed not simply against Abel but, as the Jewish tradition sees it, against all his potential offspring. 'According to a midrash, God says to Cain, "The voice of thy brother's blood . . . cries out . . . and likewise the blood of all the pious who might have sprung from the loins of Abel"', 'The talmudic principle "He who kills a single human being, it is as if he has destroyed the entire world" grows directly out of the Cain and Abel narrative' (Dershowitz 2000: 55).

Does God Govern People who make War? – Children Reflecting about Good and Evil, God and the Devil

Children are different from adults. This seems to be a truism, but hardly a thoroughly explored issue with regard to a child's religion. What we have pointed out in the preceding section about God's freedom and the fallibility of humans, and, conversely, about human freedom and God's self-restriction, is a theology of adults. But as religious educators we definitely have to look also for a theology of children – 'the religion of the child' (for the most thorough study of this issue in historical and systematic perspectives see Schweitzer 1992). Children's religious and philosophical imagination is a rich meaning-making process. They want to come to grips with the mysteries, horrors and joys of reality on roads which adults have mostly forgotten.

In the Tübingen qualitative research project on religious classroom instruction and interaction (Schweitzer *et al.* 1995; the verbatim protocols in Faust-Siehl *et al.* 1995), some insights of practical relevance can illuminate the paradigm shift entailed when taking the perspectives of children. The quality of Christian education in church and of religious education (RE) in schools surely depends on many factors. Among them the active and creative religious role of children is to be regarded as one of the most important. In accord with John Hull's (1991) more private explorations in his book about 'God-talk' with his own children, we regard children as 'young theologians' (Schweitzer in the foreword to the German edition of Hull's book, 1997: 7).

The Tübingen project, conducted from 1993 to 1995, drew on 24 lessons in RE in state schools in the age groups of 10–12 and 16–17. The lessons were recorded, marking each pupil's contribution anonymously but in a way which allowed the identification of the individual child or adolescent in order to see how his or her religious understanding might have changed during the course of a lesson.

The transcripts were independently interpreted by the team of authors from several perspectives – developmental, educational and theological. As a developmental theoretical frame of reference several structural-cognitive approaches regarding moral and religious development were combined (L. Kohlberg, F. Oser, in particular Fowler *et al.* 1986). Fowler's theory proved to be the most valid instrument for attaining coherent interpretations of the data. At the same time, we tried to appreciate the children's religious creativity and the teacher's competence from educational and theological aspects. The classroom analyses were accompanied further by interviews with the teachers.

The integrated discussion of the results followed a new path of religious education in Germany, the approach of 'elementarization' (Nipkow 1982). Elementarization is conceptualized in terms of five dimensions – the original first four (Nipkow) being enlarged by a fifth (Schweitzer) to form a multilayered frame of questions for the purposes of both planning and analysing religious education processes. The approach requires an intertwining analysis of the following aspects.

1   The *elementary structures* of the instructional content, for example biblical texts or others.
2   The *elementary experiences* involved as seen from two perspectives: first those experiences which make up the experiential background of the texts (or other materials such as religious architecture, pictures, rituals), second those which might play a role on the part of pupils' experiences today as possible presuppositions for their understanding of the past texts (or other religious witnesses).
3   The *elementary accesses* to understanding in developmental and biographical terms.
4   The *elementary truths* consisting of the ensuing truth experiences and truth claims following from them, again resulting from the two perspectives outlined in dimension 2: on the one hand, the normative implications of the religious tradition, on the other hand, those that might arise in the teaching–learning process on the part of the pupils.
5   The *elementary methods* which may support meaningful religious learning.

The selected lessons in RE were on three curricular topics: God, Justice and Parables. The following example relates directly to the main theme of this chapter. The children are concerned with the issue of God in the context of war and peace from the perspective of 'good' and 'evil' and where the evil comes from, facing the question of how to attribute the evil and thereby hinting at the issue of 'theodicy'.

In one of the lessons about 'Images of God' (age group 10–12), having asked the children to draw their ideas of God, the teacher was suddenly interrupted by a girl, let us call her Helen, asking,

> How far does God govern or guide people? If it is God who guides them, war couldn't exist, or could it? Therefore I ask myself: is it the people who do these things by themselves alone?

Helen is bothered by an issue that parallels Cain killing his brother Abel, with God neither stopping Cain nor war. In both cases he does not intervene. This points to a fundamental issue, long since recognized: 'Why is there evil in the world at all?' Those who believe in God are confronted with the issue of theodicy; they are painfully urged to modify the question: 'Why does God allow the evil?' 'How can God be justified?' 'How can his love and almighty power be compatible with the suffering of the innocent?' In an earlier Tübingen empirical study (Nipkow 1988) the issue of theodicy showed up as one of the most serious temptations of faith (alongside death and the issue of the afterlife) to which adolescents (and adults) are continuingly exposed. The German dramatist Georg Büchner (1813–37) called the issue of theodicy 'the rock of atheism'.

Helen's question and the ensuing classroom conversation can be interpreted along the lines of the elementarizing approach with its five dimensions. In a way, Helen is 'elementarizing' by herself by putting a difficult theological issue in plain words, with a double focus, first by concentrating on the 'elementary structure' of the relation between God's action and the action of human beings, and second, relatedly, by posing the question of who causes the evil. What is the characteristic nature of 'elementary experiences'? It is their elementary impact by which we are confounded, perplexed, puzzled, or alternatively happily overwhelmed, in any case affected in an unusual way. So were Helen and her classmates in those days of the Bosnian war. They were confronted with daily TV reports on killings, fugitives, victimized people, crying children, photos of atrocities. As in Genesis 4, the war appeared as a war between brothers, between Serbs, Croats and Bosnians who in spite of their ethnic and religious differences had lived together for decades.

Can we describe the 'elementary structure' more precisely? According to her pattern of religious thinking, for Helen it seems to be an 'either/or' structure, either God is responsible for everything or human beings are. If it is the latter, God cannot be blamed for having directly caused the war. But even now he is not 'justified', for why did he not stop the killing? His indirect responsibility is painfully left open.

As to the 'elementary experience', Helen does not mention any details of war; it seems the word 'war' is sufficient for everyone to know what is meant, the 'elementary' impact of facts harshly contrasting with the children's learnt image of God. The elementary core concerns a possible self-contradiction in God himself – a frightening idea. This is the puzzling problem Helen wants to come to terms with and to share with the class.

The religious dilemma has a rational and an emotional side. For a girl like Helen, and other children of her age who for developmental reasons tend to a dualist thought pattern, there are only two answers logically left – and both are destructive to faith. Either God himself is directly or indirectly responsible, which contradicts the teachings about him as a 'good God' and our 'dear Father', or human beings are autonomous with the sad consequence of God being absent or, in the worst case, not existing at all.

As already indicated above, Helen's reflections also throw light on her cognitive development as one precondition among others: we are advancing what I have called the educational 'elementary accesses' to understanding, the third heuristic aspect of 'elementarization'. To use Piaget's theory and its more recent theoretical elaborations, by opposing cognitive alternatives Helen is approaching thinking in 'formal operations'. Dualistic oppositions belong to them, playing a dominant role both in daily life and in modern digital information technologies. Helen is far from having developed 'post-formal operations' such as dialectical, complementary and paradoxical ones (Commons *et al.* 1984). These much more complex categories are necessary to grasp a theological idea such as the paradoxical linkage of God's almighty power and voluntary self-restriction. The other statements above about the co-existence of a free human will and, at the same time, of human dependence show a similar dialectical cognitive structure.

What is true? Facing controversial issues, religious educators have to be aware of students' widespread interest in clear-cut answers. The dimension of 'elementary truth experiences', respectively 'truth claims', as the fourth dimension of 'elementarization' is the most difficult one. The teacher in Helen's class was wise enough to give the children the lead as he had done before by first letting them draw their own images of God. In keeping with his child-oriented approach he asks Helen,

Could you draw it? (that is, her problem)

This was an adequate step for it passed the issue on to the class and their own religious creativity, and it immediately turned out to be successful, an appropriate 'elementary method' within the fifth dimension of elementarization. Such a style of interaction is not found everywhere. As we discovered in the project (dating from the mid-1990s), the teachers in the sample schools tended to teach 'above' their students' heads, thus often failing to gain their comprehension. In situations blocked by misunderstandings or helplessness they escaped to their ('adult') theological knowledge and academic language, without much regard for the children's development. To take children seriously, one should systematically apply 'learning by discovery'. What discoveries were made in the next minutes? Why was the teacher's confidence in his class's own abilities justified?

Pupil: How can you draw it? That God . . . that some people stand in the way, so that he can't see anything, or something like that.

Unlike Helen, this classmate is thinking in 'concrete operations', for he explains the lack of divine intervention in the Bosnian war by a physical hindrance, maybe people standing around (or clouds hovering above) fatally blocking God's perception of what is going on. A second student comes up with another idea.

Pupil: No, he may have a remote control in his hand or something like that. (Laughter) Yes indeed, don't laugh!

This explanation evidently remains within the framework of concrete operations too. What the pupil is thinking of is not quite clear. Does God use a remote-controlled vehicle on the battlefield which he has lost control of? Wars getting out of control or escalating beyond a tolerable limit? Not a stupid idea at all, if so. Teachers should not tolerate other pupils' poking fun; any contribution deserves attention. In our lesson the teacher did not ask for further clarification. He should have done. He got confused, as he confessed later in an interview after the lesson. Being at a loss to know what to do with the remote control, he rejected the proposal slightly ironically:

> *Teacher*: God with a remote control? You know something better. Let me help you.
> *Pupil*: Puppets.
> *Teacher*: Yes indeed! [We hear his sigh of relief!] And how could you draw them? Such a puppet, the puppet master and your problem?
> *Pupil*: Maybe the strings are broken.
> *Pupil* (another one): I would put it a little differently . . . God has his puppets, and then the devil, well, a Punch and Judy Show, puppets, and those (of the devil) do something different, just the opposite (of God's puppets). – Well, here is a line, and this is above and that's below. Up there is God with his puppets or something like that. And there are the (puppets of the devil) who will do just the opposite of what God's puppets are doing.
> *Pupil* (another one): Now the devil also has a pair of scissors separating God's puppets from God.
> *Teacher*: (drawing a pair of scissors) This is a pair of scissors attacking the puppets.
> *Pupil* (another one): Or maybe the strings are breaking and the devil catches them up with his hands.

After this last remark the teacher continued his original plan for the lesson. He did not realize the unique opportunity for building on the pupils' creative religious imagination.

What integrating commentary can be given, first from *theological* perspectives? When using a personification of evil as a counterpart to the good God the children were recapitulating an old (and still present) dualistic pattern of thought that was traditionally supposed to solve the problem of theodicy. Attributing goodness to God and evil to the devil enables children of that developmental stage to explain the evil in the world and to escape Helen's dilemma, for the solution avoids a self-contradiction in God's nature and actions. It is the shrewd wickedness of the devil who, by cunningly separating the puppets from God or by catching those which had become lost when the strings got broken, deprives them of moral orientation. Now the war is caused neither by God nor by human beings alone. Helen's tentative idea of human autonomy is not taken up; people remain 'puppets', the opposite of autonomy. Instead of following the path of her question, the other pupils play with mythical 'explanations': either it is the numinous power of another transcendent entity that accounts for the evil in the world, or it is a mysterious corrosion of the ties between God and human beings that will lead to the breakdown of goodness in the cosmos.

In *developmental* terms, the structure of the dualistic cognitive God–devil pattern is less complex if compared with the structures of complementarity (present already in the Chalcedonian formula), with paradoxical (Kierkegaard) or dialectical (Hegel) thought patterns. Leading systematic theologians today are accustomed to interrelating opposing aspects in order to approach the mysteries of God, not in order to rationalize them. Thus, man's free will and human dependence, or, with respect to the issue of theodicy, God's love and almighty power and human suffering, are, so to speak, 'bound together' 'beyond' our usual logical comprehension. The empirical developmental side of the issue of theodicy has been broadly investigated by Johannes A. van der Ven (1990, chap. V; van der Ven 1989). The most sophisticated research on 'thinking in complementarity' is published by K. Helmut Reich (Reich 1989; 2002).

From an *educational* perspective we should not devalue children's interpretations prematurely; instead, we have to appreciate them as adequate attempts at understanding according to their age, and full of religious wisdom. However, we can predict some difficulties in both directions, in Helen's 'solution' and in that of the 'puppet group'.

For many people belief in God is totally replaced by the idea of human autonomy with no religious comeback. 'Once the gap between immanence and transcendence has been opened up, it is extremely difficult – if not impossible – to expect help and support from God in situations of concrete emergency arising in daily life' (Döbert 1991: 170). The 'deistic solution' (Oser and Gmünder 1984, stage 3) of God having created the world once upon a time, but now only looking at it from a distance without effectively intervening (see Helen's question as one option), presumably leads to 'developmental impasse' (Döbert 1991: 173). Subjects at stage 3, which Oser and Gmünder have called 'deistic', operate with a 'two-kingdom doctrine'. They attribute 'great responsibility for planning and decision-making to themselves' and 'separate the ultimate . . . completely . . . from their own sphere of action' (Oser and Gmünder 1984: 94). If so, for Döbert 'atheism represents one extreme variant of this stage' (1991: 173).

The mythological dualistic 'solution' of 'two Gods', the good God and the bad one, the devil as powerful opponent, is risky too and can in adolescence lead to satanic cults, another extreme variant, or later in life to infantile dependencies of many kinds. Hence the task of religious education must be to help change ideas about God and evil along the lines we are going to pursue. It is the *one* God who knows about evil and looks at the badness and sin of humankind. There is no terrible second godlike power, except for that wickedness done by human beings themselves – here Helen is on the right path. But humankind is not devoid of any knowledge. God grants us knowledge as he did Cain, and he supports us paradoxically as he did Cain.

When we draw a comparison with the story of Cain and Abel, we observe that the children are sensitive to the fallibility of human beings and to the idea of sin 'lurking at the door' like a 'demon', as Alan M. Dershowitz translates. In order to express their ideas they use the language of mythology as an authentic vehicle of their attempts to come to terms with a very difficult issue. Myths belong to the oldest means of religion in forming a 'narrative memory'.

We cannot say whether other students in that classroom thought like Helen, who seems to have left mythology behind and started developing the idea of human autonomy. Those who took part in the discussion did not. The idea of a relative autonomy is a true one, as everyone knows. But believing (as Cain did) that one has absolute command of oneself (autonomy as complete self-possession) would be a self-deception and wrong. So would be the assumption (like the one made by Cain) that one is able to use one's own free will without misuse (autonomy as moral self-security). What seems very positive in terms of philosophical ideals and enlightened human reason looks very different when it comes to working it out in the real world. The quest for the good in moral and religious education needs to be based on a realistic anthropology such as we find in biblical stories like that about Cain and Abel. A serious and thoughtful view of human nature is a characteristic of moral and religious maturity.

Crime, Guilt, Human Manoeuvres and Children's Notions of Justice

> The LORD said, 'What have you done? Listen; your brother's blood is crying out to me from the ground! And now you are cursed from the ground, which has opened its mouth to receive your brother's blood from your hand. When you till the ground, it will no longer yield to you its strength; you will be a fugitive and a wanderer on earth.'
>
> (Gen. 4: 10–12)

Crime deserves punishment and atonement. If offenders are not prosecuted, the victims and their suffering are not respected. This view should not be confused with revenge. There are two reasons for a serious reaction: the public expression of moral consciousness and, above all, the respectful public memory of the victims. A culture of memory of the sufferings is a service to human dignity.

Punishment, atonement and memory are not identical. While blind punishment is morally without value, true atonement is a profound reflective act through which the victim becomes reconciled and the offender regains his own dignity as a self-responsible person who is ready and capable of repentance.

As mentioned earlier, there is a justified emotional and moral resistance against a God who punishes, while, ironically enough, the same people sometimes ardently advocate capital punishment, a deliberate killing of a human being by other human beings. Religious educators want to transmit to the young generation 'a human image of God' (Ziebertz *et al.* 2001). Against the background of a history of Christian education that has misused the Bible for the political purposes of oppressing souls and minds, aversion to an image of God as a gigantic policeman is more than understandable. However, we also have to be aware of possible hypocrisy, projections of guilt onto others and an illusionary image of human nature.

To begin with the last of these, one fails to pursue a realistic moral and religious education by clinging to anthropological illusions. In the long run, they will leave children helpless in our world. To include empirical knowledge about self-deception and guilt is necessary and something quite different from the former doctrine of God as a judge looking for 'satisfaction'.

A typical psychological manoeuvre is to shift guilt to others by projection. The most famous biblical example is to be found in Genesis 3 when Adam is reported arguing against God, 'The woman whom you gave to be with me, she gave me fruit from the tree, and I ate' (Gen. 3: 12). 'Why did you not prevent me from being as I am? From having done as I did? Why did you create such a miserable world at all?' These manoeuvres distort the truth and ground education in lies. To lie is the business of the devil, lying is another barrier to an adequate moral and religious education in a time that continuously tends towards camouflage and hidden corruption.

Hypocrisy pretends to serve ideal values, but in reality betrays them by deceitful behaviour and language. 'Oh, that nobody means death when he says life!', Nelly Sachs remarks in one of her poems ('Völker der Erde').

Cain is a murderer. What should the punishment he deserves look like? What is just? Is it the kind of justice which is usually thought of as appropriate in society? Even in many civilized countries people think that a murderer like Cain deserves the death penalty. Is it permissible to derive the 'human' image of God's righteousness and justice from such ideas among us 'humans'? Or is it God who defines what is 'truly human' (cf. Chapter 2)? Again, teachers are well advised first to ask their pupils what they have in mind when they hear or speak about justice.

In an RE lesson about Matthew 18: 23–35 with children aged 10–12, as part of an older research project conducted by G. Stachel (1974), the issue of forgiving played a crucial role.

'Then Peter came and said to him, "Lord, if another member of the church sins against me, how often should I forgive? As many as seven times?" Jesus said to him, "Not seven times, but I tell you, seventy times seven"' (vv. 21–2). The following parable told by Jesus is about a slave who owed the king an extremely large sum of money ('ten thousand talents') (v. 24). As he could not pay, he fell on his knees and prayed for mercy, and the king 'released him and forgave him the debt' (v. 27). The same slave came upon one of his fellow-slaves who owed him a small sum ('a hundred denarii'); 'seizing him by the throat, he said, "Pay what you owe"' (v. 28). The fellow-slave fell down as he had before and pleaded with him, but he refused to release him and to forgive the debt; he threw him into prison (v. 30).

In the preceding lesson the teacher had collected the children's notions about justice taken from their everyday experiences. Now, at the beginning of the new lesson on the parable, he asked his students to sum up what they had remembered. This preparatory step was to prepare for the confrontation between the biblical answer and their own ideas. The children recollected the following views.

- For one child retaliation was the only reply, the form of which was left open.
- One boy proposed a balance between rewarding the good and punishing the bad. His idea of justice seemed to approximate an equal distribution (*iustitia distributiva*).
- A girl emphasized a different treatment such that social status and income differences would be taken into account. Her notion of justice made her vote for punishing with 'individual consideration', justice as equity (*equitas*), which allows unequal punishments.
- The children revealed a rather broad spectrum of views. It was Verena who alone in the class reflected on the sad consequences of an incessant reciprocity in the form of unmitigated retaliation. She pleaded for a merciful interruption of the spiral of violence, irrespective of whether it was illegal or legal. 'If someone has killed another person, you can't simply go killing again. That is a never-ending chain . . . which would never come to an end.'

Verena envisages an escalating spiral of violence that for her will never come to a peaceful end. Here a new perspective is introduced that contrasts with the principle of proportional punishment as such. Verena does not explain her opinion. Maybe she would concede a certain degree of punishment, but she clearly shrinks from taking another person's life, even if it were to be executed in the name of the law. She would understand God in our Old Testament story while I suppose the majority of the class would be less ready, or not ready at all, to accept God's weak indulgence.

In line with the basic educational principles of this book, teachers would do well to ask their pupils to find out for themselves what is just. I would also suggest stopping telling the story of Cain and Abel after verse 8, and asking the group how they would react. Collect the answers and discuss their substantive moral before you continue. The story is a provocation. Why does God not impose proportional judgement? Why is he so soft on Cain? Or the teacher might interrupt after verses 13 and 14.

God's Life-preserving 'Not so!'

'Cain said to the LORD, "My punishment is greater than I can bear! You have driven me away from the soil, and I shall be hidden from your face; I shall be a fugitive and a wanderer on the earth, and anyone who meets me may kill me"' (Gen. 4: 13–14).

Cain has spoiled the soil: Abel's blood cries out 'from the soil'. Now he is driven away from it. Cain has destroyed human community; now he is going to lose community himself. He who has taken life must be afraid of his own life being taken away. Cain has acted against God; therefore he is worried by the prospect of 'being hidden from God's face'. Doesn't he deserve it? Isn't it just? How many in our world would agree. But the Lord said, 'Not so!' '"Not so! whoever kills Cain will suffer a sevenfold vengeance." And the Lord put a mark on Cain, so that no one who came upon him would kill him' (Gen. 4: 15–16).

God speaks his life-preserving 'Not so!' – hereby interrupting the usual human schemes of retaliation as Verena wanted. The 'human' image of God is different from the ways in which 'human' beings are accustomed to think. Ours is to comply with moral standards, God's is to reveal undeserved grace and to be satisfied with a lenient punishment. For Eberhard Jüngel the story of Cain and Abel throws a first light on God's deepest intention, 'the justification of the sinner' (Jüngel 1998: 7–11).

God keeps loving his creation from the very beginning until the day when he again will be 'all in all' (1 Cor. 15: 28). His will is directed to the preservation and renewal of life in eternal fullness. The emerging of God's different humanity – God's shalom as peace through justice as it is meant as all-embracing saving reconciliation – will next be pursued in the Psalms with the cry for justice of those who suffer and, through the mouth of the prophets, with the promise of God's coming messianic kingdom of peace and justice (Chapter 4).

In Jesus' preaching this 'Kingdom of God' broke forth as a visible reality which could be experienced together with him, in his actions and parables, in his life and his death, until the wonder of Easter beginning in a garden ('The new creation, like the old, begins in a garden', Douglas Webster, as quoted in Slee 1990) suddenly made it clear to the disciples that it was Jesus *himself* who embodied God's righteousness, justice and peace as living ('resurrected') truth (see Chapter 7). The miracle was to take place in each of them individually, as was to happen with unexpected force in the life of Paul, where God's quite different, surprising way of reconciliation, in absolute contrast to Paul's firm convictions as a ruthless persecutor, was to create a biographical breakdown and a revolution that led to a message of hope for the whole world (1 Cor. 15: 20–28) (cf. Chapter 8).

Cain's crime was not a sudden act, but a deliberate one. He cannot argue that he did not know about the wrongness of his deed, for he had been told that it would be 'sin' (Gen. 4: 7). Abel was his own brother at that. The more one realizes these facts, the more odd and paradoxical God's subsequent action is. He strongly warns those who might take the opportunity to kill the homeless fugitive, and he puts a mark on Cain for the purpose of protection!

A crucial task of spiritual Christian renewal and of Christian education in schools, churches and amongst the public is to present the true image of the biblical God. We recall the fourth dimension of elementarization which deals with 'elementary truths'. From the very onset of the biblical tradition God appears as the Lord of life and the incarnation of love. His intentions are directed to peace in the form of a reconciled world.

Lamech and the Demon of Retaliation

One of Cain's descendants is Lamech. He took two wives, Adah and Zillah. The Bible has handed down a song of Lamech,

> Adah and Zillah, hear my voice;
> you wives of Lamech, listen to what I say:
> I have killed a man for wounding me,
> a young man for striking me:
> If Cain is avenged sevenfold,
> truly Lamech seventy-sevenfold.
>
> (Gen. 4: 23–4)

In sharp contrast to God's intentions recorded just before, a certain Lamech dares to play God's role in a strongly distorted form. God's role as creator and protector of life is usurped by Lamech. The results are disastrous. In his hands the rules of 'justice' become instruments of blatant, arbitrary injustice. They no longer even offer an equal balancing of proportional rewards and punishments as a matter of symmetry, let alone reflecting any spirit of mercy. No memory is left of God's protection of life. Vengeance – not justice – is extended to the extreme, retaliation exercised beyond any limits – a matter of sheer asymmetry. (On the problem of symmetrical or asymmetrical violent reactions see in the context of theories of cooperation, Chapter 10, pp. 177–8). A man is slain by Lamech for nothing but a wound; a young man who has only struck him is robbed of his life. The 'sevenfold' is multiplied to 'seventy-sevenfold'. Many years later Jesus will respond to Peter's question, 'How often should I forgive? As many as seven times?' with the words 'Not seven times, but seventy times seven' (Matt. 18: 21–2), opposing the multiplication of revenge with the multiplication of forgiveness.

Between the story of Cain and Abel and Lamech's song we hear about the growth of civilization, about towns which were founded, with urban professions. Some further chapters later the legend of the city of Babel is recorded, speaking about 'a tower with a top in the heavens to let us make a name of ourselves' (Gen. 11: 4). In between, the story of Noah is told (Gen. 6–9). This composition records a sinful deterioration. 'The earth was corrupt in God's sight and filled with violence' (Gen. 6: 11). 'The crime rate was skyrocketing' (Dershowitz 2000: 58).

In the eyes of the Swedish author Ellen Key the twentieth century would become a 'century of the child', expressing human care of the weakest, the most innocent and most creative. In fact it turned out to be the century of the most widespread mass-killing in human history with no mercy for the weakest, neither for the old nor for children. Without doubt in the course of time the human species has learnt a lot about humanity, but unfortunately not enough to provide effective peace, justice and reconciliation.

Cain Looking for Who He was Before He Became the War – a Story about the Story

> When War had
> already reached
> a high age –
>
> it always
> had existed,
> the people said –
>
> the mighty in the world
> became afraid of
> the day when it might be
> all up with War.
>
> So they met,
> friends and enemies,
> consulting together
> what to do.
>
> However different
> their opinions were,
> in one thing they agreed:
>
> Without War
> We cannot manage.

With these verses a moving story of timeless relevance begins, written by Irmela Wendt and fascinatingly illustrated by Antoni Boratyński (1991; the extracts are translated by the author; the English version, 1995, is a very free translation). It was published for use in religious education in schools and churches on the subject of War and Peace (see also the working map, Hinnecke 2000). Again and again the mighty had been devising new plans, systems and most of all weapons to keep War running by rejuvenating him. War was very pleased with this, until one day he was bothered by the strange idea that before he had become War he might have been someone else. But however much he pondered upon it, he could not remember who he had been.

Therefore he asked for leave, and wandered back through time right down to its origins in the remote past.

> He let the clock
> run backwards
> and left behind
> the missiles,
> the bombs,
> the tactical aircraft,
> the tanks,
> the machine-guns,
> the motors.

Even when he had hurried back through many millennia and had returned to using the bow and arrow, and eventually even throwing a stone with his bare hand, he still did not know who he was before he became War.

One day he met a man. Never before had he been afraid of anyone, but now a hot shudder shot through him.

> 'Who are you?' War shouted.
> The stranger did not answer,
> but came nearer.
> 'Who are you?'
> War shouted again.
> 'Who are you?'
> echoed the stranger.
> It sounded like an empty echo,
> and War became afraid of his own voice.
> He dropped stone and club
> and stood up
> with staggering knees.
>
> The stranger
> had now come so close
> that each of them could feel the other's
> breath.
>
> 'Who are you?'
> War asked for the third time.
>
> 'Who you were!'
> the other answered.
>
> 'And your name?'
> War asked lowly,
> 'I don't remember your name.'
> But the other kept silent.
>
> They walked across the heath,
> the one beside the other,
> and no word passed their lips.

Fog was hanging in the air
touching the grass
and the flowers, and when it lifted,
a man was lying,
and his blood
had soaked
the soil
and the flowers
red.

'Abel! my brother!'
War cried.
He fell on his knees,
was no longer War,
was who he was,
was brother,
was Cain,
was no longer strange to himself.

Tears
unwept for millennia,
poured down like rain
weeping away all the gore.
And the brother Abel stood up.

Afterwards the two collected dry brushwood and made a fire. They prepared a meal and Cain related what he had experienced among the mighty in the world. Then Abel said:

At the time when everything began,
each of us was standing alone by his fire.
If we had given our offerings together,
you would not have slain me.
And everything else
that happened afterwards
would not have happened in the world.

The story ends with a funeral. The mighty had waited in vain for War's return. As they thought that the old man must have died, they prepared a huge coffin and filled it with all the things War had liked most – tanks, tactical aircraft, machine-guns, missiles, also medals and decorations, everything nicely scrapped so that there was room for a lot of it. Then the funeral procession set out, the mighty political leaders ahead, followed by the generals, silent and with sad faces, after them the people – and they were merry.

At the end they gathered
around a man
who called himself brother,
he told
how the War was redeemed.

Chapter 4

God and the Cry for Justice in the Psalms and Prophets

God and Justice – a Public Issue

Martin Luther called the Psalms 'the little Bible', because they contain the whole of the Bible in sum, and he believed that the Holy Spirit had assisted with the composition. We use the Book of Psalms in public worship and as a book of personal prayer and meditation. We do the latter because the Psalms speak the language of the heart in a moving non-academic spirituality. In this chapter we shall show that they can also play an important role as part of the curriculum of religious education with children in exploring roads to peace through justice.

The Psalms sound the notes of complaining to God and praying to him, of thanking him and praising his goodness. In the Psalms the faithful remind God also of his promises by insistently crying to him for help.

> To you they cried; and were saved.
> (Ps. 22: 5)

> O Lord my God, I cried to you for help,
> and you have healed me.
> (Ps. 30: 2)

> When the righteous cry for help,
> the Lord hears,
> and rescues them from all their troubles.
> (Ps. 34: 17)

In other cases all the crying seems to be in vain:

> I am weary with my crying;
> my throat is parched.
> My eyes grow dim
> with waiting for my God.
> (Ps. 69: 3)

> O Lord, how long shall I cry for help,
> and you will not listen?
> Or cry to you 'Violence!'
> and you will not save?
>
> (Hab. 1: 2)

The issues raised in the Psalms and in the books of the prophets are misery and suffering occasioned by violence and injustice.

> Destruction and violence are
> before me;
> strife and contention arise.
> So the law becomes slack
> and justice never prevails.
> (Hab. 1: 3–4)

All expectations are focused in the cry for God's justice and righteousness:

> In you, O Lord, I take refuge;
> let me never be put to shame.
> In your righteousness deliver me and rescue me.
> (Ps. 71: 1–2)

In this chapter the relation between peace and justice is the outstanding new perspective, following on from that of violence and murder as the most obvious opposites of peace in the previous chapter. Unjust human relationships are less easily identified as factors frustrating peace, but very often social injustice is the main root of growing and lasting conflicts. From an educational perspective we will again apply the approach of elementarization, beginning with the 'elementary structures' of justice.

Justice means, first, legal justice, second, social justice, third, a proportioned balance in respect of life and fate, good and evil. In the biblical tradition the first two aspects are mostly linked and dealt with together. The first aspect relates to honest application of the law in contrast to judges who are corrupt and partial in court. In this legal field justice aims at *fair judgement*: 'How long will you judge unjustly and show partiality to the wicked?' (Ps. 82: 2). What is expected instead is 'a just cause' (Ps. 17: 1), 'to judge people fairly' (Ps. 58: 1).

Another concern is justice as economic fairness and basic subsistence for everyone in contrast to exploitation of the poor and needy; now justice stands for *fair sharing*: 'May God defend the cause of the poor of the people, give deliverance to the needy and crush the oppressor' (Ps. 72: 4).

In the Middle Ages the classical Christian ethic was embodied in the two interrelated values of pax and iustitia. The same connection is found in the Psalms. In awaiting God like a political ruler the days of his coming kingdom are praised with the words:

> In his days may righteousness
> flourish
> and peace abound, until the
> moon is no more.
> (Ps. 72: 7)

> Righteousness and peace will kiss
> each other.
> (Ps. 85: 10)

God's justice or righteousness is the fundamental source of peace, of his all-embracing 'shalom'. Although both English translations of the Hebrew term(s) 'saedaeq/sedaqa' ('justice' and 'righteousness') are adequate, they are semantically not identical. The term 'justice', the verb 'to judge' and the noun 'judgement' point to the forensic field describing God as a judge who presides over a legal court; the translations focus on his *just acting*. The adjective 'righteous' and the noun 'righteousness' are broader in meaning, covering the basic attitude underlying God's acts of judging; they mean his *just being*. Now the translations point at the very characteristics of his nature: God's just judgements are rooted in his righteousness, which represents his essential divinity. The theological and educational task is to prevent the isolation of the purely forensic aspect.

His righteousness is his truth, and God is fervently urged to manifest himself as truth. To reveal himself in his divinity, majesty and holiness is nothing more than the relevation of his justice. When the wicked as the embodiment of injustice boast of their deeds and of escaping God's punishment, God's very existence is at stake. Is his truth a self-deception, a lie?

> In the pride of their countenance
> the wicked say
> 'God will not seek it out',
> all their thoughts are,
> 'There is no God'.
>
> (Ps. 10: 4)

Two features are remarkable. First, the issue of God is basically not a moral issue of values; the presence or absence of justice and peace is an ontological issue of being or nothingness. Second, if the 'wicked' will triumph in the matters at stake, namely justice and peace, they are more than just evildoers. In 'renouncing the LORD' (cf. Ps. 10: 3) they are people without God which means that they stand for a universe without meaning at all. Here the third semantic aspect of justice comes into sight; the basic truth of the universe as such is being questioned. This possible ontological crisis is hinted at in the words,

> If the foundations are destroyed,
> what can the righteous do?
>
> (Ps. 11: 3)

Through this last aspect (we will come back to it later) the issue of justice becomes a question of religious certitude (and, therefore, religious education) which transcends the question of morality (and moral education). Nevertheless, the encompassing religious truth of the biblical God is concrete and needs to become visible in everyday life; therefore, the religious issue implies moral consequences (and still today moral education on biblical grounds). In the Psalms and elsewhere, the absence of God is the source of painful lament again and again. In the eyes of the Old Testament believers God will have to take the side of the sick, poor, oppressed and suffering. Hence, notwithstanding the distinction made between the moral and the religious dimension, the close link between the religious and the moral state of affairs is also true, as all biblical texts and our own experience of faith prove.

The language of the prophets and the Psalms is not vague but is precise in naming the offenders who resist God's will and in proclaiming hope for those in need. Biblical teaching and learning in churches and schools has also to be precise. It is not permissible timidly to draw a veil over the moral disasters of our wicked planet. It is necessary to face up to the brokenness of human nature in both its moral and religious foundations. 'God's righteousness' consists of a soteriological message of salvation which later in the New Testament was to be conceptualized in the doctrine of 'justification' (see Paul, Chapter 8), and implies a moral Christian commitment. Reviewing the course of our analysis so far, it is now imperative to add these perspectives to those of the preceding chapter.

God's revelation is taking place in time and space, in short, in history. The educational tasks of childhood and adolescence and the spiritual paths to religious and moral maturity in adulthood cannot appropriately be defined by a timeless spirituality or, even less, by a privatized, self-content, religious individualism added to the many other forms of esoteric escapism apparent today. Positively speaking, Christians who have experienced the biblical tradition in its moral human potential to promote a just and peaceful society are called to be present in public life.

Spheres of Relevance: Private, Political, Public, Global

There are two main possible patterns for regulating the relationships between religion and the state or, more generally, between religion and public life. These patterns may be typified by the two classical historical patterns in the western world.

The first is a *state church system*, which in the past used to exert a strong political influence on the whole of society. This system has become obsolete because of its negative effects for both sides: it neglects plurality in society and it robs the church of its freedom. Where it still exists, it has been considerably modified in order to meet the standards of liberal democracy. The opposite pattern is a *separation of church* and *state* and of other religious organizations from the state, with the possible negative consequence of a public marginalization of religion. This can occur if the separation is reinforced by an attitude of hostiliy to religion and is accompanied by a rigid privatization of religion.

On the one hand, a certain limitation of religion to the 'private sphere' is based on sound reasoning, for the 'sphere of polity' has to be independent of any religious bias and of pressures from religious organizations, as well as itself refraining from political interference with religions. According to political theory, the modern state has to restrict itself to religious neutrality by providing a secular legal frame of rights that leaves personal religious preference to individuals and to religious communities.

However, on the other hand, this so-called 'negative religious freedom' as a right of the individual who is to be protected against (hence 'negative' freedom) governmental authorities does not reasonably exclude the so-called 'positive religious freedom' which allows for promoting religious life in both the private *and* the public sphere alike. It makes no sense to debar religions from the dynamics of public life as a matter of principle. The effect might easily be what Richard John Neuhaus in his book on religion and democracy in America has called 'the naked public square' (1984), a decay of the discourse on common public affairs.

The distinction between the 'sphere of the polity' and the 'public sphere' (Neuhaus 1984: 141) helps to clarify the issue. While the former, as the sphere of constitutional law and political administration, is not allowed to favour specific religions, or to permit them unduly to influence the democratic institutions which are to serve all citizens, since privileges granted to one religion alone might harm the rights of others, the sphere of public affairs needs the joint efforts of all social groups to explore the common good. The public sphere ought to link political and moral reason on behalf of social justice and peace within our own society and also globally. This view is supported by P. J. Palmer,

> When we remove faith from public discourse, the dialogue stops, and society is forced to find its common ground elsewhere. The ground it finds may be common, but it will be necessarily lower ground than that provided by the great religious traditions. The public expression of great religious truths gives us our best chance to find the framework of love and justice within which true pluralism can thrive. Perhaps our problem goes deeper still. Perhaps we resist true public worship because worship in private allows us to emphasize that which makes us different, that which divides us, rather than that which unites. In private, in the company of 'our kind', we can laud our uniqueness and even denigrate others without being checked against reality, without being called to account. But public expression is accountable. Under the pressure of accountability religious discourse may be forced to reach for the essentials which unite us.
>
> (Palmer 1981: 138)

The Psalms are texts not only for individual prayer, but also for worship, for congregational and for 'public worship', as Palmer urges in favour of the contribution of Christians to 'the renewal of America's public life' in his book *The Company of Strangers*. Although the language of the Psalms is that of the individual crying to God, its content transcends individual religious needs. Lack of justice is a public scandal, the vision of 'shalom', of all-embracing peace, is a common good. This will become immediately evident by linking the Psalms to the message of Old Testament prophets like Isaiah and Jeremiah, Amos, Micah and Habakkuk: the last we quoted above, envisaging the consequences of a lack of public justice: 'the law becomes slack'.

We have distinguished three spheres of relevance: (1) the individual spiritual meaning of the Psalms and the prophets ('the private sphere'); (2) their public importance for the welfare of all (the public sphere); and (3), more indirectly, the possible influence of the prophetic ethos on the form of 'good governance', that is, the constitutional relevance in 'the sphere of the polity' (R. J. Neuhaus). Surprisingly enough, a fourth sphere of relevance can be added, namely in respect of the biblical contribution to a peaceful and just global community; we call it the sphere of international politics and global ethics.

In the eighth century BCE, the prophet Amos accused several nations neighbouring Israel of sinful 'transgressions' against God's will, drawing on norms of behaviour that can be regarded as a transnational moral code. Amos described several 'covenants' under which God had led some of those nations under his guidance as he had led Israel. This view permitted the limitations of a separate and closed moral 'internal solidarity' (*Binnensolidarität*) to be overcome, and can be identified, according to the Jewish philosopher Micha Brumlik, as a preliminary pre-modern step towards a Law of Nations (Brumlik 1999: 19), at least for the Canaanite–North-Semitic cultural sphere (p. 14).

> 'O people of Israel', says the LORD.
> 'Did I not bring Israel up from the land of Egypt,
> and the Philistines from Caphtor
> and the Arameans from Kir?'
>
> (Amos 9: 7)

With these 'covenants' as divine governance, including, as well as Israel, Egypt, the Philistines and the Arameans, a broader moral law comes into view which can be interpreted in theological terms as reflecting the universal character of God's care. It consists of six moral prescriptions against severe phenomena of injustice, thus reflecting God's justice.

> Thus says the LORD:
> For three transgressions of Damascus,
> and for four, I will not revoke the punishment;
> because they have threshed Gilead with
> threshing sledges of iron
> . . .
> For three transgressions of Gaza,
> and for four, I will not revoke the punishment,
> because they carried into exile
> entire communities,
> to hand them over to Edom.
>
> (Amos 1: 3, 6)

We need not quote all the relevant verses. In the name of the Lord Amos forbids (cf. Brumlik 1999: 15):

- totally destroying the agricultural infrastructure of a country (Amos 1: 3)
- enslaving and deporting whole communities (Amos 1: 6)
- waging an implacable civil war (Amos 1: 11)
- ripping open pregnant women in order to enlarge one's own territory (Amos 1: 13)
- and dishonouring a corpse, in particular of foreign rulers (Amos 2:1)

Israel is accused of further crimes of injustice with the famous verses,

> because they sell the righteous for silver,
> and the needy for a pair of sandals,
> they who trample the head of the poor
> into the dust of the earth,
> and push the afflicted out of the way,
> father and son go into the same girl.
>
> (Amos 2: 6–7)

Although the prophets could not yet think of the modern notion of individual human rights, the moral consciousness of Israel has became universalized (Crüsemann 1992).

Their approach was different and less abstract in that it started from both the social integrity of the community as a whole, which is based in mutual (reciprocal) solidarity, and from the overall vision of the preservation and cultivation of life, including animals and plants. God is believed in as the creator and Lord of life. Thus, what we are about to explore in this chapter about the notion of justice is linked to the previous chapter's emphasis on protecting life against violence and devastating war.

Moreover, the warning against destroying agricultural infrastructure also throws light on our practice of wasting the life of animals and wasting natural resources. The link between human beings and animals is deeply distorted. The balance between humankind's needs in the face of hunger and starvation, on the one hand, and a just sharing and caring, on the other hand, gives way to a growing social disjuncture as well as to a dichotomy in nature. We have completely lost sight of the interrelationship between animals and humans as partners within a common creation.

Lamenting, Protesting, Praying, Thanking

For the purpose of religious education the Psalms should not be dealt with each in their entirety, except for some famous ones like Psalm 23 or Psalm 103. What counts educationally is to respond to their impressive language and content in a corresponding language which allows them to resonate in pupils' hearts and minds. The language of the Psalms is their best teacher.

Again the 'elementarization' approach (see Chapter 3) can help us to introduce the texts and to open up their meaning. While in the first section of this chapter our point of departure was a look at elementary definitions and categories of justice, let us now illustrate what 'the cry for justice' and 'God's justice' are about by highlighting some Psalms themselves. The focus shifts now to the way the 'elementary structures' of the Psalms relate to 'elementary (faith) experiences' as their living background. The following recurrent themes are mostly selected from Psalms 7, 10 and 13.

(1) The feeling of the absence of God is a general heavy burden and temptation.

> Why, O Lord, do you stand far off?
> Why do you hide yourself
> in times of trouble?
> (Ps. 10: 1)

> How long, O Lord, will you
> forget me forever?
> (Ps. 13: 1)

The absence of God is felt in time ('you forget me forever') and space ('you stand far off'). The modern mind is overwhelmed by the vastness and autonomy of the universe which ever since the so-called Big Bang has expanded at an ever increasing speed, obeying, as it seems, laws of its own. Three hundred and fifty years ago the Protestant Moravian bishop, theologian and philosopher John Amos Comenius (1592–1670) interpreted this movement as a curve, starting as a centrifugal process in the beginning of creation and, since Christ's resurrection as the first act of a new creation, as a centripetal one back to God. The Psalmists do not yet elaborate this eschatological perspective. They are expecting God's interventions in their present time, here and now.

The beginnings of the Psalms vary. Often they start with a description of utter loneliness. Children and adolescents can share this feeling. We know about the childhood anxieties of losing the way, being left alone in the house or in the dark, being without someone to keep you company as daylight turns to night, sitting beside your bed for a while. Adolescents feel their loneliness differently, more self-reflectively, sometimes nourishing thoughts of suicide.

The special approach in RE of linking the experiences in religious traditions to analogies today has been called the 'correlation' approach (a term coined in Catholic religious education in Germany). It remains controversial. In my view, one element concerning the similarity of basic human experiences throughout the ages as a precondition of understanding is valid. But whether children can actually realize the full impact of a situation of 'God-darkness' (*Gottesfinsternis*, Martin Buber) is questionable. There is some empirical research about 10-year-old boys and girls already seriously doubting whether God exists at all, but we do not know enough about what that really means to them.

(2) The second recurrent underlying theme in the Psalms is deep distress and growing anger because of the blatant injustice that casts a dark shadow upon God in all the cases where he does not intervene. His apparent absence seems to allow the wicked to triumph and encourage a denial of his very existence.

(3) Thus, understandably, the third elementary theme in the Psalms is thoughts of revenge creeping up in the heart, or at least the expectation of a just punishment of the wicked, so that 'their mischief returns upon their own heads' (Ps. 7: 16).

(4) These feelings are the stronger the more one regards oneself as innocent. God is fervently asked to acknowledge one's own righteousness.

> O let the evil of the wicked
> come to an end,
> but establish the righteous!
> (Ps. 7: 9)

(5) Contrary to what might normally be expected, the theologically important fifth feature leaves the restoration of justice to God alone, for his is this role everywhere on earth and in the heavens. It is in this line of tradition that Jesus will see the Kingdom of God being sent to the poor who regard themselves in need of God. The longing for 'establishing' the righteous has little to do with self-justification.

> The LORD judges the peoples.
> (Ps. 7: 8)

> . . . take it into your hands,
> the helpless commit themselves to you.
> (Ps. 10: 14)

He is 'the Most High' (Ps. 7: 17), a statement that has to be taken literally, for as judge God will be sitting on his throne in the heavens. Therefore he is summoned to 'rise',

> Rise up, O LORD; O LORD, lift up
> your hand,
> do not forget the oppressed.
>
> (Ps. 10: 12)

(6) Surprisingly enough the urgent appeals to God are phrased in the form of an insistent reminder, sometimes in a blaming tone. God is accused of not having intervened and, as it seems, having forgotten his people. He is ironically addressed, 'But you do see!' ('don't you?') (Ps. 10: 14).

(7) The last elementary theme in this type of Psalm, which usually begins with deep lament, is gratitude and praise of God's righteousness and justice. Psalm 7 concludes with the words

> I will give to the LORD the thanks
> due to his righteousness,
> and sing praise to the name of
> the LORD, the Most High.
>
> (Ps. 7: 17)

Psalm 10 concludes with unbroken confidence in God despite all oppression and terror (vv. 17–18).

Justice – a Category of Universal Order

What is the deepest motivation for the longing for justice in human history? As has already been pointed out, the category of justice refers to the realm of law and political order (just judging), to economic conditions of livelihood and survival (just sharing), and to the general meaning of the cosmos (just being). The first two aspects are still burning issues today. We meet countries with a corrupt system of law and crippling poverty, people without enough food and shelter, lacking clean air and water, inadequate health services and sparse care for the aged. The gap between rich and poor countries has widened. A country may be deemed to be an unjust system if the following two aspects together generate general misery: the lack of a principle of equality both in respect of at least a relatively fair balance of the conditions of social life, and in justice in court. Hence, justice is a public affair of the highest order (see pp. 45–51). What about the third, ontological dimension of justice? What does it mean? What is the 'elementary experience' behind the texts in this respect? Is this still a relevant question today?

The original pattern is found in Ancient Egypt as the idea of a just cosmic balance, expressed at that time by the term *ma'at*. In all ancient cultures of the Middle East, not only in Egypt,

> justice was a central term beyond the juridical sphere aimed at the centre of political and social life and thinking as such. Terms like ma'at in Egyptian, kittu and mīšaru in Akkadian, ṣaedaeq/ṣedāqâ in Hebrew, and dikaiosyne and themis in Greek, were related to the social, political, and cosmic contexts. What they have in common is that they always also imply the world-order: just actions are actions in accordance with the meaning inherent in the world.
>
> (Janowski 1999: 220)

If so, the phenomena of injustice in life erode nothing less than belief in the foundations of the whole universe, so that the question already raised above must be repeated, 'If the foundations are destroyed, what can the righteous do?' (Ps. 11: 3).

Bargaining and Reciprocity

The background expectation of the Psalms is belief in God as the final guarantee of the just cosmic order of the universe. Its logic requires that the righteous are rewarded and the wicked punished; 'the mystery of lawlessness' in humankind (2 Thess. 2: 7) needs a final answer. In crying to the Lord for justice believers want God not only to intervene on the moral level, but to overcome wickedness and to restore the order of the world on the ontological level. Old Testament theology discusses this issue as the concept of a correspondence between 'doing' and 'faring' (*Tun-Ergehen-Zusammenhang*); 'good deeds' are to be followed by 'faring well', 'bad deeds' by 'faring badly'. 'The reward of a person who does [acts], lies in that something is being done for him. This [correlation] God holds to be ma'at.' This inscription on a stele in honour of King Neferhotep in the period of the Middle Kingdom (13th dynasty, *c.* 1700 BCE) sums up the principle: what a person does, is done to him in return. This law of reciprocity becomes effective 'by virtue of the "communicative structure" of the world', into which people expose themselves in speaking and acting, as the German Egyptologist Jan Assmann has put it (Assmann 1990; cf. Janowski 1999: 168).

At the bottom of reciprocity lies the idea of justice, on the one hand, concerning the wicked and lawless, on the other hand, concerning the victims; their sufferings are ridiculed if they are left without atonement. For this purpose, the pattern of reciprocal thinking, which is widespread in all religions from very early on, has generated numerous rituals in order to reconcile the deities who are regarded as the guarantors of the cosmic order as a just balance. In this context the idea of a Last Judgement after death was to gain a prominent place; it was developed in Ancient Egypt.

The final status of the dead was believed to depend on the outcome of a test before a court, with an actual balance and a pair of scales in the room. The dead person was accused of his or her sins. In a later description, the dead person's heart as the symbol of his or her conscience was put on the one scale, while ma'at, the divine universal justice, was symbolized and put on the other scale. Each lie would make the scale with the heart on it dip deeper (Janowski 1999: 223, 227).

In the more recent history of humankind religions differ in many respects, but by and large we usually still come across the pattern of reciprocity. It seems to be repeated in ontogenetic development, where the Swiss psychologist Fritz Oser has identified and named stage 2 of the development of religious reasoning as the *do ut des* stage (Oser and Gmünder 1984). Some years previously Lawrence Kohlberg described the same pattern in moral development. It may be assumed that the idea of possible bargaining with the deities was rooted experientially in the economic sphere, being applied from there to the image of weighing in the balance morally and religiously.

Bargaining in terms of reciprocity has been observed in Chapter 3 when we looked at children's notions of justice. The dominant idea was that of equal distribution; everyone earns what he deserves in a strict symmetry. In adulthood such symmetrical thinking is not necessarily replaced by more mature patterns. It can survive as a lifelong cognitive means of striving for a just equilibrium. People who unexpectedly fall heavily ill will often ask, 'What have I done to deserve this?' 'Am I responsible for my illness?' Other people try to pay in advance with 'good works' to make sure that God will repay them with his goodness later, in situations of emergency.

An eloquent example is the description of the life of Millie by J. W. Fowler (1981), with her instructive 'commitments to reciprocity and fairness in God's dealing with humans'. Millie is dealing with God in a sort of give and take, thereby illustrating the characteristic structure of Kohlberg's stage 2 (p. 142). Another woman, a Mrs W., in her fifties, also 'constructs her understanding of God and the world in terms of reciprocity. Daily, or even hourly prayers and acts of praise enable her to "put money in the bank" – to store up God's good favor against times when special help or forgiveness may be needed' (pp. 147–9).

In the New Testament, when seeing a man blind from birth the disciples ask Jesus, 'Rabbi, who sinned, this man or his parents, that he was born blind?' (John 9: 1–3). Jesus replies: 'Neither this man nor his parents sinned' (ibid.). Jesus overcomes the pattern of reciprocal 'bargaining' and 'balancing'.

Towards the end of the Old Testament traditions, a similar lesson is given Job's friends who, according to the author, fail in God's eyes with their reciprocal assumptions. They were looking for the sins through which Job must have deserved his misery. There are also some psalmists who discard the pattern of bargaining because they know about God's free grace, although they remind God of their righteousness (see pp. 52–3).

Today belief in a personal God has declined, in particular amongst younger people. To a certain degree it is replaced by a more or less vague belief in 'higher powers' or a 'higher destiny' (see the representative data in Jörns 1997: 51, 64). However these transcendent powers might be conceived, they mirror the old need for a balanced cosmos, for a world in just equilibrium, for the chance to 'bargain' with fate.

God's Justice as His Caring Faithfulness – a Community of Mutual Solidarity

'To care for justice' – this continuing human longing was answered by prophets like Amos by prefiguring transnational and anti-imperialistic moral norms (see pp. 49–51). Amos regarded God's will as being directed to care for life as such. Today we are faced afresh with the need to preserve the very basis of life on our globe. The Jewish philosopher Hans Jonas has proclaimed the basic moral rule 'that life may exist and be maintained as such' (Jonas 1997). This moral principle of 'global survival' is linked to the other principle of caring for 'a good life'. In Old Testament times a good life was envisaged as a life of all-embracing justice, and in Egypt and Ancient Israel it meant more than a mere fair sharing of goods and the survival of the poor. These particular goals needed as their foundation a vision of society as a whole, a quasi-theoretical concept that enabled a just practice of life. According to Jan Assmann (1990: 58, 283) such a vision existed as 'connective justice' in a community of mutual solidarity.

In Israel the common solidarity was rooted in God's 'covenant' with his people, understood as a lifelong relation of mutual obligation. Therefore prayers reminded God of his self-obligation as they remembered Israel's obligation in return (cf. Hosea).

Far from being an abstract idea justice was a matter of personal and collective relationship between the living God and his concrete people. The story of God's covenants goes back to the covenant with Noah, determining the integrity of nature and humankind as a whole, followed by the covenant of Sinai as the starting point of the preservation of Israel in particular, and later by the renewal of creation itself through Jesus' coming. He became the first new-born being. With him and through him the promise of the never forgotten restoration of the whole creation set in (see Paul's summary at the end of the First Letter to the Corinthians, 1 Cor. 15: 20–28). The universal process of salvation encompasses the 'justification' of humans (see Paul's letters to the Galatians and the Romans; Chapter 8), as well as of animals and all other life, for until now 'the whole creation is . . . groaning in labour pains' (Rom. 8: 22). From the beginning until the end of time, according to Christian belief, God's intentions are directed to proving and implementing his righteousness as everlasting caring and faithfulness.

In the light of this general perspective the theological understanding of God as 'judge' needs a basic reinterpretation. When the poor and oppressed in the Psalms cry for the judgement of the Lord, they cry for a 'saving judgement' as proof of God's righteousness, a *'saving* justice', not a condemning one (Janowski 1999: 220). The former image of the God of the Old Testament as a fierce God of vengeance and retaliation is wrong. It has produced terrible religious prejudices against the Jewish people. The God of the Hebrew Bible (the Old Testament) and of the New Testament is one and the same as the Lord and protector of life, individually and socially, locally and globally.

But what about the wicked and lawless and their victims whose blood 'cries out' like Abel's? Shouldn't there have been an answer to their prayers so that they were not in vain? Notwithstanding God's basic intention to save, or, theologically more precise, just because of it, Israel's relationship to God in the form of a covenant necessitated, indeed, a remaining emphasis also on a 'saving *justice'*. God's paradoxical kindness could not mean to let injustice triumph, to make a fool of the victims before the world and to turn the idea of justice into an empty word. Thus, Israel 'could not easily endure without a world to come in which God could keep His promises out of the view of humankind' (Dershowitz 2000: 238) as a lasting source of hope. God's love and justice belong together. We shall come back to this in the light of the New Testament (see Chapter 7 on Jesus' death).

Discovering the Psalms with Children

How can the traditions of faith experiences in the Psalms and the prophets be opened up to the younger generation of today? In the preceding sections we have been dealing with the 'elementary structures' of our issue (justice *and* God – God *as* justice), in conjunction with 'elementary experiences' in the past (Ancient Israel, Egypt), with only a few hints at the moral and religious situation today. What about the 'elementary accesses' that open up understanding in children and adolescents? And what about the 'elementary truth claims' that are at stake?

It is the great merit of Ingo Baldermann to have experimented very successfully for many years in the field of religious education based on the Bible, with special emphasis on the Psalms (summarizing Baldermann 1996). His specific interest was in introducing the Psalms to young children, to make them familiar with biblical language in general. His findings are based in on a sort of qualitative classroom research in religious education in schools.

Like many religious educators Baldermann wondered whether children can make personal contact with the Bible which as a document of faith was written for and handed down to adults. The telling of biblical stories already has a longer tradition, though; the first attempts to use them in catechetical instruction in Europe go back to the eighteenth century (Johann Hübner). However, there have been no attempts to deal with the Psalms with young children. They are documents of 'existential' prayer by and for adult believers, whereas for a child, so we are inclined to assume, his or her own 'self' as a whole seems not yet to be of particular concern. While this may be true in the specific sense of the term 'existential' as used in philosophical and theological contexts, it would be a premature conclusion from the perspectives of child psychology and education. To use the words of Jerome W. Berryman (1991: x), which Baldermann would underline, it could well be 'that children *do* have an awareness of the existential limits to their being and their knowing and that they are crying out in ways we do not often recognize for the language tools to help them build a life that takes such ultimate concerns into consideration'.

This perspective differs slightly from that of the well-known development theories although they remain valid and will have a specific role to play later (Chapter 6; see also Chapter 3). What I mean now is that children do, indeed, already participate in the basic emotional core of human situations independently of developmental cognitive stages. They do so, of course, in modified ways, in particular in how they work through their emotions cognitively. Their religious understanding differs from that of adults; their underlying emotional experience much less so.

To give an example, adults would not feel lonely where children would, because adults '(re)construct' and handle the possible situations differently by taking into account rational factors from previous experiences which the child has not yet had. They also draw on mechanisms of self-control which might alleviate the situation, but which a child has no command of; but the feeling itself, of being lonely, may be similar. Even if 'children do not use adult language to speak of their encounters with the existential boundaries to life', and even if they 'certainly do not divide their ultimate concerns into such neat concepts' as we adults do (in particular as theologians), this 'makes it all the more important for us to notice such issues in the lives of children and to give them religious language to name, value, and express their ultimate concerns so they can cope with them now and prepare for a more healthy and creative life later' (Berryman 1991: x).

Ingo Baldermann found this language in a book of the Bible where language is used to describe basic situations of life in an imaginative way that bridges the differences between adults and children. Baldermann recalls his starting-point: 'If biblical teaching were to make any sense, I had to find the point where biblical words address them as directly as they do me' (1996: 26). In his search he looked at biblical sentences which might speak to the children 'directly'; he found them in the Psalms.

> I sink in deep mire where there is no foothold.
> (Ps. 69: 2)

I am weary with my crying.
(Ps. 69: 3)

All who see me mock at me;
They make mouths at me, they
shake their heads.
(Ps. 22: 7)

(1) As a first feature, sentences like these are close to everyday speech, they do not belong to the academic theological 'language-game' (Ludwig Wittgenstein).

(2) At the same time they are not flat or 'small talk', for they tend towards, or represent, poetical language, an emotional and imaginative language. This feature is of importance in both recurrent foci of this whole book: the children on their journey to spiritual maturity in adulthood, and the issue of the biblical God. Children like to play with images and imaginative language, and the Psalms provide a concentrated, elementarizing access to God by showing a lived faith.

(3) Baldermann started with words of fear and anxiety. These words not only awakened sad feelings within the children; speaking about their fears to others and in particular to God helped them to leave the dark shadows gradually behind (Baldermann 1996: 27). In later lessons (and corresponding steps of his research programme) Baldermann turned also to biblical words of joyful experiences with God.

(4) How did the children generally react when they were confronted with statements from the Psalms which were introduced to them without any commentary or verbal stimuli? In hundreds of lessons the result was the same: They started 'a thoughtful discourse among themselves' (p. 27). They often began, 'Maybe there is somebody who . . .'. That sounds as if it were being said from a distance to the text, but this assumption would be wrong. The children were soon able to identify with the fears in the Psalms in their own way. They evidently had experienced similar fear and distress. However, as they needed a sort of protected space for speaking about the issues, they did not address their private experiences directly. They concealed their personal intimacies behind the language of the Psalms by speaking about the statements of others.

(5) The children showed no difficulty in understanding the imagery of the Bible as far as the selected verses were concerned. When the teacher put a sentence on the blackboard such as 'I sink in deep mire', the children would speak 'of fear of death, of a bad conscience or of hostility. It scarcely happened that the dialogue stuck to the flat literal meaning of the image' (Baldermann 1996: 27). If the imagery appears strange to children for whatever reasons, we know from a mass of data that they do indeed have difficulties in adequately grasping the meaning of religious expressions (see Chapter 6). This fact limits Baldermann's optimism. Nevertheless his discoveries remain valid too, for they refer to an imagery that is near to nature (water, mire or swampy ground, rocks), situations of everyday life with well-known feelings (weeping, crying, becoming 'weary' and tired), in short, imagery that is easily understood if used metaphorically. Thus, by his methods Baldermann was able to discover 'elementary accesses' to the rich heritage of the Bible similar to our Tübingen approach of 'elementarization' (Schweitzer *et al.* 1995).

Children and Truth – Evident Experience and Familiar Language

Are children able to grasp the complex theological aspects of God's 'saving righteousness/justice' in relation to 'wickedness' as separation from God and, even more, the ontological crisis in the understanding of the world as a whole? Are they able to distinguish between the moral aspects (which refer to acting) and the soteriological aspects of the issue of God (referring to being)? The doctrine of the 'justification of the sinner' is a matter not of values (*Werte*) and meaning (*Sinn*), but of being (*Sein*) and, therefore, truth (*Wahrheit*). In defining the term 'truth' I am going to concentrate on two perspectives, one of hermeneutics, the other of language. In the final section below we shall return to a normative theological perspective.

Truth and the Sensual and Hermeneutical Frame of Reference

Throughout the first three chapters, the realm of human experience appeared as the living context of our understanding of the theological, anthropological, social and educational perspectives of the issue of God. Previous and present experiences constitute the reality of the human universe, that is the 'world' as we perceive, interpret, comprehend and judge it. Other species have another realm of perception. What we speak of as being 'true' depends on our specifically human sensual and hermeneutical frame of reference. Thus, truth is always concrete truth.

If so, it is much more adequate to speak of 'truth experiences' within contexts of shared meaning which help us to conceptualize and formulate even what an individual experiences as quite new, that is a divine revelation. Truth claims are rooted in those truth experiences. Religious truth as doctrine is the attempt to express their general binding character. We recall the sentence from the beginning of Chapter 2 that 'faith is an experience with our experience'. The truth of faith 'happens' amidst our other experiences, rectifying or falsifying our usual human experiences.

Truth and Understandable Language

In the same way, faith experience as a possible truth experience is also bound to language. If nothing in our life resonates semantically to the new relevation as experience of 'disclosure' (Ian T. Ramsey), nothing can be understood and expressed in communicable ways. To speak of God's 'love' depends on at least some elements which have been met in this field and called 'love', so that the phrase 'God's love' also can become a part of our language and universe of meanings. Although God's relevations may be something wholly new, sometimes shockingly new as we will paradigmatically see with Paul's conversion on the road to Damascus (Chapter 8), the new experience is related to the existing old experiences. With Paul they were those of his life as Saul of Tarsus, being educated as a Pharisee by Gamaliel, having become an ardent believer in the Torah and a fanatical persecutor of Christians. He had had to know about the 'law' in order to gain a completely new estimation of its 'true' meaning.

If the given universe of meanings in language is rooted in experience, and we look at the children's present environment, they will probably be able to grasp, at least to some extent, the 'truth' of the following situations in the Psalms and elsewhere in the Bible, since there are elementary overlappings:

- the experience of loneliness and abandonment
- fear of others who are about to harm them
- reactions of just anger
- the longing for just punishment and
- the restoration of a just order
- feelings of revenge
- the relief of not having been overwhelmed by revenge
- the blessings of forgiving
- the feeling of gratitude to God.

In all these situations truth 'happens' immediately, when the children cannot but think, feel and say, 'Yes, that's how it is!', and, complementarily, 'Yes, that's how it should be!' Truth has to do with evidence and acceptance: on the one hand, with evident facts from the world as directly experienced ('Such is life!' 'Such are human beings!'), which are to be honestly admitted; on the other hand, with the evidence of God's view of these facts and his corresponding acting in view of them: 'It is good that God is not acting in the same way as we would.'

Methodological Approaches

There are proven methodological approaches in religious education which promote a thoughtful discourse about texts like the Psalms without bracketing the dimension of truth claims. As a first approach Baldermann mentions 'associative talk' (1996: 41–3). Such talk seeks to evoke a symmetrical conversation between teacher and pupils (and also, of course, among the pupils): no teaching any longer from above! Children welcome being left by the teacher to work out their own observations and questions. The teacher may invite the group to keep quiet for a while, in order to encourage everyone to reflect on important topics independently. At other times the group may recall previous conversations, and draw on their memories.

The statements of the children should not be prematurely evaluated, unless necessary. Since the Bible itself is not value-free – the Psalms being full of evaluative statements – the children, of course, want to evaluate too. You cannot be neutral if the issues are good and evil.

Another approach of indepth religious learning is meditation combined with 'silence-exercises' (Faust-Siehl *et al.* 1990). The teacher proposes a period of sitting in complete silence. Children like it very much because they are discovering the comfort of physical and spiritual rest: 'I could only hear my own heart beating, it was so good to my ears.' In such an atmosphere the words of the Bible address both the head and the heart.

A third way, which is gaining appreciation among religious educators, is to let the children write their own texts. They are asked to write stories about the beginning of the world, about seeing and not seeing God, about speaking of God in a paradoxical way ('God is far, but near to me'), to outline thought games and prayers about the phenomenon of time, to write about God and suffering, about justice and injustice and, most excitingly, 'Speeches to Humankind' about peace, starting with 'Listen to me!' (see Oberthür 2000: 71).

Listen to me, people!

Try to do good instead of evil.
Share what you have got.
Don't listen to those people who say, 'War, war'.
Abolish the whole of the military.
Don't punish people who committed crimes 20 years ago,
be kind to them.
Let all children grow up in peace.
Let all mothers educate their children peacefully.
Don't believe that there are underlings.
Don't overlook anyone, but include them.
Try to cure sick people,
even if they look horrible.
Give all people time to consider.

(Niklas, 10)

'Courage to Change the Things I Can' – Education for Justice with Young People

Shortly after the end of the Second World War an anonymous Canadian soldier brought the following prayer to Germany,

> God, grant me the serenity
> to accept things
> I cannot change.
> Courage to change
> the things I can
> and wisdom
> to know the difference.

Young people are hardly gifted with patience and serenity. However, the most promising of them, although not the majority, are seized by a burning desire to change things for the better, socially, politically and ecologically. They assist international non-governmental organizations like Greenpeace, Amnesty International and others. The young Christians among them share the goals of the 'Conciliar Process for Justice, Peace and the Integrity of Creation' that was launched at the 6th Full Assembly of the World Council of Churches in Vancouver 1983.

The Israelites who in the Psalms cry to the Lord for justice, and the prophets who accuse their societies on the same grounds, could hopefully become partners of today's youth. RE in schools is a small, but necessary forum for resistance-learning against the lies, cynicism and egoism that dominate minds. Where, as in some countries, state schools do not provide for RE, education in the churches will have to seize the opportunity to deal with the issue of God, human nature and education for peace and justice.

Amos belongs to the classical units of the curriculum in RE in German schools, which are mostly state schools. I would propose that the topic be treated twice, at the beginning of the secondary level (age 13/14) and in later adolescence. The pupils should be introduced to the phenomenon of religious prophecy as an outstanding event in the history of humanity. The impact of the Old Testament prophets in shaping moral consciousness right down to today can hardly be underestimated.

The first encounter with a figure like Amos at the beginning of the secondary level should focus on his person. Amos represents the dilemma of a prophet who is compellingly summoned by God to proclaim what the powerful elites don't want to hear. The pupils learn about personal religious and public courage. In the second reading emphasis should be given to the moral content of the prophetic message, to the Bible's option for the weak, sick, poor and oppressed.

Since about 1970, in Germany the so-called 'contextual approach' (developed by the author) has been introduced successfully into RE, and partly into confirmation classes too. The new concept was implemented in the German RE curriculum within a few years. The central idea was (and still is) to contextualize biblical content by linking it to the important issues of our own time and also by comparing it with competing responses given from non-Christian standpoints – a double context!

The frame of reference can be widened, and hence become more complex, in RE with older teenagers (age 17–19) by highlighting global economic and political causative factors that add to social injustice and the violation of human rights. In reviewing 'the four spheres of relevance' mentioned above (see pp. 48–9), Amos' elementary moral rules can be presented as the beginning of a road that has finally led to the documents of an international and global ethic of today with human rights as the main focus. Incidentally, from a methodological point of view, analysis according to the 'contextual approach' can start either with the biblical text or with the similar problems of today.

From a theological point of view, it is also possible and necessary to explain the belief in a Last Judgement, the history of its misuse included. This concept can be interpreted as (1) necessary in order to prevent the victims from being mocked at, (2) as a protest against the wickedness of the lawless, and (3) as a democratization of rendering account of one's own actions, for, as opposed to the heavenly privileges of the mighty in other religions, kings would now have to expect equal treatment. Later, in Christian times, paintings showed hell populated also by bishops, cardinals and popes.

A decisive factor in any successful religious and moral education is the personal experience and competence of the teacher. Have those who teach suffered from any deprivation themselves? Or have they been eye-witnesses of injustice to others? Are they aware of their own possible failures of submission to those altars on which the idolatries of today triumph? Are they informed by relevant sociological and psychological analyses of the plight of deprived people? Are they able to speak responsibly and unobtrusively of their own relation to God? 'O LORD our God, other Lords besides you have ruled over us, but we acknowledge your name alone' (Isa. 26: 13).

I grew up under Hitler who 'ruled' as a diabolic 'Lord' of life replacing God as the true Lord of life. We were exposed to the poison of ideas that despised the dignity of human beings. Most parents and most state education failed to resist because of collective ideological indoctrination, enforced compliance and cowardice. Bearing this in mind, in my view religious education should not be restricted to education *about* religion, as a more or less descriptive exercise, but has to be primarily education *from within* religion, thereby resisting historical forgetfulness and present forms of human oppression, both for the sake of the younger generation and also for the sake of a common human future.

III
RECONCILIATION THROUGH LOVE

Chapter 5

Young People, God and Jesus – Towards a Culture of Compassion and Care

What does the central figure of Christianity, Jesus Christ, contribute to peace in the world? His appearance on earth is celebrated as the coming of God's peace: 'Glory to God in the highest heaven, and on earth peace among those whom he favours' (Luke 2: 14). Jesus preached love – 'love of neighbour' and 'love of enemy' – and he embodied love through his life and his death on the Cross. He started 'proclaiming the good news of God' (Mark 1: 14), for now 'the time is fulfilled, and the kingdom of God has come near' (v. 15), by describing God's kingdom as a revolution of values (see this chapter) and a feast of joy (see Chapter 6). The core was God's reconciling love, therefore we speak in Part III of peace as 'reconciliation through love'. People experienced this love as the power of forgiveness: 'Father, forgive them; for they do not know what they are doing' (Luke 23: 34) (see Chapter 7). Jesus' death meant (and means) new life: 'So if anyone is in Christ, there is a new creation: everything old has passed away; see, everything has become new!' (2 Cor. 5: 17) (see Chapter 8). In the eyes of faith, God's promises concerning 'peace through justice', through 'God's righteousness' (see Part II) and the appearance of his righteousness in Jesus belong together. It is this perspective of God's paradoxical love that we have been pursuing.

But how do people today react to the good news, to this loving righteousness and forgiving justice, to this way of 'justification of the sinner' as a message of peace?

'It's Annoying, Simply Unjust!' – Youth Protesting Against the Improbable and Impossible

> I think it's annoying!
> Simply unjust!
> Hey, that's, hey, I am lost for words!
> I'd never dare look into the eyes of those who worked hard the whole day!
> That's absolutely unbelievable!

These statements from students aged 16–17 in our Tübingen empirical study (see the complete lessons in Faust-Siehl *et al.* 1995) refer to the parable of 'The Workers in the Vineyard' (Matt. 20: 1–16). The story is told by Jesus to illustrate God's generosity as a feature of 'the Kingdom of God'. For many people, even some Christians, this biblical terminology has become strange. While adults may politely just shrug their shoulders at the metaphor of a 'kingdom', young people are much more direct in their reactions, as those quoted above show. They can also feel angry at such a text and reject it harshly.

Surprisingly enough, they are not protesting because of the obsoleteness of royal dynasties still serving as religious imagery. Nor do they object because a so-called 'God' – an idea that for quite a few is in itself already strange enough – is presented to them as a 'king' with connotations of authoritarianism. Instead they regard the story as crazy because it is foolish; there are values accompanying it which do not fit in at all with their familiar experience of life. And provocatively enough, it is precisely from daily life that the Jewish Rabbi Jesus of Nazareth, whom the church believes to have been the 'Son of God', takes his examples. The protestors ridicule the kindness of the landowner and thereby ridicule God's kindness.

> The kingdom of heaven is like a landowner who went out early in the morning to hire labourers for his vineyard. After agreeing with the labourers on the usual daily wage, he sent them into his vineyard. When he went out about nine o'clock, he saw others standing idle in the marketplace, and he said to them, 'You also go into the vineyard, and I will pay you whatever is right.' So they went. When he went out again about noon and again about three o'clock, he did the same. And about five o'clock he went out and found others standing around, and he said to them, 'Why are you standing here idle all day?' They said to him 'Because no one has hired us.' He said to them, 'You also go into the vineyard.' When evening came, the owner of the vineyard said to his manager, 'Call the labourers and give them their pay, beginning with the last and then going to the first.' When those hired about five o'clock came, each of them received the usual daily wage. Now when the first came, they thought they would receive more; but each of them also received the usual daily wage. And when they received it, they grumbled about the landowner, saying, 'These last worked only one hour, and you have made them equal to us who have borne the burden of the day and the scorching heat.' But he replied to one of them, 'Friend, I am doing you no wrong; did you not agree with me for the usual daily wage? Take what belongs to you and go; I choose to give to this last the same as I give to you. Am I not allowed to do what I choose with what belongs to me? Or are you envious because I am generous?' ['Or is your eye evil, because I am good?' – Luz 1997: 139] So the last will be the first, and the first will be the last.

Unemployment and disparities in the labour market, a strong propensity for fair wages and a sharpened awareness of the alleviating or aggravating conditions of specific work situations – all these features of today are factors of that old story too. 'Unemployment already seems to have been a problem of that time' (Schröder 1979: 91). In Palestine we find workers and day-labourers (p. 90). They were unpropertied persons, often smallholders, who had lost everything and had to make their livelihoods day by day, living from hand to mouth. They were usually totally dependent on the market (Fiensy 1991: 85–90). Young people today are very sensitive about social discrimination; youth unemployment is quite high (in eastern Germany the average unemployment rate is 18 per cent). No wonder then that the strategies of employers are regarded with suspicion. Today the smell of exploitation hangs in the air, as it surely did at that time too. How can such a story promote social peace?

Admittedly, comparisons with modern social issues in a sort of backward-projection may be problematic. But young people do not bother; from their perspective the employer's opinion that the labourers were standing around 'all day' in 'idleness' is not empathetic; a landowner should know. In the story the unemployed react with a mixture of resignation and mild reproach, pointing to what for them is the naked truth of the matter: 'Because no one has hired us.' Surely our young people will take the side of the unemployed.

The pay of one denar was normal it seems, but not too much (Schröder 1979: 90). Other exegetes question the landowner's behaviour and speak of a bad contract (Derrett 1977: 51). The minimum living wage was about 200 denars for a family per year. If one considers that most of the money had to be spent on food, many families lived in poverty. As such, the payment for the day-workers of the late afternoon is 'generous' indeed (not just!), as young people will concede. Admittedly, it's a minimum for a day's living, but they obtained it without having done very much for it. However, what about the annoying payment of all the others, in particular those who worked from early morning? The original agreement between the landowner and the workers can no longer count. All that matters is justice, as the early workers clearly state as a matter of fact. As will our young people, in understanding justice rigidly as equal distribution, mirroring the universal 'balance' (cf. Chapter 4). Maybe the specific working conditions of the early workers as another point of comparison add to the angry reaction. Hadn't they had to work under 'the burden of the day and the scorching heat', suffering from the hot winds of the sirocco?

But is there not a more deep-seated explanation for the young people's reactions? Results from a special pilot study (Nipkow 1997: 924–6) on the attitudes of young people towards Jesus himself (not only towards the content of the stories told by him; we will come back to this point) indicate a much more basic frustration than just the irritation caused by the unfair payment and social injustice as described above. It is the creeping general feeling of lost hope, that there is no chance of a greater justice in the world such as that depicted in the New Testament parables of the 'Kingdom of God'. There are some reasons to assume that to a considerable extent the background of the anger is a hidden sadness. The objective facts of life undermine alternative images of human life, producing frustrations which are articulated by some youngsters in the guise of ridiculing the improbable and unbelievable.

Religious Diversity in Young People

If the churches want to contribute to a peaceful world, they have to know about the younger generation and their religious attitudes. The situation has become more diffuse and pluralistic than ever before. Even if the moral aspects of the issue of peace and justice are of interest, are young people also interested in the theological focus of our approach: God?

In the last 15 years, I have been developing a hermeneutical theory of practical theology in the field of Christian and religious education that I have called a 'pluralizing or plural hermeneutic'. It is meant to cope with the radical religious diversity among adolescents today. A detailed presentation of the results has been given in my study on pluralism (Nipkow 1998, 2: chap. 6). In my view the time for pursuing one 'approach' only is gone. It is difficult to say whether the high degree of religious 'individualization' allows a typological description at all. The following one, presented here only very briefly for reasons of space, has been informed mostly by my own empirical studies (see Nipkow 1987, 1988; cf. also Schweitzer *et al.* 1995). The samples included adolescents and young adults; therefore the results also question the traditional methods of Christian adult education in church and society.

1   A Shared Understanding of Faith

A situation of a shared understanding of faith rests upon, and expresses itself by, the tacit agreement that the Bible self-evidently is the 'Holy Bible' as 'God's Word' and a source of meaningful and necessary knowledge for Christian life. The attitude appropriate for approaching it is 'to listen' to the word of God, not (only) to historically explore and criticize it. Exegetically seen, a one-sided historical exegesis is transformed into (not simply replaced by) a 'hermeneutics of consent' which interprets biblical texts in the light of, and promotion of, faith (Stuhlmacher 1979: 206–8; see also Fuchs 1958: 135–7). In educational practice, prayers and hymns open and end lessons in confirmation classes (and even in RE lessons in state schools) without questioning. This pattern presupposes the believing congregation that unites younger and older church members. A frame of a given spirituality constitutes the shared (or at least assumed) common consent that is welcomed and lived by all. Still today all over the world millions of baptized Christian children and young people are conducted along a path devoted to disseminating, nourishing and promoting faith according to the above pattern. We are accustomed to speaking of 'Christian nurture'. The appropriate methodological approach of religious learning by a shared religious practice is best known from church Bible Study Groups. The Bible is the centre of a serious and committed in depth approach of common exchange, shared learning and mutual edification. The approach is still valid under the hermeneutical preconditions delineated above. However, if the churches stick to it as the only path to follow, they may run the risk of religious self-exclusiveness and, because of this, of failing adequately to communicate with secular contemporaries.

2   An Open-ended Critical Search for Faith

Since the period of the Enlightenment another attitude has become more typical in European countries than the approach discussed above. It is that of critical religious search and assessment, rather than religious certainty. At best it is a quest that is open to the Christian faith, although today the spiritual moves are also directed towards other religious or psychological and esoteric alternatives as functional equivalents. The search is open-ended because the general tendency is to avoid a premature religious decision or a clear decision at all.

   The typical mode of education cannot any longer be that of positive and unquestionable 'nurture'. In the following statement (from a collection of my own), Sascha, aged 10, is very honest about his early religious doubts, which require similarly honest attempts at clarification from any religious educator.

   I think God is only a legend. But in the next moment I believe in God. That wanders around in my mind. I don't really know what to write about the topic 'God'. In church I am always getting an odd feeling in my stomach. When they start and go on telling about God, I also start believing in him. But the next day I don't believe in him any longer. So I keep changing. When you go to an old people's home, you often see pictures with God on the Cross. But in the story about Daniel God is said to have rescued him from the cage of the lions. Whether it's true nobody knows.

Sascha drew a picture underneath, with two crucifixes on a slightly curved part of the surface of the globe. One of them he crossed through, the other not. Do they symbolize his irritations? God is letting Jesus die, although he cries to his father, 'My God, my God, why have you forsaken me?' (Matt. 27: 46). That is a shocking story for a young boy or girl in view of the normal behaviour of a father. God does intervene, indeed, but later; 'too late', Sascha would perhaps say. I do not know whether Sascha is able to approach the mystery of the Cross in its 'true' theological meaning. We will come to it in Chapter 7. 'God-talk' in relation to 'peace through justice' (see Part II) and 'reconciliation through love' (see this Part III) becomes difficult.

3   A Lost Understanding of Faith

What sort of hermeneutics is required now? Cognitive clarifications alone are not sufficient; usually the problem lies deeper. People suffer from the clash of two realities: the reality of life refuting the promised reality of God's presence: 'Where is God?' 'Why is he absent, as it seems?' 'Where do we find justice in the world?' 'Why does God allow evil?' These questions of the psalmists and of Job constantly recur (cf. Chapter 4). If the protected faith of childhood is contradicted by the same despising cynicisms today as the Psalmists were confronted with in their days, no wonder that it is these 'temptations of life' even more than the 'temptations of thought' which in most cases lead to loss of faith (on both forms of temptation in more detail cf. Nipkow 1990: 287–98).

In the following statement, quoted by Schuster, a young apprentice painter in an RE lesson at a vocational school (age 17), writes down anonymously what he thinks about God:

> What do I think when I hear the word 'God'?
> The Third World. Injustice. The fear of losing my faith in him. An invention of humankind. All sorrows and hopes having been collected to form a God. A sort of escape. Emergency exit. The unjust punishment that he has imposed upon us. His strange way to peace. Believing Without Fatal Theses! God instead of religion. Was God a racist? Once having the luck of hearing him speak in a dream. Knowing how it was in fact. In spite of everything God is a fine invention I keep to. THE FEAR TO LOSE MY FAITH IN HIM!
> (Schuster 1984: 131, capitals in the original)

The young man lists those aspects of life which seem to contradict God's loving nature and which, eventually, may lead to a denial of God's existence. Therefore, they are 'fatal theses' to faith. The salient factors relate to social injustice concerning the gap between rich and poor, the lack of peace and racism. There are also basic religious doubts, mainly the suspicion that God might be nothing but a human invention and projection of human fears and hopes. At this point the text repeats the nineteenth-century critique of religion of Ludwig Feuerbach, Karl Marx, Ernst Haeckel and others. We do not know whether the young painter has ever heard of Feuerbach, but you do not need to be a philosophically informed, educated person to hit upon this 'fatal' possibility. In short, the statement confronts us with the principal issue of this book: God, justice and peace are topics of young people, but in the perspective of radical questions.

4   The Complete Lack of Understanding of Faith and New Curiosity

The three preceding types of religious attitude are not new. Today they must be complemented by two other patterns. The first has many causes. In the former East Germany it resulted from a systematic anti-religious indoctrination of the young generation for political and ideological atheistic purposes during the forty years of Communist rule from 1949 to 1989. Statistical data (Tiefensee 2000: 88) reveal that between 1946 and 1990 the number of those not belonging to any Christian denomination was ten times higher than in the years before. The eastern provinces of Germany show a majority of about 65 per cent of religiously non-affiliated persons. The new situation has been described as 'a vast heap of ruins after an earthquake' (p. 89).

The result is a 'denomination' of its own, without name and based upon stable, taken for granted atheistic certainties. It is a set of convictional assumptions as a sort of belief system delivering the comfortable feeling of belonging to an atheistic community where one feels 'at home' (Tiefensee 2000: 91). The atheism is a practical one, rather than one that has been thought through theoretically, and largely tending to grow into a total religious 'indifferentism'. Religion is regarded as a field where it is of no use posing fundamental questions because you know beforehand that you will not get answers anyway.

Nevertheless, although the young people (like the adults) display what Eberhard Tiefensee in his study calls a 'religious unmusicality' (p. 93) and they are left without a language they can use to give their existential experiences shape, a broad empirical survey in Saxony in the early 1990s (Hanisch and Pollack 1997) about the (voluntary!) participation in Protestant RE in state schools produced interesting numbers and other data. Of the total number of students 46 per cent came from a non-religious background. They chose RE (instead of 'Ethics', the alternative choice) out of 'curiosity', in the first place, second because of 'interest in the issue of God' – the main focus of this study – and, third, for 'the climate of open dialogue'. Atheistic young people appreciate the non-prescriptive style of modern Protestant RE, but even more important is their even stronger interest in learning about God. Belief in God is the basic content of religion in European history. At least for a minority of non-religious young people, it seems to be difficult to leave the issue of God completely aside.

5   'God in the Subjunctive'

The following religious phenomena are hardly explored. They form a spectrum of a postmodern religious search. Sometimes it is the questions of an interviewer that serve as a catalyst for becoming aware of one's own religious position during the actual course of an interview, by helping to clarify what is going on in oneself. The following hesitant, tentative, twisted argument of an undergraduate at a German university is a telling example. The statement is taken from an empirical study of the early 1990s (Kirchenamt der Evangelischen Kirche in Deutschland 1991: 108).

> Yes, as to my faith, that's something, hey, man, that's not easy to explain . . . If I were to tell you now that I don't need to go to church, then what I really mean is, if I do have a real

problem, which I don't want to bother other people with or if I think that nobody can help me, that in such a situation I do sit down and try to think it through anyhow, quite by myself, quite alone . . . But sometimes I think, if there were a God or some such being who could help me, then it would be a matter which you might definitely need . . . Well, if he did exist, then he would now be the only one who could be of any practical help.

The broken syntax conveys a message in a somewhat odd, stilted manner. The language oscillates awkwardly between self-justification and pride of autonomy on the one hand and signalling the need for help from God on the other hand. Religion is given not a real, but only a 'hypothetical relevance'. The vagueness of language reflects the vagueness of understanding; the subjunctive mood prevails – God in the subjunctive.

Teachers in sustained contact with adolescents over many years speak of 'a belief in transitions' that can be characterized by a hesitant expectation 'hovering' between commitment and indifference, by being afraid of insistent authoritarian religious institutions and by a definite interest in a standpoint of their own.

Another new phenomenon is an as-if attitude (*als ob*). One wants to hedge one's bets with belief at least in a fictitious religious orientation. Although they seem to be quite certain that God is an illusion (an 'invention', as the young painter said above), quite a few hold this idea to be a 'fine' invention. 'If I am in trouble', a 17-year-old student in a vocational school tells us, 'it is not the imagined "God" who helps, but belief in this God, and one's will' (Schuster 1984: 313). An odd distinction is being made between God and belief in God. While God is either supposed to not exist at all, or at least is not expected to really help, the belief in him fostered by one's own will(!) helps a lot. It is one's own will and one's own belief which are regarded as the truly effective sources of support, not the imagined God. Subjective factors replace God in his objectivity without dropping the term 'God'. Strangely enough, this self-contradictory cognitive operation does not bother the youngsters provided it serves to relieve them of their troubles. A girl aged 15 remarks, 'Frankly speaking, I am glad that there is God, though only in my ideas and in the ideas of other people' (Nipkow 1998, 2: 255). For these young people it is all the same whether God as the 'object of reference' exists or not; their faith refers to itself as a sort of 'self-referential faith', a belief in a belief, not in a living God – a strange game of self-deceiving make-believe.

Another phenomenon can be named as a new religious sadness: 'I should like to believe, but unfortunately I can't.'

Other pupils have become so alienated from Christian faith that some elements of it obtain a fresh fascinating quality; these religious features appear to them as too different from what they are accustomed to in the practical orientations of their life.

To sum up, the extreme diversity of preconditions demands unusual ways as our response. It also requires a resolute concentration on the essential themes; together with the focus on God it demands a focus on Jesus as person, his life and death, and the meaning of his resurrection.

Jesus – a Fascinating, Ambiguous and Annoying Figure

At Easter the followers of Jesus gained a new knowledge, although it was basically the knowledge that the people of Israel had experienced from the beginning. In a way, therefore, the new revelation was an act of memory. Israel had learnt about God in Egypt and in the desert, later in their new hilly land and in the founding of David's 'kingdom' (hence the notion of a 'kingdom' of God). They had experienced God and struggled with him in their daily life in their prayers and through the prophets, in captivity in Babylon and after returning to Jerusalem, to the Zion. They had already learnt a lot about God's paradoxical love and loyalty in spite of human disloyalty, envy, hate, violence, murder, destruction of peace, in sum, in spite of their own sin (see paradigmatically Cain and Abel, Chapter 3). They knew well everything necessary about God's justice and righteousness. They had 'cried for his justice' as God's saving justice and restoring judgement (see the Psalms and the prophets in Chapter 4).

The followers of Jesus had forgotten very soon too. After the crucifixion they had hidden themselves in low spirits and sadness, with nothing left in their hands and hearts – having lost their faith, confidence, hope and knowledge. It is essential to realize that still today it is not sufficient just to get the information that others have experienced Jesus and God. The women who had seen Jesus 'told this to the apostles. But these words seemed to them an idle tale, and they did not believe them' (Luke 24: 10–11).

They had to receive a new knowledge that was to enlighten their old knowledge. Each of them needed it individually, sometimes against their stubborn nature, as the story about Thomas shows – and this, indeed, happened. The apostles and others happily regained and renewed their memories of the Jesus who told parables and healed, and thus they regained their faith in him as someone who had lived and shared his faith with them before; the memories came back together with the new 'revealing' interpretation of them. Jesus had been, indeed, not one of the usual rabbis. Now, eventually, they clearly saw 'in the face of Jesus Christ' 'the glory of God' himself (2 Cor. 4: 6), the appearance of the kingdom itself, different in actuality from the way the parables had told of it. Therefore they could speak of this Jesus as the 'Messiah of God', the 'Christ': they had received 'the light of the knowledge of the glory of God in the face of Jesus (as the) Christ'.

So, ever since, for Christians the issue of God has become identical with the issue of Jesus Christ. Therefore, it is of the greatest importance for Christian education and spiritual growth to find out what the younger generation know and think about Jesus. Here, as indicated in the preceding section, we meet a promising new situation: young people are challenged by the unusual strangeness of Jesus compared with their own social surroundings. He is discovered as a man who has presented to the world the strongest contrast image of God among all other images of deities that have ever been devised. Jesus appears to them in his inconvenient, revolutionary, radical nature. As theologians and religious educators we are responsible for withstanding a polishing, harmonizing distortion of the true image of Jesus (and God), for avoiding any form of 'policing the sublime'' (Thatcher 1996). It is just those among modern youth who have been brought up in atheist families, or have become alienated for other reasons, who are seized by a new amazement which can help us to regain new elementary approaches to Jesus. They are caught by surprise and open up new surprising paths of religious education, and Christian adult formation too.

As for the empirical background, I draw on several studies. Although our Tübingen study about 'elementarization' (Schweitzer *et al.* 1995) was to explore the pupils' views on the issues of 'God', 'justice' and 'parables', and not specially Jesus, there were interesting hints about him.

A pilot study (Nipkow 1997) with a sample of 113 students in vocational schools in the urban region around Stuttgart, where pupils were asked to put down their views of Jesus in an anonymous written form, allowed a close look at attitudes towards Jesus in addition to the data above (cf. also Nipkow 1998, 2: 260–63).

A Bavarian study (Schmid 1989) in the same field of vocational schools, conducted by a Catholic expert in religious education with the instrument of group interviews, served as a third source of data. It must be added that my focus is selective. In the meantime a broader description can be studied in some special investigations (Büttner and Thierfelder 2001).

The Fascinating Jesus (a Stuttgart Study)

According to the results of the Stuttgart study, following the instruments of the 'grounded theory' of Glaser and Strauss (1968), the positive comments could be put into six categories. In descending order, Jesus was appreciated in the following ways:

1 First, as a person of unselfish love ('he is good to all', he is 'peace incarnate') and because of his commitment to others ('he lived for others and died for others').
2 Second, as someone who had acknowledged everyone on equal terms.
3 Third, as a person who had been ready to suffer for others.
4 Fourth (but only marginally), he was associated with the classical Christian interpretation of the atonement of Christ ('he died for us').
5 Fifth, he was praised for not having any need of big and loud media presentation.
6 Sixth, some admired his courage and intrepidity.

All in all he appears as a fascinating extraordinary personality. Some confessed very personal ties. A future electrical engineer in applying metaphorically the activities of his profession remarked, 'he is my line to God'. Another one who was complaining about the unjust treatment Jesus had to suffer added, 'although he had opened the eyes of the people, the same people executed him'. Only one of the students commented that Jesus went too far, when he 'always[!] turned his right cheek to others'.

Jesus fascinates as a human being in his humanity; the deeply human traits of his behaviour, including his death, form the elementary approaches for appreciation, while the theological attributes in the Creed, glorifying him as 'risen' and 'sitting' at the right hand of God in the 'Last Judgement', are not mentioned.

The Ambiguous Jesus (a Bavarian Study)

For other young people Jesus is a deeply ambiguous presence as is God himself ('the two of them up there'). In his Bavarian study Hans Schmid (1989) administered group interviews with students from vocational schools. His methodology of speaking with a 'clique' was based on the plausible assumption that the dynamics of peer group processes will most probably influence the attitudes of the individual group members. Beside other factors this assumption could be illustrated by the role of the group speaker. In the following statement such a 'speaker' not only answers the interviewer's question, but simultaneously addresses his clique by signalling to them how he wants them to react. He even tries to influence their expressive reactions ('let us smile!').

The interview is about God; the specific issue being God's absence in the time of the Second World War, focusing on the massacre of the Jews. In referring to what they have learnt about the Nazi regime, the speaker comments on God's and Jesus' behaviour with bitter cynicism.

> Yes, yes, it was at the time when Hitler lived when God was active so much . . . He was shooting around in the heavens like a singed sow in order to undertake something against Hitler, well, and then there is the Bible where we read that Jesus, that ambiguous one – he who is said to have raised somebody from the dead, that's what it says, doesn't it? hey, hey, let us smile! (strong gestures) . . . he himself is also said to have risen – but then (with emphasis), in the Third Reich, neither of them has done anything.
>
> (Schmid 1989: 44–5)

Jesus is proclaimed by the church as the embodiment of love, as caring for and saving life. He is called the 'saviour', which not only means eternal salvation, but also overcoming death in real life. The Bavarian adolescents have heard about the biblical stories which report that people have been recalled by Jesus from the dead. As in the Old Testament, the saving righteousness of God is expected on earth. But now both God the Father and his Son seem to have been helpless in the face of the most atrocious annihilation of life.

The Annoying Jesus (a Tübingen Study)

Among the lessons analysed in the Tübingen study (Schweitzer *et al.* 1995) were some about the topic of justice. For this purpose the teachers had chosen the parable of 'The Workers in the Vineyard'. At the beginning of the chapter we quoted some angry reactions of students (aged 16–17) to the generous behaviour of the landowner. However, their protest was not limited to the plot of the parable. In other contexts it was also directed against Jesus himself as a crazy figure who in their eyes did not fit the realities of the life they were used to. Some of them could not understand at all why Jesus behaved liked that, unselfishly helping all the people he met. Some statements read,

> (Speaking emotionally), Well, either I am an idiot or that Jesus . . . he's a bit off his nut, isn't he? (laughter).
> Ha, it's impossible that he has always been doing good and never retaliating, for instance against the Pharisees or the rabbis . . . continuously accepting everything that happened to him, always helping others, you can't keep that up.
> Well, I think – he was not quite normal.
>
> (Faust-Siehl *et al.* 1995: 387)

In a post-Christian arena like ours, with the Christian institutions having lost their former reputation and attraction, the figure of Jesus is still exciting, although very controversial; Jesus appears as an *annoying* fool. But it does make very good theological sense that it is in just this way that he should regain his proper place in the consciousness of the younger generation, given the actual agenda of issues in our time. Speaking properly about Jesus means speaking about his provocative and therefore risky life, which necessarily led to the conflicts conducive to his death. In the context of the statements quoted above, three features can be identified which explain why Jesus is exciting in terms of present-day value systems (quite apart from the specific scandalizing effects in his own lifetime 2000 years ago).

- For the students he is a simple man who does not need what most young people and adults in our affluent, consumerist societies claim as their legitimate amount of goods, income, money, social reputation, amusements, fun, glitter. He is a provocative exception as to his personal life style.
- Jesus' life is not centred on his ego. Although he lives and acts in a way wholly consistent with his convictions, thus proving his identity, this self-identity is not one of self-interest. His centre of gravity is nothing but God, in exclusive trust in him alone. 'My food is to do the will of him who sent me and to complete his work' (John 4: 34). 'And the one who sent me is with me; he has not left me alone, for I always do what is pleasing to him' (John 8: 29).
- And what will please God? To be with others and help them. Surely, this is something that is experienced in everyday life too, with friends or in the family or wherever. But unlike the usual humanitarian conventions, it is the extreme phenomenon of a loving existence with a total refusal of violence against others, and of any form of retaliation in response to suffering caused by others, that makes young people view him as almost crazy (an 'idiot'). Jesus renounces the 'culture' of all Lamechs in the world.

The issue of Jesus (and together with him the issue of God) is at stake particularly in those situations in which suffering from injustice and violence surpasses all our imagination, that is in the midst of triumphant wickedness. For the Bavarian young people this satanic power had found expression in Hitler's regime. In their scornful laughter ('let us smile!') they not only repeated the mocking of the soldiers beneath the Cross, they also participated (in their way) in the despair of the disciples who had fled and left Jesus in the hour of his crucifixion. Thus the disciples and all Christians manifest the guilt of all human beings who capitulate to the power of evil and fall prey to doing something that they do not want to do (cf. on this point the life of Paul Chapter 8).

How are we to respond to this situation? The cynicism of the Bavarian students is adressed to an interviewer who is a theologian. In a shocking way they articulate the question of whether the Christian faith can provide somewhere where evil and wickedness can be explained and understood. In the Christian view this place is the suffering of Jesus on the Cross. As a Christian educator I do not know how to respond without speaking of the paradoxical appearance of God's love as sharing the suffering of the sinners and overcoming it. In the light of the experience of Easter the new creation springs up in this way. As the first new human being, Jesus was born out of suffering and death as a unique event in the history of humankind (cf. Chapter 7).

The context above has been illustrated by statements and attitudes of young people who reflect experiences of resistance and protest against Christian faith. Hence, the word 'experience' becomes ambiguous, compared with its hopefully typical use in religious education. This prompts us to revisit the experiential approach that has so far been our guideline.

The Concept of 'Experience' Self-critically Revisited

In the past decades the practice of RE in schools and in Christian education in the churches has been impressively enriched by a huge variety of wide-ranging methods, covering classical textual studies and narratives, as well as methods using drama and painting, new songs and media, the exploration of nature, examples drawn from art, ethnographical findings, community experiences and much more. In order to implement a plural approach in religious education, based on a plural hermeneutic (see pp. 69–73), we can fortunately also draw on a variety of procedures.

In all these respects and perspectives, religious educators hope to be successful by adopting an experience-oriented theory and practice. In this book we also started with a general appreciation of the category of experience, for several good reasons, theological, anthropological, epistemological and educational (Chapter 2). 'Experience' appears to be a very promising term.

- First, it promises to free us from the bonds of tradition, in particular from the cognitive burden of unintelligible church doctrine and the authoritarian threats of dogmatism. Experience links world and self by integrating the inner and outer world to the living reality of our daily perception.
- Second it appeals to all the senses, and makes possible a fuller knowledge that includes emotions and the imagination. It overcomes rationalistic narrowness.
- Third, historically seen, with the connotation of autonomously generated individual knowledge, the term has accompanied the process of emancipation that has occurred in the modern period since the late Middle Ages. The new experience of one's own self fostered self-reliance and self-determination; it encouraged new ways of self-realization with no other forum to decide on truth than individual inner certainty.

The modern understanding of experience differs considerably from the earlier understanding of the word in European history. For Aristotle 'experience' was 'memorized practice' from which flowed reliable knowledge as wisdom in moral affairs and maturity in political action (Herms 1982: 89). The term 'experience' was a keyword in respect of matters of general human and public relevance. If today someone is called an 'experienced' person, the older understanding comes into view: it indicates a person who is well informed, who knows the world and who is thoughtful in his or her decisions.

Strangely enough, religious education today features neither the classical meaning of the term nor its current common usage. Instead the term 'experience' (in German *Erfahrung*) emphazises a holistic concept involving cognition, the emotions and social interaction. Sometimes it also overlaps with, or approaches semantically, what in German is called *Erlebnis*, an emotionally moving event or encounter. Religious education has widely become an 'Erlebnis pedagogy', a concept with its historical roots in the first two decades of the twentieth century. It was developed as one stream of the 'Reformed Pedagogy' (see in the United States John Dewey and the 'Progressive Education') and to some degree influenced by the *Lebensphilosophie* (Philosophy of Life, see Henri Bergson).

For education generally as well as for religious education in particular the understanding of 'experience' as 'Erlebnis' and as a basic aspect of 'Existenz' is certainly valid too. In Germany *Existenzphilosophie* (M. Heidegger) was to influence the so-called *Existential-Theologie* (R. Bultmann and many others) which after the last war gradually took over large areas of theological thinking. Almost all issues of theology were redefined and expressed in anthropological terms. As the term 'experience' referred to what deeply affected the individual in a time of secularization, when the religious tradition was to be rejuvenated hopes were set on procedures by which the past could regain a personal meaning for people in the present. The preceding chapters have reflected this development on several levels, most conspicuously in the approach of 'elementarization' with its dimension of 'elementary experiences'.

However, this modern meaning of experience, be it that of aiming at the experiences 'behind' the faith tradition, or at that of children and young people today, conceals three important aspects.

First, the concept of a religious education keen on the interplay of the cognitive and affective domain in a 'living learning" cannot be of much help in matters of moral and religious content. Our concern for social injustice, violence, paths to reconciliation and peace, ecological catastrophes, racism, hostility to foreigners, antisemitism etc., just to name some of the substantial issues today in moral education, cannot be adequately dealt with by the instruments of modern learning theories alone.

Second, the concept of experiencing one's own self leaves open the question of how to escape the 'prison' of the self. The name of 'God' indicates a horizon that transcends the self. Furthermore, we can by no means be sure that our own experiences will always open up hearts and encourage the mind to turn to God. What about experiences that resist God? If these questions are put aside, we fail to take seriously important theological dimensions of religious education.

The Old and the Radical New – Human Experiences Resisting Faith Experiences

While the educational assumption that the realm of experience favours religious learning is generally true, it suffers from a certain illusion with respect to a rather crucial religious phenomenon, the natural limitations of human beings to grasp transcendent reality and overcome evil. The hermeneutical logic of 'experiential' religious learning is based on the assumption that if religious items are linked to familiar human experiences their religious content will become familiar too. The hermeneutical argument follows the equation that 'like' supports 'like': speaking of 'God's love' will become intelligible by reminding people of experiences of 'human love'; 'God's faithfulness' will be understood if one recalls 'human faithfulness' as it has been experienced in warm social relationships, and so on.

This classical hermeneutics of human similarities, as developed by Wilhelm von Humboldt, Wilhelm Dilthey, Hans-Georg Gadamer and others, remains of course valid as religious language itself shows by using comparisons and metaphors (see Chapter 4). However, what about the 'non-similar' or, even more, the completely strange? What about the relation between 'old' experiences and 'radically new' ones? Can everything easily be assimilated to the familiar? Can it happen at all? Let us consider the question from several angles.

According to Jean Piaget's psychological view, the first limitations are given by developmental cognitive human structures. When confronted with something new, its 'assimilation' to one's own cognitive 'structures' runs against developmental barriers that render an assimilation difficult, or even impossible if the new is too strange. It is the 'structures' of the organism that now will have to change, in a process Piaget has called 'accommodation'.

In the field of social and cultural relationships, the strangeness of strangers or the otherness of others can also frustrate learning if something is too strange or too different. To a certain unbridgeable extent the otherness of the non-human, that of animals and plants, will ever remain an unknown world, although close empathetic relationships to animals may surely bring humans and animals together. Or can humans understand the otherness of inorganic and organic nature? Certainly not at all.

What about God and his intelligibility? Again experience is regarded as the key that opens the doors to all religious mysteries. In fact, human experience suffers from several constitutional handicaps which are rooted in specific features of human nature. To name just three:

- Humans cannot transcend the sensory limits of their perceptional apparatus. They live in a mesocosmos with clear limits to the macro- and microcosmos, and even in this mesocosmos our perceptions can be illusory, as we all know.
- Second, we have to take into account the historical dependencies of human interpretations, and the epistemological deficiencies of knowledge. Human self-consciousness seems to be a matter of absolutely clear and immediate cognition, but in fact it only exists within a process of context-bound reflection which is open to many influences that distort what one thinks to be 'pure' and therefore 'true' reality. Experience is deceptive, and the ensuing knowledge epistemologically uncertain; therefore it always ought to be open to improved knowledge.
- Third, social routines reduce our capacity to reflect upon and interpret our experience so that often it hardly deserves to be called experience at all. It is only if the stream of sensations and observations flowing through our conscious being is reflected upon or pondered that an experience will be formed. If we are nothing but 'drifting' through waves of feelings and associations an experience will not gain shape.

It is against this general background of human limitations that the effect of faith-resisting experiences must be considered. Faith and experience can come into 'sharpest contrast'. A prophetic message in the Old Testament or the radicality of Jesus preaching the 'Kingdom of God' in the New Testament, let alone the meaning of the Cross and Resurrection, can contradict much of what we are used to regarding as reasonable or holy. Cherished habits of behaviour and familiar values prevent us from becoming open to the new; old experiences block new experiences.

Presumably, the main hindrance to developing trust in God stems from the offences to our self-esteem. We will never feel comfortable if our weakness is laid open, if our guilt cannot be concealed any longer, or if our dependency is a bare fact. We speak of 'not losing face'.

Education for Justice and Peace and the Culture of Compassion and Care

In the parable of 'The Workers in the Vineyard' the workers who had been hired at six o'clock in the morning lost face when, having observed to the landowner, 'these last worked only one hour, and you have made them equal to us who have borne the burden of the day and the scorching heat', they received the answer, 'are you envious because I am generous?' ('is your eye evil [bad] because I am good?') (Matt. 20: 15).

God does not want human beings to lose face, either on earth or in heaven; his intention is to restore them by lifting his face upon them. But human resistance to God's goodness is also a fact, resistance to the unusual, to the 'incomprehensible interruption of the usual' (Jüngel 1986: 164) as a matter of grace. We are usually interested in self-security and self-assertion within a framework of values we hold to be absolutely valid. This framework can become a 'cage' which imposes its laws upon us. Max Weber has spoken of the 'iron cage' of capitalism. The idea of justice in the egalitarian form of equal distribution is another cage in the form of an iron law.

Our parable revolutionizes our values, and breaks open that cage. The fact that the landowner hires unemployed day-workers at the eleventh hour, only one hour before the end of the working day, is itself most unusual. Why does he do it? Are they old or sick people whom nobody wants? His action does not follow the usual economic logic. The storyteller does not explain; but the listeners are to be motivated to pay special attention to those employed last – and of course also to God behind the landowner. Those who were familiar with the biblical tradition knew that the imagery of the vineyard hinted conclusively at God himself. 'And now I will tell you what I will do to my vineyard' (Isa. 5: 5). The time of sunset used to be the time for paying wages, not only on earth. 'You shall not keep for yourself the wages of a laborer until morning' (Lev. 19: 13); 'you shall pay them their wages daily before sunset, because they are poor and their livelihood depends on it, otherwise they might cry to the LORD against you, and you would incur guilt' (Deut. 24: 15).

The word 'wages' further reminded everyone of God as the righteous judge who will pay the righteous in the future life. Moreover, the term 'landowner' (v. 1) is now changed to the 'LORD of the vineyard' (v. 8). The attention is enhanced so that everyone expects that something unusual is going to happen, and it does, indeed! 'That those employed last to whom God had promised nothing would also receive a whole Denar is completely unpredictable' (Luz 1997: 148). It is still totally contrary to economic logic today.

Then the moment comes when those employed first are paid. They expect more, of course; and readers of the parable today will agree with them. But they also receive only one denar each – and protest. In an arbitrary way – without considering the work they have performed, and without taking into account at all the particular working conditions ('the scorch of heat' for those employed first, the much more comfortable temperatures for those employed last) – the landowner violates the principle of justice by equalizing according to his unusual criteria.

The protests are well grounded and have to be taken seriously. The landowner is open to argument and addresses the speaker in a kindly condescending voice, 'Friend, I am doing you no wrong.' No harsh rejection, but a calm self-justification. Hadn't they negotiated for 'the usual daily wage' (v. 13)? It is a formal argument according to the idea of justice that the spokesman of the early workers had himself invoked. In sum, according to the broadly accepted social norm no violation of the concept of justice 'as usual' had occurred.

Then the landowner defends his right to act in this way in his position as proprietor, 'Am I not allowed to do what I choose with what belongs to me?' (v. 15). Only after rehearsing these well-known arguments does the landowner reveal the central motive of his action: 'He is good although he is not under any obligation to be good' (Luz 1997: 150). And it is this unusual reality of goodness that causes envy, the envious eye, literally (in Greek): 'the bad eye', which also means the 'evil, hostile eye', the well-known source of conflict and war.

We have to draw theological conclusions unencumbered by a long history of distorting exegesis. The parable does not place 'goodness and God's righteousness against each other antithetically. Rather, the story tells of the miraculous goodness of a landowner who fulfils the claim of justice in each respect' (Luz 1997: 151). Nor is there any opposition of grace and reward. 'On the contrary, the grace towards those employed last consists of the fact that they do receive their wage, from mere grace' (ibid.).

We have already dealt with the issue of justice in Chapter 4, and tried to highlight the point that God's justice, according to the faith of the psalmist, is a 'saving' justice that expresses God's option for the poor and suppressed, and restores the just order of the world as the order of his original creation. Now the time has come for this new creation. The Old Testament and the New Testament, the faith of the Jewish tradition and the Christian tradition, cannot be separated in that in the Old Testament there is only distributive justice, while in the New Testament there is only astonishing pure grace (Luz 1997: 152–3). As we have seen already in the discussion of the story of Cain and Abel in Chapter 3, both stories show the free and faithful intention of the just and righteous God to prove who he is – a good and loving God. His righteousness (justice) is his love (see the title of Part II: 'peace through justice', and the corresponding title of this Part III: 'reconciliation through love').

What is the precise difference compared with the human criteria of acting that we are used to? The notion of egalitarian justice is no longer allowed to be the dominant norm for all people and all human activities. The character of this norm in its absoluteness, by which it excludes and rejects the unusual radical attitude of loving, gracious goodness, is refuted. However, this does not mean that God is obliged to grant goodness as if human beings were entitled to claim it.

Those young people in our time who get frustrated by the 'fatal theses' in 'religion' as they experience it (see the young painter) have to be told that in exactly the reverse way God contradicts the 'fatal laws' ruling the 'iron cage' of meritocracy which ruthlessly divides winners and losers, the successful and unsuccessful, the gifted and the handicapped, devaluing all who fail to meet its egalitarian standards. Jesus as the incarnation of the biblical God has not come to abolish the classical understanding of justice, or to weaken the necessary efforts of each of us in our professions. But he accuses his contemporaries of their lack of radical solidarity with the weak and poor. In the parable those get more who need it. Likewise the churches have to be the advocates of those who need 'neighbourly love' in the broadest sense of this term, aiming both at those near at hand and also those far away on the other side of the world. Many young people have lost their belief that a 'better' justice might ever appear on earth. Christian education will have to show them that it is not impossible.

For this goal Christian education for peace and reconciliation through love as a new justice has to be pursued in two directions. They encompass

- promoting responsibility for social justice and legal justice alike, as a moral issue, in struggling against social injustice and corrupt practice in law, and
- highlighting justice as the expression of a culture of caring on a transmoral level, resisting the absoluteness of the sphere of morality as such.

In the first perspective, the advocacy of equal rights is opposed to unequal treatment, while in the second, unequal treatment is defended against the egalitarian. Christian ethics cannot be adequately understood if restricted solely to the former. Knowledge of faith about 'justification by grace only' simultaneously *includes* the former perspective while also *transcending* it in a culture of compassion and care that does not rely exclusively on the capacities and achievements of the individual. Where people come in touch with, and are hopefully seized by, this liberating message, life becomes a feast, and a feast is never celebrated alone, but in a new community, as it was in the famous story of 'The Prodigal Son' (or 'The Two Sons') in Luke 15.

Chapter 6

Christian Education Revised in the Spirit of God's Reconciling Joy

'Let us eat and celebrate; for this son of mine was dead and is alive again; he was lost and is found!' And they began to celebrate. When the older son protested, the father responded, 'But we had to celebrate and rejoice, because this brother of yours was dead and has come to life.'

The Joyless Character of Traditional Christian Nurture

The quotation above is taken from a New Testament parable which in the past used to be called 'The Parable of the Lost (or Prodigal) Son'; today exegetes speak also of 'The Parable of the Two Sons'. They do not entirely disregard the word 'lost', but they remove it from the heading. In my own childhood Christian education tended to warn of bad manners and guilt; the glory of the biblical stories was refracted through windows tinted with pale colours. Relatedly, participating in the Lord's Supper was for all of our family an awe-inspiring event pictured in black. I used to approach it with trembling knees. Christian nurture was dominated by an atmosphere of fear, as was the life of the church as a whole. Our anxieties had much to do with forms of conduct; the religious path to God was paved with moral stumbling blocks. The doorway to God, who was always referred to as 'der liebe Gott' (the German word 'lieb' meaning 'dear', 'kind', 'loving'), was a bad conscience.

Almost any biblical story can be related to the issue of conscience. The 'lost' son, we were told in RE in school, was only welcomed by his father after he had repented and 'came to himself' (Luke 15: 17) stung by remorse: 'I will get up and go to my father, and I will say to him, "Father, I have sinned against heaven and before you; I am no longer worthy to be called your son; treat me like one of your hired hands"' (vv. 18b–19). If these sentences are emphasized in religious education, the parable becomes a story primarily about sin, repentance and penance. The focus is on the threatened loss of salvation, and as the remedy all attention is drawn to a path that leads through self-humiliation: 'treat me as one of your hired hands'.

Such a focus is surely backed by the wording of the text, but is it the only possible or the most important reading? Interpretations of biblical texts are shaped by generalized traditions of reading habits which depend on still broader trends, on the self-understanding of the church in connection with the moral and religious temperature of society. During the longest period of Protestant education – we leave the Catholic tradition aside – the general view of the correct theological interpretation of the Bible was in accordance with a certain relation between 'law' and 'gospel': the 'gospel' followed the 'law'; the father's acceptance of the lost son followed his repentance and decision to return. Although the doctrine of law differed between the various Protestant denominations, the impact on children was basically the same. Whether God was threatening the young soul via the more indirect authority of God's law, incorporated in the surrounding secular institutions of the family, the state and others (the 'politicus usus legis' of the Lutheran tradition), or through the direct authority of Christ's law (the 'tertius usus legis' according to the Calvinist view) (on the understanding of law see Chapter 2), the stern demanding face of God prevailed over his gracious and loving character. God acquired the role of the very highest policeman.

The two traits of Christian education in the past, a) rigidity and b) the sequence of repentance, that is submission and – then – forgiveness, have a very long historical background. In Jesus Sirach (the author, Ben Sira, lived around 190 BCE) we find the classical illustration of the first characteristic. The following prescriptions of moral education were valid in Jesus' lifetime and have been absorbed into a long tradition of Christian education.

> He who loves his son will whip him often,
> so that he may rejoice at the way he turns out.
> He who disciplines his son will profit by him,
> and will boast of him among acquaintances
>   (Sir. 30: 1–2)

> An unbroken horse turns out stubborn,
> and an unchecked son turns out headstrong.
> Pamper a child, and he will terrorize you;
> play with him, and he will grieve you.
> Do not laugh with him, or you will have sorrow with him,
> and in the end you will gnash your teeth. . . .
> Bow down his neck in his youth, and beat his sides while he is young,
> or else he will become stubborn and disobey you,
> and you will have sorrow of soul from him.
>   (Sir. 30: 8–10, 12)

In later history this rigid pattern was modified and softened, until in the relatively liberal Middle Ages the process of moral and attitudinal 'civilization' as internal control of one's own impulses and emotions gradually set in (Norbert Elias), in particular from the late Middle Ages onwards, when the moralist movement in France and Germany gained ground (Ariès 1960). The religious movements of the Reformation and Counter-Reformation added to this process. The habit of secluded education in boarding-houses developed. The history of physical punishment between the fourteenth and the seventeenth centuries shows that punishment aimed at humiliation, the intention of degrading becoming the characteristic element of the new attitude towards childhood. The intimidating character of the Christian education continues although it weakens in some aspects in the eighteenth century, the era of the Enlightenment and of humanitarian ideas. In the nineteenth century the rule of obedience was strengthened again. Why?

The logic of rigidity, the first trait of traditional Christian moral education, can easily be explained by three factors: (1) by the dynamic natural energies of uneducated children, whose impulses to move around and play can be observed in young bears and foxes as part of a common ancient evolutionary heritage (hence the correct observation and comparison between young horses and young humans in Sirach); (2) by the necessity of getting children under control and taming this anarchic nature in order to integrate offspring into the general efforts for survival and prospering (the 'profit' of 'inclusive fitness'); and (3) by the other sociobiological fact that success is dependent on age, on shaping the body and soul of the male child 'while he is young'. Humans are the creatures with the greatest capacity for, and need of, learning, and the most capable of effective and rapid learning at an early age.

The logic of the second trait of traditional Christian moral education (the sequence of repentance, submission, forgiveness) is evident too, for it implements the law of learning by reinforcement, by adults who punish, ignore or reward actions. Moral behaviour becomes the product of the interplay between expectations and fulfilment. To switch back to our case: the behaviour of the younger son is described as a breach of given moral standards, 'he squandered his property in dissolute living' (Luke 15: 13b). The older brother adds, 'he has devoured your property with prostitutes' (v. 30). Consequently, according to the logic of expectations generalized over generations, he should expect punishment. Still today the logic of this temporal sequence of steps is convincing to everyone. It was and still is a matter of daily experience that mother or father react to their children's conduct, in the case of bad behaviour by respectively ignoring them, or in more serious cases by a withdrawal of love, or in the worst cases by punishment; in cases of good behaviour, by contrast, they react with indulgence and forgiveness, thereby healing the damaged relationship. For this positive reaction usually at least a certain signal of repentance is expected, and the child knows about this expectation as a law of mutual reciprocity. Children learn how to deserve their parent's benevolence.

What about the Reformation standpoint of God's grace by faith only? It is truthfully transmitted from generation to generation, but with a questionable result. Although in confirmation classes some years later I learnt the difference between Catholics and Protestants – the emphasis on 'deeds' there and on 'faith' here, a lesson admittedly cast in terms of a crude opposition – this lesson in doctrine was not personally convincing. The actual content of the lesson remained a purely external matter, it did not become an internal conviction with tangible effect on behaviour. The 'Catholic' standpoint still exercised a natural attraction in practice, and for good reasons, as indicated above: in order to heal interpersonal relations special efforts were needed, concrete moral achievements, visible moral progress in conduct.

The preceding chapter concluded with the distinction between the moral sphere, with its well-known inherited reciprocities, and the much less definitely known nature of a transmoral sphere, where it is not achievements that count, but gifts. How can the latter become an effective force in education as a convincing and lived truth if in general children learn the 'iron law' of 'do ut des'? We may assume that our parable evokes ambivalent reactions at the very least, as happens within the story itself with the older brother: the father is not fair! His much too lenient behaviour offends the natural feeling of justice. Cain and Abel come to mind, as well as the paying of the labourers in the vineyard: God's incomprehensible difference remains part of the ongoing challenge to a radical reconstruction of religious and moral education from a biblical perspective. His difference as a logic of love and forgiveness disturbs the logic of retaliation and war.

'The Parable of the Two Sons' – a Feast of Reconciliation

We need to look at the parable itself from a fresh standpoint with a focus on joy and a reconciled community. From another angle, we might elaborate our theme of unreconciled humanity and the reconciling ('saving') justice of God's shalom. The aspects of joy and community are relevant for educational and spiritual practice, for both the 'educational ethos' of a school and the 'spirituality' of church life. In many countries schools suffer from bullying and violence among the pupils.

The parable is about a wealthy farmer who has many workers (Luke 15: 17) and slaves (v. 22). Of his two sons the younger wants to get his portion of the inheritance (v. 12), which is not unusual, or rebellious, or against the rule of morality, for quite a few Jews in those times had to emigrate into the diaspora, since the Palestinian soil could not feed the population.

After a while the young man had 'squandered his property in dissolute living' (v. 13), a negative commentary, and is surprised by a severe famine at that – a factor for which he is not to blame (v. 14). His social decline is surpassed by his religious one, for he loses his religious identity, first, because he is forced to work for a gentile (v. 15), second, because he constantly has contact with pigs, animals which were regarded as 'unclean' (Lev. 11: 7). In this new environment he abandons his faith and lives under the curse of apostasy. The lowest level of living is reached when he would be glad to 'fill himself with the pods that the pigs were eating; and no one gave him anything' (v. 16). A saying goes that 'when the Jews are forced to eat the pods of carob, they will do penance' (quote in Wiefel 1987: 289). 'The younger son has become a non-person' (Schweitzer 1982: 161).

When he 'was dying of hunger' (v. 17) he decided to return to his father and to confess his guilt (v. 18). His motivation comes from comparing his misery with the wealth and comfort at home. Since the listeners knew what the parable was about, namely not simply a tale about any father anywhere, but about the heavenly father, it was the recollection of the glory of heaven that prompted the son to return. Therefore, one can perhaps say that in this moment the father was already with him, in his 'recollection': 'conversion being remembering' (Schweitzer 1982: 161). This was how Israel was when it had cut itself off from God. The son felt not only guilty, but also that he no longer had any right to be called son. He would be happy to be one of his father's workers (Luke 15: 19). 'So he set off and went to his father' (v. 20).

The return is told in great detail; the parable approaches its climax, the father and his reactions. He seems to have waited for his son; with strained eyes he must have looked out for him, for he noticed him when he was already 'still far off' (v. 20). It is added that at once he was 'filled with compassion' – a strong hint at the inner feelings for his son, feelings of love. What now follows is quite unusual as it breaks the rule of fitting conduct: the father 'ran' out to his son; in terms of the relationship between young and old, to behave like this went against all custom. 'To an Oriental, for an elder person to run quickly is itself undignified' (Schweitzer 1982: 161). The father embraced the son: 'he put his arms around him and kissed him' (v. 20). Forgiveness is expressed not in words but in action. Moreover, this action precedes that of confession. When the son articulates his sin the father seems not to listen, the next sentence beginning with a quick, as it were, interrupting 'but': 'But the father said to his slaves, "Quickly, bring out a robe – the best one – and put it on him; put a ring on his finger and sandals on his feet. And get the fatted calf and kill it, and let us eat and celebrate"' (vv. 22–3).

Each item is an eloquent proof of joy and reconciliation without words; no formalized pious ritual of 'repentance', 'confession', 'absolution' or whatsoever is necessary. The ring and the gown restore the honour of the son, by the ring the son obtains the right to seal. The sandals mark the difference between the free man and the slave who went barefoot. Eventually the 'fatted calf', always at disposal for an unforeseen event like this, transforms everything into a feast. The reason why is given in the sentence, 'for this son of mine was dead and is alive again; he was lost and is found!' (v. 24). These words clearly indicate the level of salvation, 'death' meaning separation from God the father, being 'alive again' referring to resurrection which is identical with communion with the father. At the end of the parable these words will be repeated in order to emphasize them when addressed to the elder son (v. 32).

He had been in the field and falls aghast when 'he heard music and dancing' and asked what was going on (vv. 25–6). 'He became angry and refused to go in' (v. 28). And again it is the father who approaches his sons, now the elder son, in order to persuade him to change his mind and join in the joyous feast. But the elder son resists. In the light of what we have said about 'human experience' blocking off God's coming, rather than being a bridge to him (as is generally supposed in modern experiential religious learning), the reasoning of the elder son represents precisely the old pattern of 'bargaining' (cf. Chapters 3–5). This pattern rests upon a notion of 'justice' as, first, tit for tat in equal terms, and, second, as something that ought to be deserved by achievements. The elder son accuses his father of never having killed even a 'a young goat' for him in spite of his working 'all these years . . . like a slave' (v. 29), whereas he now had killed the fatted calf (30), the one reserved for special purposes. His own daily life had been nothing – as it seems to him – in comparison to what was happening now – itself, in the view of the elder son, a crying injustice. He exaggerates the unworthiness of his younger brother by calling into the father's mind that 'this son of yours . . . has devoured your property with prostitutes' (v. 30), a fact (?) that had not been mentioned before. The rules of a just world order (cf. Chapter 3), justice as equal proportions and as a balancing of good and bad deeds, are doubly broken.

Again the father's line of argument is radically different from customary logic. His response highlights something quite different to one's conduct, namely one's being. 'Son, you are always with me, and all that is mine is yours' (v. 31). It is not the deeds of humans that constitute their relationship to the living God, but rather their simply being with him, and this being together with him is God's selfless richness: 'all that is mine is yours!' Nothing only for me, everything also for you.

The elder son does not agree. He does not join the feast and hence fails to participate in the sacrament of new community. Instead he refuses to come, avoids addressing his father with the name 'father', and speaks of his younger brother in a distancing way as 'this son of yours', no longer regarding him as his brother. Community is dissolved in both directions, spiritually speaking, to God and to other human beings. This is the image of the unreconciled world – even in what we are accustomed to rely on as the most intimate community, that of our own family.

The most severe reproach of the elder son concerns the father's kindness, his gracious love, as we saw earlier with the reproachful looks of the vineyard labourers who had been working from early in the morning (Chapter 5). The confounding truth the Bible tells about humans is their resistance to something that ought to be for them the most desirable good on earth. This good creates, expresses itself and is in a way identical with community. Its refusal because of the stubborn clinging to one's own merits, is, in theological language, the core of the doctrine of the 'justification of the sinner' (see Chapter 8). From an educational perspective, it marks the dark reverse of all optimistic educational efforts and the reason why we have to base moral and religious education on a disillusioned, realistic picture of human nature (see Chapters 9 and 10). But is what follows from this not that kind of Christian education we described above, with the sombre face of penance? Yes and no, for in the light of our parable the overwhelming joy of the father is the dominant biblical message. It cuts through the thought pattern of 'bargaining', either with the younger or with the elder son. The spirit of Christians in educating children and young, be it in churches, in schools or wherever, should be the joyful spirit of the gospel – the 'good news'.

Broken and Restored Community

As in the preceding chapters we are going to continue weaving together theological and educational perspectives in order to form a coherent, convincing context in both directions. Our specific educational interest is to ask how to deal with the parable with young children. For this purpose we will again align hermeneutical methods and empirical data and apply the elementarizing approach. Its five dimensions ask for elementary structures, experiences, developmental accesses (entrances) to understanding, truth experiences and methods.

To start with the elementary structure, 'The Parable of the Two Sons' can be summed up doctrinally as an illustration of the 'doctrine of justification'. It concerns 'the righteousness of God and the justification of the sinner'. These terms belong to a well-known academic theological language game. But if teachers use them in the classroom without explanation they will fail. Empirical observations (Schweitzer *et al.* 1995: 51–4) have shown that in critical situations, when pupils' understanding is blocked, teachers take refuge in dangerous theological abstractions. They activate the university knowledge which they had once mugged up for examination purposes. This material is still quite ready to hand – but falling back on it is completely the wrong solution. Consequently, throughout this book the topic of God's righteousness and shalom as the context for an education for peace and justice today has been expressed in quite different, more accessible language (the Bible itself helped us), such as narrative language (Cain and Abel), poetical imagery (Psalms) and the plain condensed language of parables. Let us continue exploring understandable language.

To look for an elementary structure one has, first, to look for the plot. In Luke 15 several parables share the same structural plot. Usually they are put together under the heading of 'what was lost is found' – a sheep (vv. 3–7), a coin (vv. 8–10) and now a son (vv. 11–32). To speak of something that was lost and could be found again is plain common language, which every child easily understands. Another chief characteristic elementary feature is clear too: finding something that got lost is a reason to rejoice. Hence, not the loss as an isolated fact, but finding again is the elementary crucial event which 'structures' the plot of the story. The parable conspicuously elaborates the joyful event of a reunion: a family reunion, a new belonging together. In a way, this even takes place twice. First, the 'lost' younger son comes back and the father takes him up in the old community with him. Second, we see the father's attempt to include his elder son too in the joy of the new being all together again, an attempt, however, that fails, but does not alter the governing 'structure'. Twice the father pursues the same intention.

A further elementary structural item communicates a remarkable theological message. On both occasions the father (God) wipes away all negative aspects of previous separation. He does not refer to the younger son's past – no mention of it any more. Nor does he blame his older son for his behaviour. He 'began to plead with him' (v. 28), which is quite different from reproaching him; using again common language, we may say that he bears him no grudge. That's something even young children understand very well, both as to language and as to substance. They know the difference between people who do not bear unfriendly feelings towards them although their behaviour may have upset them, and those adults who habitually bear grudges. Thus, the elementary structural core consists of both these two main traits: on the one hand, no grudging, on the other hand, new community and, indeed, both of these are definitely strong reasons for joy.

By retranslating this ensemble into theological language, we can say that 'The Parable of the Two Sons', in its narrative plot, not only speaks about, but actually brings what is spoken about into life. It is the 'Good News' of 'forgiving' without 'charging' the 'sinners' (both the younger and the elder son) for their 'wickedness'. The offenders are not punished. Educators should notice with particular attention that the father is far from any moralizing. In New Testament parables of the Kingdom of God we do not find any justification for a moralizing Christian education.

A final theological point refers to the image of God who, indeed, does not appear as a 'judge', but as the fatherly 'host'. God's way of interaction with human beings is to 'invite' them kindly. His 'pleading' to the elder son shows that he puts his trust in asking, requesting, kindly urging, not in violent force. One might think of quite a different story about a son who has squandered his property and, moreover, violated everything his religion holds sacred, and a father upset and reacting harshly to this. Pupils might be asked to devise a plot along these very different lines. God the Father Almighty might even have mobilized his men to fetch the son back from abroad; at any rate he might demand 'satisfaction', as was and still is the case everywhere on earth, and in the practice of the churches too. But in Luke 15 there is no hint of the doctrine of satisfaction.

Jesus Celebrating – Children Celebrating

With regard to 'elementary experiences', the elementarization approach distinguishes between, and coordinates, two perspectives, the quest for the experiences expressed in the faith tradition, in this case those 'behind' the parable, and the corresponding experiences of children and young people today. What were the experiences in Jesus' time such that parables like the one we are interpreting made such an impression that they were handed down to subsequent generations of the Christian churches? We do not have to look far. If it is true that the 'structural' core is one of joy and celebration, then this is the way Jesus himself had been experienced. The person who told this parable was the person his disciples and adherents knew as the one who had entered the house of Levi, son of Alphaeus, who had been 'sitting at the tax booth' (Mark 2: 13), and had asked him to follow him and with whom afterwards Jesus was sitting 'at dinner . . . with many tax collectors and sinners' (Mark 2: 15; cf. Luke 5: 27–32). It was the man from Nazareth who had on many other occasions also sat together with 'lost sons' in order to celebrate a feast. Jesus and his followers are compared both with John and his disciples and also with the disciples of the Pharisees. "'John's disciples, like the disciples of the Pharisees, frequently fast and pray, but your disciples eat and drink." Jesus said to them, "You cannot make wedding guests fast while the bridegroom is with them, can you?"' (Luke 5: 33–4).

The 'Kingdom of God' is present in Jesus' actions as it is present (and happening) in 'The Parable of the Two Sons' and other parables, all of which form one wonderful coherent manifestation of 'reconciliation through love' as the road to peace with God and among people. Jesus brings himself, and with him the Kingdom of God, that is, God himself, through the parable as an event: This whole event is truly a feast. We have to add this new dimension to the discussion of God's righteousness and peace earlier in this book. In its nature as a feast God's 'righteousness' and 'justice' manifest their character as the loving kindness of the Creator to his creatures, in stark opposition to the dark, frightening spirit of earlier ways of Christian education and life (see pp. 85–6).

What are the corresponding 'elementary experiences' of children today? What images and feelings will be evoked by 'The Parable of the Two Sons' when it is introduced to them? How can we avoid a trivializing handling of the text and how can experiences of today contribute to rejuvenating encounters with texts from the past? Children and young people are very fond of all sorts of celebrations. They are accustomed to speaking of 'parties', with birthday parties at the top of the list. That is a wonderful bridge to stories in the Bible dealing with festivities. However, often we tend to forget important differences. It is our responsibility to enable children and teenagers to be sensitive to at least some of these differences. Words like joy can cover several things and meanings. Youngsters today 'enjoy' fun, but the joy in the parable has nothing to do with mere fun. We can find an answer by recollecting the elementary structure of the story, the joy at having found something that had been lost, and of returning home after having suffered from being away. These traits, which are central from a theological perspective, can be understood very well by children from their perspective. Children can be very sad about something they have lost, and from which they have been separated. Equally, they can share the son's joy. Similarly, they can be deeply disturbed when a friend moves or, worse still, their mother and father divorce and one of them leaves the house. If they rejoin children will be full of joy, and from this perspective they can also share the father's happiness in the parable.

Is it possible to open up to their understanding and their feelings the other important aspect, Jesus sitting with and celebrating with what the New Testament calls sinners? They are the socially outcast and marginalized. Who are the outcasts in our societies whom children and young people come across? This question will need to be answered according to the different circumstances in different countries. Yet some typical situations are likely to be expected almost everywhere on earth. In a plural world minorities will typically be people living separated in various ways from mainstream society, and suffering from both subtle and obvious forms of discrimination. People of different ethnic, cultural or religious backgrounds, and of course above all of different social milieus, can become strangers or outsiders whom one tends to avoid. Today the parables of the Kingdom of God have to be applied to this field of intercultural and inter-religious tensions too, as well as, of course, to the differences between Christian denominations themselves (see Chapter 11).

In Germany, as in many other European countries, celebrating together the festivals of different religions in schools is a practice that is on the increase. While this is an appropriate development and should be supported, we have to consider the character and quality of feeling that is evoked for one another. Forms of superficial community can hardly be compared with the experience of deep joy about the new sense of community in our story. The parable reminds us not to overlook the background against which joy can spring up, which may correspond to the joy of the celebration in the house of the father. Sometimes children will feel the worth of joyful community only after, so to speak, tears. This does not mean waiting for harmful conflicts to occur, but if they do, and if then they are resolved by steps of reconciliation, they make the children feel truly relieved.

Our topic has very much to do with the experience of a new freedom through forgiveness. If guilt is forgiven and sadness wiped away by being together anew, what a wonderful sigh of relief there is on both sides, prompting true enjoyment of the feeling of belonging together in the family, true enjoyment of the birthday party or any other celebration. One of the major ways towards peace that Christians will propose is to join the joyful feast of new freedom.

Learning by Surprise

In these recent remarks we have already come very close to the third dimension of elementarizing reflections, concerning elementary points of entry to understanding ('elementary accesses'). For what follows I draw on the Tübingen empirical investigation of lessons in RE with children aged 10 to 12, who among other topics were confronted with exactly our parable. While in the section above we looked chiefly at the daily life of children (parties, celebration of birthdays, fun, festivals of other religions in the classroom, conflicts with a positive outcome), we have now to turn to developmental factors. Whereas it seems easy to get children to enjoy a story about family conflicts and their solution, it appears much less easy to introduce them to the religious meaning of a parable.

In the Tübingen project the pupils in the lesson on Luke 15: 11–32 assimilated the plot to the family experiences they were accustomed to, namely quarrelling with their parents, and quarrelling among sisters and brothers (Schweitzer *et al.* 1995: 15–20). 'Well, at first, both [the younger son and the father] were angry with each other, and when the son came back, the father felt sorry and then both apologized.' The story is taken as an example of the well-known, fairly constant frictions between children and parents, but quite different in one key respect from the parable itself. For the boys and girls in the class, both son and father had regretted and apologized to each other. According to Jean Piaget's studies on cognitive development, new perceptions are 'assimilated' to what is familiar. Here it is not only assimilation to the familiar social scenery of family life as such, but, even more conclusively, assimilation to the pattern of reciprocity in domestic conflicts. All of us tend to think in the pattern of mutual provocation and mutual conflict-solving. If one person will give in, the other will mostly do so too. In the preceding chapters we have identified the pattern of reciprocity in human action as a very old one. It is central to the issue of justice as fairness, of maintaining equilibrium on equal terms. However, we have also realized that the biblical God does not fit into this pattern. In the analysis above, the pattern of reciprocal thinking was mirrored by the figure of the elder brother whose protest will presumably be well understood by everyone today. We must infer that any asymmetry in solving social conflicts is more or less unusual, in particular for children and young people.

Yet if children and adolescents see the father as a guilty party too, the reconciliation loses all its religious meaning. The parable becomes an example of a normal moral conflict with a solution on similarly normal lines. Therefore, the teacher has to reconstruct the true traits of the parable together with her class or group along the lines we have tried to indicate above. When the teacher succeeds in correcting this most basic misunderstanding, and it becomes clear that the father has to be appreciated from quite a different perspective, the children will wonder why he acted as he did, in this quite unusual way. The unusual and novel must be clarified and set against the usual and the well established. This was the starting-point of our analysis from the very beginning of Chapter 2. Indeed, it has been the leitmotiv of the whole book since.

Another factor relates to the children's comprehension of metaphorical language. In Chapter 4 we discussed how Ingo Baldermann succeeded in opening up children's understanding of the poetic metaphorical religious language of the Psalms. But the verses he used were quite selective and spoke an imaginative language with an emotional background that resonated with corresponding emotions in the children ('I am weary with my crying') or used imagery which was taken from nature ('I sink in deep mire where there is no foothold'). In our parable, the famous sentence whose meaning turns on metaphorical usage is different and meets with considerable difficulties. 'Let us eat and celebrate, for this son of mine was dead and is alive again; he was lost and is found' (Luke 15: 24, 32). The following passage reveals the ways in which the pupils in our class at their age of 10 to 11 assimilated that statement:

> *Teacher*: Great joy is expressed by the father when he says to his slave, My son was dead and he is alive again.
> *Student A*: (murmuring aside) Who will believe it?
> *Student B*: Well. His son didn't like his father any more, and wanted to go far away . . . that's what perhaps 'to be dead' means. But then he has risen so that he became alive again, meaning that he came back to his father.

Compared with the vast majority in her class this child (B), a girl, had developed a more differentiated understanding of metaphorical language compared with all the others, as we noted. She knew that a word or a statement may 'mean' something that is different from its literal 'wording'. She knew about and tried to transfer semantic content from one level to another. Going far away from home 'means perhaps "to be dead"'. When the son rose up to go back home, 'he became alive again', that means 'he came back to his father'. Immediately after this statement two other students gave their explanations:

> *Student C*: He [the son] was, for him, for his father, he was dead. But in truth he wasn't dead at all, for he had worked.
> *Student D*: The father has thought that his son was already dead, because he hadn't got any news from him. But then, when he came back, he thought, Yes, he has risen.

In both explanations the metaphorical language of having been 'dead' and coming 'alive again' is taken literally. The children think that the father assumed that his son had really died although this was not the case. These two comments were given shortly after the girl had clearly expressed her metaphorical interpretation – but it had no effect on students C and D!

This lack of reaction can be explained by the theory of structural cognitive development, according to which a structural pattern cannot simply be changed by content learning, that is by being given new knowledge; it requires structural learning, which takes place when the new perceptions cannot any longer be 'assimilated' to the old structures, instead, conversely, those given old structures have to adapt themselves to the new perceptions and their contents (in Piaget's terminology 'accommodation'). These processes take place on a level the Swiss expert in religious development Fritz Oser has called 'deep structures' (Oser and Gmünder 1984: 42). The information presented by the girl could not yet reach this level in pupils C and D.

Two levels of learning can be distinguished. On the first level, the emotional content of a biblical parable or any other biblical or non-biblical text, picture or other representation can impress children by the plot of the story and, in particular, by the emotionally moving human events that are recorded. Imagery plays a great role in this. Thus, Baldermann's findings are valid, and they and the data of the Tübingen developmental research project do not exclude each other. However, on the second level of structural changes, the children are perhaps not able to grasp the meaning of a text. Teachers have to know about this difference.

The two levels of learning are also interrelated. Emotional impressions deliver a platform of interest for further cognitive explorations, and cognitive dissonances (see Festinger's theory of cognitive dissonance) often excite the emotions, 'How can this happen?' 'It can't be true!' 'It's annoying!' (cf. Chapter 5, the reactions to Jesus from older pupils). The final result of our study concerning learning is that both emotional and cognitive religious and moral learning are propelled by surprises. This is in accordance with learning as well as developmental theories.

The Holy Sphere of Individual Religious Convictions

How are we to handle elementary truth experiences and truth claims? In his *Speeches on Religion* (1799) Friedrich Schleiermacher called the catechetical practice of his time ridiculous when it nourished the illusionary hope of being successful by means of the transmission of 'concepts', that is, by cognitive ideas, notions, contents.

'Concepts' at best penetrate the 'mechanism of the mind', but will never enter the 'organisation of the mind'. It is in this 'holy workshop of the Universe' that the dynamic interaction between divine transcendence and the individual takes place. Religion becomes alive only in the interior of a human being in 'freedom'. The word 'Universe' is used as a 'modern' parlance among Romanticists in Schleiermacher's time for referring to God.

Whether a faith tradition is experienced in a process of personally significant learning, thus becoming a certain truth, is not at the disposal of education. It may be intended educationally, but it cannot be enforced. This view forbids any presumptuous and, so to speak, 'aggressive' religious education, either in schools or as part of Christian education in the churches. Religious teachers ought to be modest in their expectations, careful in their means and informed of the situation of the souls of children, the 'holy workshop' of individual faith.

Recent theories of 'faith development' (J. W. Fowler) and the development of 'religious reasoning' (F. Oser) are not aggressive theories, although some may suspect the contrary when they hear about 'stages'. They do not presuppose strict developmental 'laws' working in a mono-causal determination. From the very beginning of dealing with them in the 1980s I have read the theories quite differently, first, as a reminder of just the opposite, the necessity of waiting, not pressing children, second, as a proof of the fact (valid at least for western countries) that the individual religious journey strives towards a stage of 'individuative-reflective faith', as Fowler has called it (1981). The developmental data also remind the religious educator to take note of what cannot and must not be planned. In short, from several points of view there is a warning against any form of religious indoctrination. The issue of religious truth experience has to be protected against a presumptuous educational as well as a theological usurpation of children.

What does this mean for the relation between children and our parable? Half a century ago a Dutch pioneer in the field of religious education, Martinus J. Langeveld (1956), was one of the first to intervene on behalf of the child from the perspective of what counts for a child as religious truth. He approached the relation of the child to religious 'truth' from phenomenological observations about the 'nature' of the child, speaking frankly in this connection of the child's 'soul'. Although being a non-psychological category, we will immediately realize that we need this phenomenological perspective as an important guideline. Langeveld's intuitive view of the child enabled him to see that for a child, when living religiously, she or he is living in the shelter of a meaningful, coherent world that is guided in the best possible way. The child wants to be absolutely certain that his or her religious world is a true world, which means a reliable world. This understanding of truth is also the biblical understanding, for God is believed in as the reliable Lord who keeps his covenant. The child also wants to be sure that parents and others are the guarantors of this truthful reality (and of course they expect it from God too). The small child 'does not live in conscious knowledge of his or her sin, nor conscious of the experience of his or her obstinacy and weakness in loving God and serving Him. Instead, it is certain of God's protection, God's kindness, God's "forgiving and renewing benevolence"' (transl. from the German edn, 1959: 27).

The background of Langeveld's defence of the child's natural needs was a declaration of the General Synod of the Dutch Reformed Church in 1949. Langeveld stated that the Synod's 'adult' theology, as I would put it, completely failed to do justice to children and their religion. This is broadly speaking also the sad practice today. What we must do is to look for that 'true' interpretation of our parable which is adequate to children. Does it mean that the child alone will deliver the criteria? No, for the answer depends also on the possible forms of a theologically legitimate reading (*Lesart*) of the parable. Are there exegetical and educational perspectives that converge? I think this is the case in some major respects, though not in all.

As children of 3 to 6 and also of 10 to 12 (the age of the group in our research project) have not yet developed a consciousness of their 'self' as a whole that has been reflected on in terms of self-identity, they will also lack the religious feeling of being a total sinner in the meaning of the word in its comprehensive singular form. What children may understand is 'sins' in the plural form. They become aware of specific concrete failures; they will not perceive themselves as living in complete religious desolation. Or to return to the parable, a child will not be able to comprehend the radical meaning of being 'dead' as denoting total failure before God. Hence, the formula of 'simul iustus et peccator' ('simultaneously justified and a sinner') cannot fully be appreciated either. The grace of the father's – respectively God's – restoring actions is not felt against the background of a penetrating and comprehensive experience of their own desperate wretchedness, as is the case with the prodigal ('lost') son. In other words, whereas in the adjective 'lost' the semantical content that comes most immediately to mind is simply that something or someone is lost; the religious connotation of the term means lost in God's eyes. However, such a view is beyond a child's emotional and cognitive reach. To tell this to children would be deadly news, not good news. It would be irresponsibly damaging to their souls. Children surely recognize when they have failed and become guilty in specific situations, but the generalization of the plural to the singular as in the abstract phrases of 'the sin of man' makes the child basically helpless, living no longer in a safe world, but being totally forsaken.

Is 'The Parable of the Two Sons' to be interpreted in this latter way? When remembering the results of our exegetical efforts in connection with the analysis of both the elementary structural core of the parable and, above all, the elementary experiences associated with this parable (and others) about the Kingdom of God, the basic message is God's unusual, unexpected kindness which overcomes any separation and grants community. The overwhelming overall note is joy; for what was lost is found – and this children will fully understand. Not only, or primarily, sin and penance, but separation and reunion stands in the foreground of the parable. The father makes no attempt at all to discuss the sinful life of his son; no attempt at all to insist on him first showing signs of repentance before forgiving him; the old game of reciprocal calculation is over. Jesus lets the father embrace his son as he himself used to embrace the children who were brought to him (Mark 10), in both cases actions without any preconditions.

> Paul has clearly seen, namely, that the better righteousness is that which God gives us freely. To children and such as these belongs the Kingdom, without any qualifications, good works or merits. Whoever wants to enter the Kingdom must receive it like children do. This is not the whole gospel of Jesus Christ, but it is the heart of it.
>
> (Weber 1979: 29)

At the end of the story in Mark 10 which tells about little children being brought to Jesus, he 'took them up in his arms, laid his hands on them, and blessed them' (v. 16).

> According to a rabbinic treatise, the resurrection of the people of Israel will happen when 'God embraces them, presses them to his heart and kisses them, thus bringing them into the life of the world to come' (*Seder Elijahu Rabba*, 17). Something like that happened to the children. They who received the Kingdom were embraced by the messianic king.
>
> (Weber 1979: 19)

In dealing with the parable with children we do not need to extend and elaborate the 'elementary truth' of God's community with us by theological doctrines which are not the focus of the text and cannot indeed be understood by children such as the doctrine of justification in its later Pauline and still later dialectical Lutheran form, the doctrine of total wickedness and total renewal, the doctrine of the expiatory sacrifice of Jesus on the cross which in the parable is simply absent. The whole emphasis can be given to the issue of joyful community against the background of separation, of belonging to God and to each other.

The Male and the Female Hand of the Father

In the Hermitage in St Petersburg visitors can admire Rembrandt's famous picture 'The Prodigal Son'. The father bends over his kneeling son, who is leaning his left temple on his father's breast while the old man covers the back of his son, who is clad in ragged remnants of pale coloured clothes, with his two hands. They reach out of the father's red gown, revealing the golden coloured shirt on his arms. The son's back and the father's two hands are the centre of the picture shining in the brightest yellow, together with the similar bright yellow on the old man's face. In the background on the right side of the picture three people watch the scene; far back in the background, on the left-hand side, a young woman dimly shows her watching face.

When comparing the two hands a fascinating discovery can be made (if I may trust my eyes): the father's left hand is a male, his right hand a female hand. The first is broader, bigger and wrinkled, the right hand is smaller, not so broad, much finer, more delicate in shape, perhaps indeed more sensitive. An elementarizing religious education requires impressive 'elementary methods' of communicative power, the fifth dimension of our approach. In religious education training centres, a broad variety of media, not only texts, is waiting to be used. A publication like this does not allow us to elaborate on what ideally ought to be given much more space. Experiments with Rembrandt's presentation of the parable have shown that in particular in upper classes the two different hands of the father's 'nature' fascinate pupils. The female hand is situated just in the middle of the back, while the left hand rests more upon the son's shoulder. Is the motherly love of God the very centre of his righteousness and reconciling peace?

Chapter 7

The Perspective of Victims – Peace and Justice in the Light of Jesus' Death

Jesus' Death as the Consequence of his Life

In spite of the ephemeral character of much that surrounds us, certain fixed points remain. Although daily frustrations make people adapt to the world as it is, there is a global longing for justice and, mostly among young people, hope for a better world. But what has justice to do with 'justification'?

Alongside the topic of justice, this book deals with peace, and their mutual interconnectedness. Against the background of continuing wars and the propensity of human beings to aggression, the chapters reflect on ways to overcome violence. Again children and young people are involved, either as victims or as offenders. But will they understand talking about Jesus' death as a 'propitiatory sacrifice' for the sake of man's 'sins', in order to 'justify the sinner'? We have good reasons to assume that to them the term 'justification' may be connected with a sophisticated 'ecclesiastic doctrine' of hardly any relevance for their daily life. Similarly, Jesus' crucifixion will probably immediately make them feel uneasy because of its repugnant external appearance.

Relatedly, there is a tendency in religious education to separate the topic of Christ's passion from stories about his life. Similarly, on the whole, Paul is separated from Jesus. Paul's theology is regarded as having left the plain path of intelligible Christian faith almost completely. While the stories about Jesus in his lifetime are welcomed, the report about Jesus on the Cross appears either as referring to a brute, deplorable fact without meaning, or as something that is rendered mysterious by theological experts. Paul's letters meet with the same objection. They take no notice of the records about Jesus' life. Instead, they refer merely to his death and resurrection as the basis of salvation. It is this soteriological frame of meaning that has been the prime focus of academic attention, with, at its centre, the doctrine of justification gaining pride of place, particularly from the emergence of Reformation theology onwards. However, even very faithful church members can no longer grasp the meaning of 'justification'. In a sort of sleepy state of subdued awareness, as it were, talking about Christ's death as a sacrifice for the sinner is being dismissed from the agenda of Christian practice completely, most of all in religious education and in modern forms of spiritual quest.

One main reason for this development seems to lie with the church itself. The church's invested interest in a timeless truth has generated more or less abstract cognitive theological concepts quite separate from biographies. However, knowledge arises in the context of life. As Saul of Tarsus, Paul had a provocative biography before he was to have an experience of such extraordinary power as to eclipse even Martin Luther's discovery, John Wesley's conversion, or Blaise Pascal's revelatory experience. It was out of this biographical revolution that his theology developed. We shall try to trace back Paul's theology of 'justification' to its roots in the next chapter. In pursuing the same intention, Jesus' death is to be appreciated as the consequence of his life.

God Delivering His Son to Death as 'the Lamb'?

The question in the heading of this section is, admittedly, a crude point of departure. God appears as simply inhumane; even more, he is accused of sadism. In the 1970s, Tilmann Moser, a German psychiatrist, caused a heated debate when he recollected his childhood, which he had spent in a sectarian-like, narrow-minded pious parental surrounding. In a powerful rhetoric he addressed God ironically in a sort of 'prayer'. His harsh attacks drew from insights taken from the field of psychology.

> As your servants used to recommend, I admired you because of your kindness in not letting Isaac be slaughtered by Abraham. He surely would have done it *for you*, and the remainder of human dignity in your elected people would have looked only a bit more horrible than it already did. Or was it only your impudent good luck that in the last second you had the idea of sending an angel to the location of the planned carnage? . . . With your own son you were less scrupulous in giving vent to your feelings. I was made to believe that by the sacrifice on the cross you wanted to ring in your new covenant of love. And again, in obeying the general invitation, I made the attempt to admire you, because you had sacrificed your only son for me, wretched sinner. That is impressive, indeed: I must be a very bad person to have caused you to take such a fuss about saving me! Only what was really odd was that none of your ministers ever had a suspicion that perhaps there is nothing wrong *with us*, but *with you* when you felt like slaughtering your son for mere humanitarian purposes. And now you give him to us to drink and to eat, for reconciliation, as they say.
>
> (Moser 1976: 20–1)

Sadism is the first focus of Moser's psychological analysis of God's intentions: here the submissive slave, there the absolutist emperor. Another trait is added: like an offended army officer God seems to need satisfaction. He wants to become reconciled by good deeds that will appease his wrath. The uproar within himself must be quelled. The main target of this cynical criticism is the image of a vengeful and merciless God.

Complementarily, Christian faith and church life, including educational practice, are denounced for suppressing the human self; people develop a lack of self-esteem. Moser had a permanent sense of being a bad, wretched creature; there was nothing left that in God's eyes might really count as good.

> At all times and everywhere I felt guilty . . . There was a fundamental insecurity in me . . . In my view, your chief characteristic is mercilessness. You had forbidden so much in me that I could not be loved any longer . . . In my eyes you were the personification of hostility to life . . . You used to grow in the hollows of my social powerlessness and ignorance.
>
> (Moser 1976: 16–23)

In short, the interpretation of Jesus' death as a sacrifice for the sinner is accused also of destroying human autonomy because it manifests a necrophile attraction to the morbid instead of supporting one's strengths and the beauty of life. At this point, feminist theologians tend to agree too, and not only those arguing from a psychoanalytic background. A theology of the Cross which revolves around the ideas of dependency and sacrifice for others falls under the suspicion of (a) cherishing sad memories of authoritarian patriarchal structures, and (b) preventing wholeness and integrity.

Moser features next a dilemma of a specifically theological nature, namely the contradiction, as it seems, between Jesus' death and God's love. Does the proclamation of love by the church necessarily require the idea of a restitution of life through death? Is Christ's suffering needed for forgiving guilt? Does a new relation to God depend on suffering and death, even if these are meant only metaphorically, as for example in Paul's Letter to the Romans,

> Do you not know that all of us who have been baptized into Christ Jesus were baptized into death?
>
> (Rom. 6: 3)

> For if we have been united with him in a death like his, we will certainly be united with him in a resurrection like his. We know that our old self was crucified with him so that the body of sin might be destroyed, and we might no longer be enslaved to sin. For whoever has died is freed from sin.
>
> (Rom. 6: 5–7)

Here Jesus' death is meant as the final end of all (bloody) cults, but why did this intention have to be implemented and interpreted again in terms of 'sacrifice'?

Another questionable aspect is the interpretation of a 'propitiatory' sacrifice, as atonement for human sins. Those who have sinned 'are now justified by his grace as a gift, through the redemption that is in Christ Jesus, whom God put forward as a sacrifice [or place] of atonement by his blood, effective through faith. He did this to show his righteousness' (Rom. 3: 24–5). Theology has failed to explain intelligibly what statements like these really mean. Furthermore, from the perspective of modern philosophy, such a stance, if advocated today, seems to ignore autonomy. A 'vicarious' sacrifice is considered as replacing, or at least weakening, the autonomous individual.

Difficulties in Becoming Aware of Guilt Today – Human Responsibility at Stake

The critique must be taken seriously, but are we simply to stop talking of guilt and sin? Furthermore, are we allowed to discard the fact of injustice and the 'cry for justice' (see Part II)? Does the belief in God's righteousness/justice and the interpretation of his justice as all embracing paradoxical forgiving love mean that God is forgetful of the victims of blatant injustice? Let us start with the issue of guilt.

Human guilt is a sad fact. On the one hand, evolution paved the way for long-lasting affiliative interaction and love between individuals generating social bonds and moral norms and rules for the survival of one's own group. On the other hand, the development of aggressive and agonistic dispositions was to serve to protect one's own resources against others, even at the expense of their lives, which could create feelings of guilt. 'Agonistic and affiliative behavior are simultaneously aroused' (Eibl-Eibesfeldt 1998: 33). Hence both needed regulation by moral rules and legal conventions (on the perspectives of evolutionary ethics in more detail see Chapter 9).

Without the existence of law and morality we cannot understand those dimensions of religion which in early societies (and also still today) were supposed to help maintain moral and legal functions. No wonder that religious language uses legal terms too (God as a 'judge', salvation as 'justification'). Religion and ethics are closely interconnected, and, again, to speak of 'justification' as a theological issue with essential moral implications ('For we hold that a person is justified by faith apart from works prescribed by the law', Rom. 3: 28), would make no sense if one could not assume general feelings of moral obligation present in human relations. Such feelings certainly do exist, but change as well, or they become eroded and even disappear. To a large extent present difficulties in dealing with human features such as moral obligation, responsibility, guilt and sin are due to the different situation today compared with biblical times, and indeed with most of history since then. But change as to the feelings of guilt cannot make the objectivity of existing guilt disappear. It is true that the following factors complicate the situation, but can they force the church to shut the eyes and stop speaking of the 'mystery of lawlessness' (2 Thess. 2: 7)?

A first factor refers to personal accountability. Sociological analyses (Sennett 1998) question the extent to which, in specific contexts, people are still accountable for what they do. Who exactly is responsible when under the pressure of economic competition there is a merger of multinational companies, with the side-effect of ten or twenty thousand workers being made unemployed? Managers will defend the steps by pointing to unavoidable globalization. Or, again, who is to be accused when people are killed in traffic accidents, if one considers that traffic on roads cannot simply be stopped? Difficulties in identifying responsibilities have grown, but the scandal itself is a simple reality and calls for an answer.

Second, structural guilt presents a new challenge to moral theory and practice. Societies lose control of global processes. In the case of emissions that damage the global climate we face the biggest future threat to creation. The New Testament speaks of 'things visible and invisible, whether thrones or dominions or rulers or powers' (Col. 1: 16), which are exerting a destructive influence on people's life. We are facing new forms of what Paul has called the 'law' and need to know how to interpret this new character of the 'law' in relation to the 'gospel' (see Chapter 8).

Third, to speak of human guilt or even sin doesn't seem any longer to fit in with the general climate of affluent societies. Technological optimism, consumerism and probing ever new lifestyle options in a 'multi-optional society' weaken moral reflection.

Fourth, along these lines international youth studies on value change reveal new 'codes' of valuing by which earlier moral categories are gradually being replaced. It is not necessary to describe all five 'value types' of the last but one nationwide survey in Germany (Deutsche Shell 2000, 1: 93–156, N = 4546). The new codes drawn from the data are (a) 'success' versus 'failure', with the highest ranking among so-called 'modern' and 'many-sided' young people, (b) 'fun/no stress' versus 'boring/stressing' with the majority among 'leisure time-oriented' adolescents, (c) 'coolness/strength' versus 'weakness' among those who trust in their (masculine) self, (d) 'beauty/youth' against 'ugliness/old age' and, (e) 'health' against 'sickness', as the two values being found amongst all groups. The groups of 'modern' (22%), 'many-sided' (25%) and 'leisure time-oriented' young people (16%) (all of them aged between 15 and 24) comprise two-thirds of the total sample.

As a fifth factor, we observe the tendency among youngsters and also adults to screen off trouble. Under the impact of negative news from all over the world incessantly putting heavy pressure on one's mood, people long for security, comfort and distraction by amusement. Church members are no exception. The trend is towards a type of religious spirituality that provides a feeling of belonging, consolation and happiness with an inclination towards religious escapism. The image of God looked for has to be harmonious. 'Guilt', 'sin', 'sacrifice', 'atonement', need for 'forgiveness' – all of this is a vocabulary of oddities, as it seems. 'Keep away from it!'

> Even though I know that God is not present, he is for me somebody whom I sometimes can talk to. I can speak to him and he will always understand, neither critizise, nor reject me . . . He won't demand any sacrifice from me.
>
> (a young ladies' hairdresser, aged 17; quote from Nipkow 1987: 85)

> I want to associate God only with nice feelings.
>
> (another female hairdresser of the same age, ibid.)

All three trends mentioned so far, (a) the theological controversies about the adequate meaning of the Cross, (b) the erosion of moral consciousness, and (c) the longing for a 'soft religion', which greatly differs from Christian faith modelled on the gravity of the proclamation of Jesus' death, require new answers.

The Perspective of the Victims

We need to start with a shift of perspectives. The strangeness of Jesus' suffering and death through violence is not strange to those who are suffering from violence themselves, from the perspective of the victims. Jesus died through the violence of a religious and political establishment; trial and execution were triggered by people in power. It makes a great difference whether one is reading the Bible from the perspective of those in power or from the perspective of powerless people. Interpreting the Bible is no affair of innocent hermeneutics; all modes of perception depend on general social and cultural trends as well as on personal experiences and interests.

In one of his recent studies, John Hull (2000) discusses issues of Christian adult education against the background of 'money, modernity, and morality'. He is keen on describing primary and secondary forms of a false consciousness. By a gradual adaptation to 'money-culture', 'religious consciousness has become indistinguishable from it' (p. 11). 'Money has literally become the God of our culture . . . Money, a human artifact, now hangs over our culture as an almost irresistible power' (p. 12). While Jesus said that if anyone tries to serve both God and money, he or she will 'hate the one and love the other' (Luke 16: 13), we now see 'that there is another possibility: he or she will confuse one with the other, cleave to one thinking it is the other' (Hull 2000: 12). Some centuries ago, when the doctrine of providence was used to justify disparities between rich and poor, God's will shaped an 'innocent motivation' (p. 13) of human beings to strive for prosperity. What was taking place can be described as an 'innocent adaptation' because people had not yet become self-critically aware of the relationship between faith, power and social injustice. However, if adaptation to the spirit of an age becomes a way of permanently or, as you might call it, structurally discriminating against other people, we face not an 'innocent motivation', but a 'motivated innocence' (p. 14).

As a social institution the church is involved in these discriminatory processes; even more, as long as it proclaims the gospel of justification by grace, its interest in maintaining influence and power would threaten the church's credibility. Could it be that one of the more hidden reasons why we encounter difficulties in speaking of the Cross might be due to defence mechanisms that have been developed by the church itself against the inconvenient truth of Jesus on the Cross? The church is at the crossroads of failing its mandate. The truth of the Cross ought to urge the church to share the perspective of victims since Jesus was a victim. In this perspective there is nothing wrong, or odd, or strange with crucifixion – and this event ought to have something to do with the restoration of justice.

The evolution of cognitive human intelligence was accompanied by the evolution of social and moral intelligence (Allman 1994). Coping with the challenges of survival needed the shared resources of the group. Strategies of action had to be developed *with* others, *for* others and also *against* others, who were potential allies, or rivals, or both. One important human feature resulting from the gradual establishment of social, moral and legal norms to coordinate social actions for the purpose of mutual obligation was conscience. Its existence marks a sharp distinction between animals and humans. Only the latter have a knowledge of right and wrong, and it is conscience that will tell us whether we have morally failed or not. Thus, conscience displays the normative structure of mind, which from evolutionary perspectives it would be silly to deny and a public danger at that. The loss of individual moral accountability resulting from it ends up in the 'corrosion of character' (Sennett).

Paul presupposes moral structures in humans when in his Letter to the Romans he starts with the general assumption that while the Jews know about good and evil by 'law', that is the Mosaic law (Torah) as given to Israel, the 'Gentiles, who do not possess this law, [nevertheless] do instinctively what the law requires, these, though not having the law, are a law to themselves'. To this law, 'written on their hearts . . . their own conscience also bears witness; and their conflicting thoughts will accuse or perhaps excuse them' (Rom. 2: 14–16). 'Therefore, you have no excuse, whoever you are' (Rom. 2: 1).

To summarize thus far, we see that in pursuing the topic of God, human nature and education for peace, the obvious close interrelation between the religious and the moral sphere remains valid despite all changes in current moral consciousness. Against the background of wickedness, lawlessness and injustice it is constitutively impossible for the human species to do without moral responsibility; however, it is an open question which logic in moral behaviour humanity should follow in order to overcome evil and wickedness as barriers to living in peace and justice, the latter as one of the basic prerequisites of the solution of local, regional and global conflicts. The Christian faith tradition offers the message of Jesus Christ on the Cross as God's answer. What is its convincing core in intelligible language? It has to do with the shift of perspective from the powerful to that of the victims.

Three Patterns of Reconciliation – Logic of Reciprocity and Logic of Love

The sufferings of victims past and present are betrayed, summing up the previous sections, by (1) a sophisticated but incomprehensible theology separated from life and biography, (2) transformation and decline of moral responsibility together with the forgetfulness of individualistic religion, and (3) a false religious consciousness that, in adaptation to unjust structures which are taken for granted, perpetuates them, thus indirectly contributing to conflict and war.

Israel felt it when things went wrong in dealing with those who lived in misery and oppression amidst its own community. The Torah was an instrument to prevent the worst. It became Israel's gift to the world to teach all people right and wrong in basic moral issues, and not without success, as the moral reputation of the Ten Commandments demonstrates. Israel also explored paths of reconciliation when human relations broke down and God's covenant was at stake. Handling guilt became an ongoing task.

In the Old Testament there are three different patterns of reconciliation as restoration, that is of healing the broken community with God and others, the first two serving as the chief means for regulating moral conflicts and the violation of a good, peaceful order down to the time of Jesus. The three procedures were (a) legal steps, with the focus on the restitution of damage, (b) a cult with sacrifices, later centralized in the Temple, and (c) intercession by an intermediary or mediator (Jacob 1966: 2097). All three patterns reveal impressively how in Israel the problem of guilt was taken seriously. What all solutions had in common was to help to restore a 'balance' (von Soosten 1994: 103; cf. Janowski 2000: 110). As discussed above (Chapter 4), in the ancient Near East the issue of justice in all its dimensions – legal, moral, ontological or cosmological – was rooted in 'justice' as 'balance'; correspondingly, 'injustice' was interpreted as an expression of fundamental 'disorder'. The violation of each of these kinds of balanced order had necessarily to be overcome by acts of restoration. To speak of God's justice and righteousness meant to trust in his remaining readiness to guarantee the justice of (not only in) the world. This divine justice was the integral part of living together peacefully on earth, of peace as anticipating the eschatological 'shalom'.

Thus, the very intention of the biblical God was, and still is, salvation as restored wholeness,

- first, in relating to the individual who is to become 'whole' as an 'integrated' person; restoration meant living with God in intimate joyful confidence
- second, restoration was directed towards the new solidarity of broken community which meant overcoming social disintegration caused by injustice, violence, and forms of oppression which victimized the poor and weak members of the society
- third, eventually and universally, restoration aimed at a new creation as a whole.

God's revelation in Jesus also appears in a threefold sense, as an individual, social or collective, and cosmic restitution, the last as the coming of the 'Kingdom of God'.

The first two religious options – restitution of damage and reconciling the deity by offerings – display a common logical structure insofar as in both cases the act of restitution is in accordance with the idea of 'reciprocity'. In the first case, damage is repaired by compensation, the extent of which is supposed to be in accordance with the degree of harm (legal restitution). In the second case, sacrifices are expected to be offered in accordance with the weight of one's own sin (sacrificial cult).

There is a remarkable difference to be observed when turning to the third option. Now a new kind of logic seems to be introduced. In either case, be it that separation from God and others is to be restored by a mediator or, likewise, guilt and sin are to be overcome by intercession, the focus is on a person. Hope is directed towards a person's commitment, with – not to be forgotten – the possibility of the intermediary risking his or her life. A similar shift to personal relationships can occur in the field of reciprocal interaction as will be shown below.

The first and second pattern of reconciliation are steps of equalizing what has become unequal, the first reacting against inequality caused by stealing property, violating reputation, intruding upon sexual relationships, or – the worst – taking another's life (cf. the corresponding commandments of the decalogue). At each time both parties are signalled to expect the same reactions from the community if they should fail. Viewed psychologically, it is assumed that both, aggressor as well as victim, will realize that their roles could easily be reversed: at any moment either of them might become the other, suffering the same afflictions or expecting the same sanctions; hence learning reconciliation means learning mutual reconcilation.

The New Testament manifests this logic at several places, the most famous being Jesus' quotation of the Golden Rule, which is to be found in many other religions too. Obviously, this basic rule operates as an essential human regulative of universal scope. Therefore, Hans Küng regards the Golden Rule as an important ingredient of what he has called a common 'global ethic' (*Weltethos*) which, by the way, is not 'a new *invention* but *only a new discovery*' (Küng and Kuschel 1993: 71). 'In everything do to others as you would have them do to you; for this is the law and the prophets' (Matt. 7: 12). Jesus sums up what seems to him a constitutive structure of the moral consciousness of the (Hebrew) Bible. Other moral invitations of his are fully in line with the logic of that rule, as may be illustrated by some verses before: 'Do not judge, so that you may not be judged. For with the judgment you make you will be judged, and the measure you give will be the measure you get' (Matt. 7: 1–2).

The logic of the second pattern, the ritual procedure of reconciliation by a sacrificial offering, is in its immediate sense directed to reciprocity within the covenant with God. A covenant is rooted in mutual obligations: I'll serve you as you will serve me. I will be faithful as you hopefully may be too. But is God's covenant nothing but a contract? Again we meet a different understanding, surpassing rationalistic reciprocity. Hosea most impressively describes God's covenant with Israel as an affiliative community or, so to speak, a contract of love, not of balancing mutual, reciprocal self-interest. In its essence the pattern of mutual self-interest is abandoned. The description rests on images, which draw on the most intimate social interrelations in human life, marriage and family.

> I will take you for my wife forever; I will take you for my wife in righteousness and in justice, in steadfast love, and in mercy. I will take you for my wife in faithfulness and you shall know the LORD.
>
> (Hos. 2: 19–20)

In this view, God's covenant is no rational contract, but a matter of the heart and of caring relationships. The imagery draws on those experiences in human life which in the light of evolutionary research make up the core of human sociality. In dangerous surroundings, survival depended on the firm knowledge of mutual trustworthiness serving the function of social security. As already mentioned above, 'cognitive intelligence' seems to have been developed in close connection with, or, more precisely, *as* 'social intelligence' ('social intelligence hypothesis', Barkow *et al.* 1992) for two reasons, because of (a) the necessity of coping with growing social complexity, and (b) with regard to the particular nurturing attention that had to be devoted to helpless children. Within one's own group, affiliation and cooperation became the dominant human pattern of behaviour, not deceit and fraud. But – human nature also remains deeply ambiguous.

> When Israel was a child, I loved him
> and out of Egypt I called my son.
> The more I called them,
> the more they went from me;
> they kept sacrificing to the Baals,
> and offering incense to idols.
> Yet it was I who taught Ephraim to walk,
> I took them up in my arms;
> but they did not know that I healed them.
> I led them with cords of human kindness,
> with bands of love.
> I was to them like those
> who lift infants to their cheeks.
> I bent down to them and fed them.
>
> (Hos. 11: 1–4)

On the one hand, in God's view too, the logic of reciprocity is not abandoned; God expects faithfulness and gratitude in return; nor is the idea of condemning injustice and restoring justice cast aside. On the other hand, calculation of the type 'do ut des' contract, or weighing costs against benefits according to the rule 'if you take the benefit, then you must pay the cost', is ruled out. People seem psychologically prepared to recognize cheaters in social games as well as being keen to exact retribution (Cosmides 1989: 77). However, there also exists a sort of love that does not calculate. 'The logic of the heart is not the logic of reasoning' (Blaise Pascal, Pensées, Frg. 277). Now the former pattern of conditional reciprocity changes its character. It is transformed and eventually replaced by the heart's knowledge of unconditioned mutual trust. 'Faith' is nothing but another word for unconditioned trust; Luther used to translate faith with 'confidence' (*fiducia*). The emotional memory of adults keeps the cords of kindness in infancy and childhood in mind for ever, and so according to Hosea does God. Against this background, the second pattern of reconciliation, the cult of 'sacrifice', appears in a different light, the warming light of love and confidence. The ritual is transformed to expressing gratitude because of the happy renewal and hoped for continuity of community (cf. Chapter 6).

But what is to be done, if one partner in the covenant constantly breaks community? Is there a pattern left for coping with such a situation? What if the logic of legal restitution and ritual reunion both fail? People can renounce mutual promise, they can cheat and deceive each other, deny even bonds of affiliation by blood, cancel cooperation. They can declare war on others and try to gain power for themselves at the cost of innumerable victims. They can choose death instead of life. In this case, love is powerless and left alone with its powerless power. Hosea dramatically describes how, nevertheless, God intends to stick to the covenant partner, since he is unable to cancel the community with his creatures.

> How can I give up you, Ephraim?
> How can I hand you over, O Israel?
> . . .
> My heart recoils within me;
> my compassion grows warm and tender.
> I will not execute my fierce anger;
> I will not again destroy Ephraim;
> for I am God and no mortal,
> the Holy One in your midst,
> and I will not come in wrath.
> (Hos. 11: 8–9)

Mortal humans and the eternal 'Holy One' differ in that God has the freedom not to be driven (or forced) to react according to reciprocity. This principle is by no means useless in daily life; it is worth being studied in more detail below and will display important positive functions in handling social relations and avoiding conflicts (see the end of Chapter 10). In the present situation 'reciprocal altruism' serves global peace. However, the principle remains a rule of calculated mutual self-interest. Instead of the pattern of symmetrical bargaining which sets its hope on the persuasive power of a symmetrical justice, the way of an asymmetrical response comes into view according to the logic of the heart ('my heart recoils within me'). Unlike 'interest' in others which might decline, love does not dwindle, but grows ('my compassion grows warm and tender'). Instead of carrying through one's interests, maybe if necessary ruthlessly and with physical force, the road of non-violence is followed: 'I will not save them by bow, or by sword, or by war, or by horses, or by horsemen' (Hosea 1: 7).

The Non-violent Logic of the Heart – Jesus giving his Life for Reconciliation

In daily life, a quarrel can reach a point where, if at all, only a third person can help to reconcile the conflicting parties; they are not able to do so by themselves. In more conspicuous form in political conflicts diplomats are needed as skilful negotiators between hostile camps, sometimes with success, many times without. In this section we presuppose situations of almost irreversible antagonisms, marked by deep mistrust or irreparable dissent. In some cases, for instance in the face of atrocious crimes committed against innocent people with no remorse at all on the part of the offenders (for example, terrorists), one seems to have good reason to give up any hope of reconciliation as the crimes are too great to be condoned or forgiven. The only reaction left seems to be an equivalent counterforce.

The 'outcry against Sodom and Gomorrah' had become 'great' for their 'very grave sin' (Gen. 18: 20). So the Lord was about to react by severe punishment, when Abraham came near and said,

> Will you indeed sweep away the righteous with the wicked? Suppose there are fifty righteous within the city; will you then sweep away the place and not forgive it for the fifty righteous who are in it? Far be it from you to do such a thing, to slay the righteous with the wicked, so that the righteous fare as the wicked! Far be that from you! Shall not the Judge of all the earth do what is just?
>
> (Gen. 18: 23–5)

As we know, Abraham went down as far as ten possible righteous, but in vain, they couldn't be found. Abraham acted as an intermediary (mediator); 'to mediate' is to intervene between two persons for the purpose of reconciling them. The means consist of a double-sided intervention, by language, namely intercession, and by one's own person: 'Let me take it upon myself to speak to the Lord' (Gen. 18: 31). Personal intervention in dangerous conflicts is a risky enterprise. Abraham 'came near' with both in mind, risking his life, but also full of trust. His redundant appeals reminded God of one salient point, focusing on the very divinity of his nature: righteousness as compassionate love, and therefore also peace through this understanding of justice – our topic and God's response as we could pursue it. He cannot afford to be unjust, to act against his nature. The theological issue of peace has essentially to do with the manifestation of God's justice and righteousness. But how can the third pattern of reconciliation, by intercession and mediation, in this context of injustice, justice and justification, be convincing and effective in a precise sense? How will it make those separated become partners in community again? In order to be more specific, we have to return to him with whom the chapter started – to Jesus and his life.

If Jesus' death is isolated from his life, one misses the point that his death is the logical consequence of his 'pro-existence', an existence 'for others': his life and death form a whole. Every aspect of it, his behaviour, preaching, healing, community with others, suffering and death, manifests the same, God's paradoxical love. Jesus acts as God himself would act, including in his crucifixion. Better, he is God acting. Therefore it is misleading if certain feminist criticism, while appreciating Jesus' loving self-sacrifice in life, opposes it with regard to his death, as if categories such as 'sacrifice' and 'vicarious' offering, which are meant to describe actions and aspects of love, were inappropriate (Janowski 2000: 116).

Instead, three things are mutually explanatory, (a) Jesus' biography, (b) the parables told by him, and (c) his way to the Cross. His characterization as 'the Son of Man who came not to be served but to serve, and to give his life a ransom for many' (Mark 10: 45) – a key statement for the interpretation of the theological meaning of the crucifixion – is reflected in the story about the Good Shepherd where we read that he 'lays down his life for the sheep' (John 10: 11). In the First Letter of John we read similarly, 'We know love by this, that he laid down his life for us – and we ought to lay down our lives for one another' (1 John 3: 16).

Love implies a risky commitment of one's own life on behalf of others, eventually one's own death. If so, it is also a deep misunderstanding to regard Jesus' act of 'giving his life' (*Lebenshingabe*) as manifesting a sort of abstract and authoritarian rule of God over human beings. Jesus was following his own intentions; he stood for himself although, or better, because he felt his union with God as his 'Father', as the Gospel according to John vividly describes. John lets Jesus say to his disciples: 'there will be one flock, one shepherd. For this reason the Father loves me, because I lay down my life in order to take it up again. No one takes it from me, but I lay it down of my own accord. I have power to lay it down, and I have power to take it up again' (John 10: 16–18). Jesus adds: 'I have received this command from my Father' (v. 18). But this statement does not contradict the sentence speaking of his 'own' accord. The fact of being permeated by God's love made Jesus act first on behalf of his Father, second because of having come 'from the Father' (John 16: 28), and third having his Father 'with' him (John 16: 32). Neither was Jesus' life lived in heteronomy, nor are those who benefit from Jesus'death robbed of their autonomy, as was the reproach above which rested upon a misinterpretation of his death as a 'vicarious' act. People don't lose their human dignity when others take care of them vicariously. In being given basic support, they are enabled to do something that they hadn't been able to before: to lead a life in reconciliation with God and others.

The pattern of reconciliation as it is being displayed on the hill of Golgotha is a reaction to violence, not an act of violence in itself of a God looking out for compensatory satisfaction. Whoever is inclined to this interpretation has understood little or nothing. By looking at the crucifixion from the perspective of the victims who suffer from violence and are healed, new light is cast on an old issue. By letting violence occur in having his body broken by those in power, Jesus principally questions any rule of violent power over humans. In radiating God's spirit of reconciliation by non-violent love, he overcomes the spirit of hate and destruction. He forgives those who execute him (Luke 23: 34) and shares his new life with the criminal hanging beside him on the same hill (23: 43).

It is not God who needs a sacrifice for his sake, but it is the human race which needs assistance to overcome the vicious circle of destruction. The first pattern, of reclaiming and restituting, is of merely relative worth because it still leaves the reality of destructiveness per se as it is, repairing nothing but the outcome of evil, not its roots.

The second solution, directed towards restoring lost balance to divine powers by presenting offerings, easily falls back into another type of reciprocal bargaining. God may be satisfied (as one thinks), but again there is only a vague hope of the underlying structural aggressiveness of human nature being changed; the propensity to aggression, violence and war remains what it was and is.

On the contrary, in delivering animals or humans as 'scapegoats' the archaic sacrificial cult obviously reproduces and exercises a typical pattern of violence in itself. While somebody who is supposed to have caused the specific evil is selected and killed, all the others seem to be satisfied with having regained their own 'peace'. René Girard (1986) has lucidly decribed the psychological mechanisms (for theological and cultural aspects see also Janowski and Welker 2001). The victim is regarded as simultaneously 'guilty' and 'holy'. At the peak of social crises as situations of social dissolution, with the members of society becoming similar to each other in a destructive way, someone is singled out and killed. This act is so fundamental that it restrains one's own potential for violence. The restoration of 'peace' seems to become possible again, thanks to the healing power of the victim. Therefore the victim is also 'sacred'. The scapegoat mechanism is still to be found everywhere today.

Christ's sacrifice is interpreted in the Christian tradition in completely different terms. The records see Jesus die as an innocent victim, and it is just this fact that makes him become the mediator to reconciliation with God and the source of new freedom. Now sacrifice is not a new violence, but a gift of life.

Those who are in power do not possess the power of getting rid of destructive power by themselves. Nor does the individual, as Paul confesses: 'For I do not do the good I want, but the evil I do not want is what I do' (Rom. 7: 19, cf. also v. 15: 'I do the very thing I hate'). Contrary to humans who do not understand their own actions ('I do not understand my own actions', ibid.), God does have the powerful freedom of discarding the instruments of violent power. Being the 'Almighty', that is, having ultimate power, he can exercice this power in order to dispose of any concrete power. Thus, human 'sin' is also lack of freedom; feelings of failure or anger overpower us and lead us to be aggressive or even cruel. Conversely, whoever participates in Jesus' death may hopefully be overwhelmed by the intensity of Jesus' love and receive new freedom.

Jesus' death as the expression of God's love does not neglect the issue of justice and, therefore, it does not relativize the weight of the suffering of the victims. Otherwise, their suffering would be ridiculed. The idea of forgiveness without atonement for the sins of the wicked ('the hecatombs of murdered') is hardly acceptable. 'The answer cannot be merely benevolent forgetting' (Spaemann 2001: 69). Against this background we understand why Jesus' death is also interpreted as an expiatory act for the sake of justice. It is, however, no longer the task of human beings to restore the just order; they will never be able to accomplish their own atonement. It is God's sacrifice once and for all, one last atonement abolishing all human sacrifices.

In biblical traditions (which exist in plural forms from different periods of time over several centuries) the third way of reconciliation, expressing the logic of unconditioned love, is mixed up with elements of the other two ways. With the exception of the scapegoat pattern of sacrificial violence, they are not without meaning and worth of their own.

With regard to the first pattern, we may often be content if, based on reciprocal self-interest, at least a peace-preserving cooperation can be arranged, although it is different from true reconciliation. Yet it is a promising step if in situations of impending conflicts agreements on procedures of mutually repaying damages or of dispensing with violent means are kept (cf. Chapters 9 and 10).

With respect to the second pattern, 'sacrificial' theological semantics need a thoroughgoing revision. We have tried to contribute to it by focusing on the meaning of giving life for others in loving vicarious commitment, including the atonement for humanity's sins. It is this pattern that appears as God's solution for the human species, since as history shows human beings are not able to overcome the vicious circle of retaliation by themselves.

From the standpoint of Christian faith, the path to reconciliation by Jesus Christ as a mediator who risked his life for all – the third pattern – is the first step on God's final and universal way of restoration with his broken creation as a whole. The eschatological process consists of a 'double frame', that of Old Testament expectation of the kingdom of Zion for Israel and all nations (Isa. 2: 2–4; 28: 16; Ps. 87; Dan. 7) and that of early Christian expectation of the restoration of the Kingdom of God after the completion of the apostolic mission of all nations (Matt. 28: 16–20, Acts 1: 6;

3: 20). According to 1 Corinthians 15: 20–28, God's kingdom of universal peace is accomplished in three stages (Stuhlmacher 2000). Thus Paul proclaims an eschatological event of universal effect with Christ's resurrection ('raised from the dead') as the first stage ('first fruits', 1 Cor. 15: 20, 23), 'each in his own order' (v. 23). As the next order or 'stage' (see also Stuhlmacher 2001: 49–53), Paul speaks of 'those who belong to Christ at his (second) coming' (v. 23). 'Then comes the end' (v. 24), the restoration of the universe as a whole when Christ 'hands over the kingdom to God the Father' (ibid.) and eventually also death will lose its power 'so that God may be all in all' (v. 28). Similarly, the Relevation to John speaks of 'a new heaven and a new earth' (Rev. 21: 1), summed up in 'See, I am making all things new' (21: 5). Against all critical voices this meaning of Resurrection definitely confirms that Jesus' death is *no necrophile event, but a praise of life*. Easter, the festival of Christ's Resurrection, and Passover belong together: God's creative love at Easter interprets the Cross.

Jesus' Life – the Point of Entry in Religious Education and Spiritual Formation

In the Creed the second article concentrates on Jesus' Cross and Resurrection. His life on Palestinian soil is not touched, let alone described in detail, except for the hints at his birth and the hours of his last suffering. However, as we tried to prove, his life is the key to understanding later christological doctrines of the church. The latter describe Jesus' death as 'expiatory sacrifice', a concept which no longer means anything to most people. The attempt has been made above to clarify what is meant in more comprehensible categories. Three very old religious patterns of restoring broken relationships have been compared, (1) repairing something wrong or harmful by repaying, (2) atonement by offering sacrifices, and (3) vicarious intercession and forgiving sins. The third pattern includes the function of a spiritual 'mediator' in two ways, through Jesus and through the Holy Spirit who is also conceived as an intercessor (as 'another Advocate, to be with you for ever', John 14: 15).

In family and in social and political conflicts, people mostly agree that they might need a mediator while with respect to God they will hesitate. In church contexts, from the perspective of believers, feeling responsible to God might be taken for granted; in religious education in schools and in secular adult education it can't be. Does this mean that religious educators have to wait for people to develop a sort of general belief in God or in a Divine Being as a precondition for dealing with Jesus' life, death and resurrection? Certainly not, it is just the opposite, for 'Jesus is the parable of God' (Jüngel 1977); it is he who reveals God's nature. Even more, his love, culminating in the gift of his life, already represents the advent of God's kingdom itself. The Jesus story is the entry to God's story with humanity.

Certainly it may be that the general feeling that something like a 'God' exists can render the tasks of pastoral theology, religious education and adult education easier. Also, generally feeling responsible for others in connection with generally being conscious of one's own guilt and fallibility may make the language of the biblical faith tradition at least more intelligible. But there is no automatic bridge from the general to the specific. One cannot derive what the God of the Bible is really about from a vague belief in God or some such thing. A general moral sentiment does not by itself point to the specific pattern of how the God of the Bible intends and brings about reconcilation and peace. From the general to the specific, there is neither a cogently logical transition nor a historical bridge. The opposite is true, leading from the concrete to the abstract, from the specific to the general (by the way, religious studies are of course also rooted in concrete religions, not in an abstract construction of religion in the singular). Therefore, beginning with the Jesus story is the theologically adequate path to approach the mystery of the God of the Bible.

Still today, the stories about Jesus can hopefully stir young people to thought and action, despite the problems youngsters have with the church, its doctrine and language. This educational perspective converges with the theological one just mentioned above. As empirical data support (see pp. 73–7), Jesus of Nazareth appears as a 'fascinating, ambiguous and annoying' figure, the latter because of his totally unexpected behaviour. He evokes controversial emotions, challenges the dominant social values one is accustomed to, revolutionizes one's world view as a whole.

If at all, young people – and many of the older generation too – can be approached by an (auto) biographical approach via life stories. On the book market, there is a conspicuous new interest in autobiographies and biographies. In contexts of concrete life, people grasp the painful consequence of harming others or being harmed. Empathy grows if you can perceive human suffering in concrete detail. In later chapters data from the field of evolutionary psychology and ethics will provide sufficient evidence as to why face-to-face encounters with suffering individuals can arouse compassion.

Of the three patterns in the biblical tradition outlined above, two, namely the principle of reciprocity ('Golden Rule') and that of reconciliation by mediators, are also open to the understanding of children, since children become acquainted with them quite early in daily life. In linking the story about Jesus as God's mediator to concrete human situations, to human abilities and failures, to experiencing guilt and being forgiven, one can gain the attention of the younger and older generations alike as is already increasingly happening in educational and spiritual practice. In the following chapter on Paul, the focus on biography will be dealt with explicitly.

Chapter 8

Overcoming Barriers – a Biographical Approach to Paul

Saul of Tarsus – Paul, the Apostle – What has Paul to do with Jesus?

Paul is the most famous early Christian theologian. He explained the religious meaning of the Cross and Resurrection – the centre of salvation – in the categories of the doctrine of 'justification'. For Martin Luther and the churches of the Reformation this doctrine was to become the crucial hermeneutical key for understanding what had happened. This is the brief answer in academic theological terms.

In terms of elementarizing language the answer to what Paul has to do with Jesus is different: Paul's earlier name was Shaul or Saul. He hated the early Christians and he hated Jesus whom those Christian believers thought to have 'risen' from the dead. Red with anger, he brought death upon them by his own hands. In a shocking vision of light that temporarily blinded him, he was addressed by Jesus himself; he saw him and he heard him speaking. After that he soon started proclaiming what had occurred to him and what, in his new view, 'Cross' and 'Resurrection' actually and radically meant: becoming a new free person and living forever in God's love despite having done nothing to deserve it. Even more: in spite of having been a torturer, an assistant of killers and a former 'enemy of God' (belonging to those to be found 'fighting against God', Acts 5: 39), who ought to have deserved death himself, Paul was acknowledged and honoured to become an apostle.

The paragraph above is necessarily longer than the introductory academic remarks. Why? Because elementary speech needs narrative elements, and a biography has to be told. Religious 'identity' is identical with one's biography as a dynamic development encompassing interruption, crisis, new beginnings. 'Behind' doctrinal language is living experience. New religious knowledge springs into existence amidst the actualities of our lives; it is contextual knowledge. So was Paul's. His doctrine of justification originated from personal experiential contexts. 'I was far more zealous for the traditions of my ancestors' than others (Gal. 1: 14). In this situation the conversion on the road to Damascus shocked him, and the firebrand in his soul kindled a new dynamic of life, urging him to speak to everyone of his new freedom and truth: independence, peace and community in Christ, in one word, renewal.

The turning point in his life resulted from something that he had no control over and occurred to him contrary to his very intentions, which were destructive. He believed he had good reasons ruthlessly to persecute Jesus' followers. The beginnings of the Jesus community were not marked by

> sectarian quietistic calm and a corresponding missionary restraint, expecting only the parousia of the Son of Man, but were more like an unexpected powerful explosion with

successive pressure waves. Both so-called 'critical' scholarship and our domesticized church piety have lost the sense of the monstrous and – in the eyes of outside Jewish observers – terrifying offensiveness of those events which Paul has listed with the utmost brevity in 1 Cor 15: 2–8.

(Hengel and Schwemer 1997: 27)

Saul, the zealous Pharisee, reacted with a corresponding terrifying offensiveness – but Jesus didn't accuse him, instead he just asked why: 'Saul, Saul, why do you persecute me?' (Acts 9: 4). That was quite different from any retaliation; it was a paradoxical, kind invitation. He who before had felt absolutely justified in his actions, received a new 'justice' which much later he was to call 'justification'. 'Justification' is a matter of experience. Later he and others were to describe four perspectives, the famous 'particulae exclusivae' (cf. Jüngel 1998: 126–219).

- What Paul received was God's free gift, something without any merits: 'by grace only' (*sola gratia*).
- What occurred to him was also trustworthy. In a compelling way the voice that spoke to him made him trust. 'Trust' is nothing but another word for 'faith': 'justification' took place 'by faith only' (*sola fide*).
- There was also no one else who addressed him; there was no mistaking the fact that it was Jesus, the same person whose followers he had been persecuting. Therefore, from this moment onwards, Paul would owe allegiance to no one else in his life: justification 'by Christ only' (*solus Christus*).
- Last but not least, it was the voice that struck him – and convinced him: 'Saul, Saul, why do you persecute me?' (Acts 9: 4). Correspondingly, from now on he also would rely on nothing else but the power of the word, not the power of the sword: therefore, 'justification' 'by word only' (*solo verbo*).

To Saul, the Damascus encounter was something unexpectedly new, completely different from the old. Later he would call it a 'new creation': 'So if anyone is in Christ, there is a new creation: everything old has passed away, see, everything has become new!' (2 Cor. 5: 17). It is as if Paul, in uttering this statement, would lift his finger and point to himself. 'Look at me! You know me from before; I have become another person.' All the difficult terms around Jesus on the Cross and his Resurrection with which we started in Chapter 7 as puzzling background, recalling them once more briefly at the beginning of this chapter, can now be understood much better. In order to show this in more detail, we will keep closely to the texts themselves, to Paul's own descriptions and to those recorded by Luke. In a way, everyone on their spiritual journey, including teachers of religious education, are supposed to be able to check the sources by themselves. We do not need much exegetical or historical assistance.

Paul's Life Story as Key to Understanding his Theology

A new publication with materials for religious education in state schools in Germany for boys and girls aged 13 to 15 (Baumann and Wermke 2001) contains a chapter on Paul on a narrative basis (pp. 16–31). It starts with Paul in Rome as a prisoner in confinement in a house near a barrackyard before his trial is opened, which as we know was to end with his execution. In his room he is visited by Claudius, aged 13, the son of a soldier in charge of the prisoner. They make friends and Paul tells Claudius the story of his life.

Among the many-coloured pictures and illustrations accompanying the text (photos taken of locations in Palestine dating from Paul's lifetime, prints of paintings with scenes from Paul's travels, photos of boys and girls today), there is Lovis Corinth's famous painting of 1911 showing Paul preaching to people, clad in plain grey, the Bible in his left hand, his right hand slightly lifted with fingers spread. An ill looking, lean appearance with thin hands and eyes wide open directs attention to his half-open mouth. It is the word that will count, coming from a body and soul that are backing what is being said. The pupils are asked to pay attention to hands and face.

During their first meeting the prisoner and the boy speak about weakness and strength in Paul's childhood. Paul is proud of his Jewish name, Saul, the name of a Jewish king. They also touch briefly on Paul's hardships in his later life. A teacher may easily add what we know from Paul himself with regard to his physical situation. He looks ill, what is he suffering from? Paul speaks of 'a thorn' that has been given to him in his 'flesh' to 'torment' him (2 Cor. 12: 7). Does he point to painfully stinging fits? Research agrees that he was not sound and suffered from a severe sickness. The list of his daily burdens is long (2 Cor. 11: 23–33); they comprise in his own words 'weaknesses, insults, hardships, persecutions, and calamities' (2 Cor. 12: 10). Physical appearance can tell more than mere words do; the painting is an adequate point of entry to teaching in accordance with our 'elementarizing approach'. The pupils should be given enough time to reflect on it.

Phase 1

Although being a 'Jew' and brought up in a Jewish familiy, Paul was a Roman citizen. Having been 'born in Tarsus in Cilicia', a Roman province (Acts 22: 3), he had become 'a Roman citizen' (Acts 22: 25) by birth ('I was born a citizen', Acts 22: 28). This was a remarkable privilege marking him out as different from others who, even including the tribune who later examined him, had to buy this status: 'It cost me a large sum of money to get my citizenship' (ibid.). We don't know much more about Saul or Paul (his Roman name) as a child and youngster, but both the usual Jewish education as well as a Hellenistic upbringing can be taken for granted.

Phase 2

Paul was able to earn his living as a maker of tents; he continued to do so during his missionary travels. In addition he had undergone training in the study of the Hebrew Bible and other religious Jewish traditions under the guidance of one of the most famous scholars of the time, Gamaliel, 'a teacher of the law, respected by all the people', and a member of the 'council' (Acts 5: 34): I was 'brought up . . . at the feet of Gamaliel' (Acts 22: 3), 'educated strictly according to our ancestral law, being zealous for God' (ibid.). The last phrase indicates the character of Gamaliel's school; he and Paul were Pharisees (Acts 5: 34). Paul was taking faith and religious obligations extremely seriously.

Phase 3

Presumably Paul's conversion occurred about three years after Jesus' crucifixion and the events of Easter. So he became a witness of the stormy beginnings of the young Christian community propelled by the experience of the Spirit. What must have upset him was that for the first Christians the atoning death of the Messiah, interpreted in universal terms, made the sacrificial practice in the Temple obsolete. The traditional meaning of the sacrificial cult was passé. The new view of things even led to open criticism of the Temple and the ritual law – at least among the Hellenists, represented by Stephen. The Hellenists were Greek-speaking Jewish Christians who wanted to use their Greek mother tongue in worship. It was probably this interpretation which above all embittered the young Pharisaic scribe and made him a persecutor. 'Could the promised Messiah and redeemer of Israel be the one who misled the people and according to the law was accursed by his shameful death?' (Hengel and Schwemer 1997: 100).

Paul seems to have first featured publicly with the stoning of Stephen, who was dragged out of the city: 'the witnesses laid their coats at the feet of a young man named Saul' (Acts 7: 58). 'Saul approved of their killing him' (Acts 8: 1), obviously observing the execution with satisfaction. The next step was his active participation in persecuting Christians, without sparing women: 'Saul was ravaging the church by entering house after house; dragging off both men and women, he committed them to prison' (Acts 8: 3). 'I persecuted this Way [the early name for the first Christian movement] up to the point of death by binding both men and women and putting them in prison' (Acts 22: 4). He confessess (all statements according to Luke) that he 'not only locked up many of the saints in prison, but I also cast my vote against them when they were being condemned to death' (Acts 26: 10). That is, he acted as judge with capital sentences.

Then he adds, 'By punishing them often in all the synagogues I tried to force them to blaspheme, and since I was so furiously enraged at them, I pursued them even to foreign cities' (Acts 26: 11). Persecution spreads – a next stage. His attempt to extend persecution to Damascus was to bring him to the turning point in his life: he offered his services to widen the radius of persecution from Jerusalem to Damascus so that 'he might bring them bound to Jerusalem' (Acts 9: 2). His own Letter to the Galatians contains the confession that he was 'violently' persecuting the church of God in order 'to destroy it'. Paul 'advanced' in his ravaging and surpassed 'many among my people of the same age, for I was far more zealous for the tradition of my ancestors' (Gal. 1: 13–14). Paul was a chief-inquisitor, a judge and probably also a murderer in one and the same person.

Phase 4

The conversion took place near Damascus as he approached his destination. Luke reports the event several times (Acts 9: 1–9; 22: 6–11; 26: 12–18). The somewhat varying reports are, in their core, precise. The agreements are much more important than the disagreements (for the parallels within Luke see Barrett 1994: 439–59). Presumably the report had ultimately come orally from Paul himself.

Common to all three Lukan reports is a bright shining 'from heaven' and the way in which the persecutor falls to the ground; furthermore he has an auditory religious experience – he hears Christ speaking to him. Both are important, the visionary 'seeing' of the Kyrios (1 Cor. 9: 1) and the hearing of his voice, the latter even more since it includes his commissioning. Paul sees Christ in his heavenly glory as the one who was risen and exalted to God, in accordance with the blinding light of the vision. This is in line with the Old Testament tradition of God's 'kabod' ('glory') in its 'concrete' significance as 'a fiery phenomenon from which the radiance and splendour proceed' (Hengel and Schwemer 1997: 342, n. 175, with reference to Newman 1992).

We don't know in detail how Paul will have understood his visionary seeing of the Kyrios; at any rate – contrary to present-day tendencies – he regarded it 'as a real, "objective" seeing of a supernatural reality in divine splendour of light, which makes itself known as the "Lord" and is recognized by him as such. Nowhere is there any thought that this could have been an illusion' (Hengel and Schwemer 1997: 39).

Historically, it is no longer possible to clarify the details of the event, least of all by psychological conjectures about the causes. To assume an illusionary character is misleading, for Paul was not prepared to receive such a vision. He was in no way disposed to expect anything to happen on the road to Damascus. His reaction paralleled the initial response of Jesus' followers for whom his crucifixion was the end of hope. For all who knew him it was a miraculous event, most of all for Paul himself; it was to change his life in a radical way. As already mentioned Paul was physically shattered, resulting in a temporary blindness.

In Damascus Paul regained his sight with the assistance of a Christian disciple with the name Ananias (Acts 9: 10–19). 'He laid his hands on Saul and said, "Brother Saul, the Lord Jesus, who appeared to you on your way here, has sent me so that you may regain your sight and be filled with the Holy Spirit." And immediately something like scales fell from his eyes and his sight was restored' (Acts 9: 17–18).

Phase 5

Paul was baptized by Ananias and left Damascus soon, after 'several days'. In the town itself he 'immediately' began to proclaim Jesus in the synagogues (Acts 9: 20). To go back to Jerusalem was dangerous. His main motivation, however, was different and involved a mandate of revolutionary uniqueness, namely to bring the message of unconditioned grace to non-Jews, the 'Gentiles', thus starting God's mission to all people, not simply the Jews: renewal as a gift of universal hope.

Phase 6

The years between Paul's conversion on the road to Damascus and his activity in Antioch up to the so-called first missionary journey to Cyprus and south-eastern Asia Minor, or up to the Apostolic Council, that is, a period of around fourteen to sixteen years, roughly between 33 and 47 or 49 CE, have been named 'the unknown years' in Paul's life. The already mentioned brilliant book of the famous New Testament scholar Martin Hengel about these years (Hengel and Schwemer 1997, in German in much more elaborated form 1999) casts new light on this period. It also supports our biographical approach and basic thesis that it is Paul's life that explains his new faith and theology, with his conversion as the decisive event. From now on biography and theology are one.

Thus we are allowed to end the outline of his life at this point with only one further factor of general importance to be mentioned. The imminent expectation of the Lord necessitated missionary goals which could be realized in a short time. Therefore Paul went to 'Arabia' (Gal. 1: 17), presumably mainly addressing people who as 'Godfearers' sympathized with the Jewish religion and who ethnically seen were kinsfolk to Israel. Faith is going to cross borders and break down barriers.

Breaking down Barriers of Religion, Gender, Social Status and Ethnic Demarcation

Paul's 'Arabia' is the mountainous region on the east shore of the Dead Sea. It was populated by the Nabateans, the most powerful Arab people in the immediate environment of Eretz Israel. They were descendants of Ishmael, the son of Abraham; in our times this fact may be interesting. The clashes between the state of Israel and the Palestinians shouldn't let us forget that Jews and Muslims share a common tradition, both being Abraham's descendants.

The Nabateans were geographically the nearest and most important 'neighbours' of Israel, and Abraham could be regarded as 'the first proselyte, primal sage and "father of many nations"' (Hengel and Schwemer 1997: 116).

In religious dialogue with Islam today Abraham plays a leading role (Kuschel 1995). It is important to remember that, according to later theological Jewish tradition, Abraham received circumcision when he was 99 years old (Gen. 17: 24), after he had been chosen by God at the age of 75 (Gen. 12: 4). That meant, God's offer of community and blessing were not dependent on this ritual. Paul may have used this argument in addition to his new insight since his conversion. As the Nabateans also practised the custom of circumcision without believing in the God of the Bible, this fact too could be understood as meaning that the custom had lost all significance for salvation. One might practise it or not; now it was 'faith' only, as trusting in God, that counted – as Abraham had strikingly shown when he 'went, as the LORD had told him' (Gen. 12: 4). Later in his Letter to the Romans Paul exemplified faith (and justification by faith) by pointing to Abraham: 'Abraham believed God, and it was reckoned to him as righteousness' (Rom. 4: 3).

Even today the geographical step to 'Arabia', and later to Europe, is a symbol for both spiritual and universally oriented liberation. The custom of circumcision is the one particular example which highlights the great relativizing revision of all religious customs and rituals in toto in a universal sense. I doubt whether we actually grasp the revolutionary impact of a message that devalues religion that far, encompassing all 'holy' rituals together. In the next chapter we will see how, and try to explain why, human beings cling to their 'holy' ceremonies and ideas – as Paul had done before. He who had been fervently driven by his concept of 'justice' met with a different understanding of 'justice': practising religion alongside the traditions of one's ancestors (Gal. 1: 14) might at first sight be seen to deserve spiritual approval, but was futile in a final sense. It had not prevented him from doing the wrong thing. Thus Paul's holy values, not being safe from misunderstanding and misuse, were no longer a safeguard against falling into 'sin'.

Jews at that time called this safeguard the 'law', which consisted of basic rules (the Ten Commandments), together with detailed prescriptions, for behaviour in daily life and rules for worship. The custom of circumcision was a major requirement among them, but not of course the whole story. Nevertheless, in those times its social function was a conspicuous means of religious demarcation. Were Greeks and Romans (and later whatever nations one might think of) supposed to become Jews before they could become Christians? Paul was most definitely opposed to this. The same new freedom from entering obligations which had lost their salvatory function encompassed prescriptions for meals: 'Food will not bring us close to God. We are no worse off if we do not eat, and no better off if we do' (1 Cor. 8: 8).

The Jews in Jerusalem who had become Christians kept the rituals they were accustomed to, and why not? Christians neither exist without rituals nor are they against them because of a principled stand having been taken on this matter. But it would be a misunderstanding of the first order to claim religious customs, rituals, institutions and doctrines as a precondition for community with God through Christ. Paul explains the issue in his First Letter to the Corinthians in connection with the issue of whether or not members of the congregation should eat 'food offered to idols' that was sold in the market (1 Cor., Chapters 8 and 10). In solving this controversial problem he presents the new Christian identity in 'liberty' in the same sense he himself had experienced it, as being 'given' without any precondition: Act in freedom! You may eat or not, take a wife or not, and so on: look at the issue that counts, thank God for the new liberation!

Am I not free? Am I not an apostle? Have I not seen Jesus our Lord?

(1 Cor. 9: 1)

Do we not have the right to our food and drink? Do we not have the right to be accompanied by a believing wife, as do the other apostles and the brothers of the Lord and Cephas?

(1 Cor. 9: 4–5)

Paul had good reasons for refraining, himself, from marrying (1 Cor. 7: 25–38), namely 'in view of the impending crisis' (7: 26), the expected eschatological events. But his 'judgement' in this and other affairs of daily life (cf. 7: 39–40) was not to bind the conscience of others. He appealed to those who knew about their new freedom of conscience to respect 'the weak', those who tended to stick to the old prescriptions and customs. 'Take care that this liberty of yours does not somehow become a stumbling block to the weak' (1 Cor. 8: 9).

Paul's focus on care and responsibility is less concerning his own conscience; it manifests his conscience as liberated from his own self and having become a 'conscience for others' (Kümmel 1964: 274, cf. 1 Cor. 10: 29). This switch of awareness from one's own pious edification to the conscience of others indicates also the new location of ethics, of religious as well as moral actions in the Christian's life. They are no longer efforts to gain God's love but become 'fruits' as expressions of gratitude (Gal. 5: 22) because of having already received God's love. Once having basically clarified this one salient point, that of a new community (and 'covenant', Chapter 7) by grace and faith 'only', a reappraisal of doing good could follow. It is illustrated first again with respect to 'eating and drinking' and their religious 'quality'. Devaluing is accompanied by revaluing through emphasizing those fruits which are in substantial correspondence with the content of God's shalom, that is, righteousness (justice) and peace (cf. Chapters 4–5), and joy (Chapter 6).

> The kingdom of God is is not food and drink but righteousness and peace and joy in the Holy Spirit. The one who thus serves Christ is acceptable to God and has human approval. Let us then pursue what makes for peace and for mutual upbuilding.
>
> (Rom. 14: 17–19)

In the Letter to the Galatians (5: 22) the (first three) 'fruit of the Spirit is love, joy, peace'. The new life is a life guided by the Spirit, not by prescription: 'If we live by the Spirit, let us also be guided by the Spirit' (Gal. 5: 25). And what enables Paul so convincingly to demonstrate the transformation of conditions to a liberated and renewed life with God, proclaiming even 'a new creation' (2 Cor. 5: 17; Gal. 6: 15)? The answer to the question, 'Am I not free?' is simple and given as an affirmative question, 'Have I not seen Jesus our Lord?' (1 Cor. 9: 1) – it is the personal encounter as he approached Damascus. The turning point in his biography is the turning point of his theology: 'For neither circumcision nor uncircumcision is anything; but a new creation is everything!' (Gal. 6: 15).

The breaking of religious barriers includes the abolition of further separating boundaries such as gender, social and ethnic ones. Through the risen Jesus they had all equally become 'God's children' by means of the gift of the Spirit.

To begin with religious discrimination, people who had been attracted by the Jewish faith – the 'sympathizers', 'godfearers' or even 'proselytes' – had never before had the opportunity to obtain equal religious rights, but remained second-class Jews. Even more separated from God's 'kingdom' and 'shalom' were the 'Gentiles'; now these divisions and separations vanished. Next fell the walls of gender between men and women. We know about many female members of the new Gentile Christian communities, even in leading positions. The same occurred to social differences concerning rich or poor, as well as to ethnic ones. 'There is no longer Jew or Greek, there is no longer slave or free, there is no longer male and female; for all of you are one in Christ Jesus' (Gal. 3: 28).

Without the universalizing meaning of the new message Christianity would never have become a world religion. Admittedly, this characteristic feature was propelled by the unifying force of eschatological expectations – differences lost their former functions. The main theological reason, however, lay with the relevation of God's true nature and intention by means of the overwhelming, unifying appearance of Jesus of Nazareth (see Chapters 5–7). Paul was given the opportunity of 'seeing' and 'hearing' him, too, as the 'risen' Lord. It was not a vision like many others; nor was it the 'appearance' as such that was so transforming, but rather the specific way in which God's kindness appeared to his creature – to this particular person.

Sin as Self-alienation and New Freedom

At the end of his life, having been imprisoned several times before, Paul became a Roman prisoner and was put to death by execution. 'Prison' can also be used as a symbol for the imprisonment of the soul. It is a sadly generally applicable truth that Paul states in his Letter to the Romans in surprisingly simple words of everyday language, 'I do not understand my own actions. For I do not do what I want, but I do the very thing I hate' (Rom. 7: 15). The sentence is repeated some lines later, now indicating 'evil': 'the evil I do not want is what I do' (v. 19). Paradigmatically, Paul describes the human self-contradiction between wanting and doing: 'I can will what is right, but I cannot do it' (v. 18).

Against the background of Paul's biography, these statements are all the more intelligible. It is not only mistaken and misguided knowledge, but also the basic fragility and weakness of human will that causes human guilt. How can it be explained? Is human nature – now taken literally as our *biological* frame – unable to implement our *spiritual* good intentions? The tension between body and soul was the idealistic insufficient answer over the centuries from the time of Greek philosophy (Plato) onwards. Biblical anthropological wisdom is different. It avoids the dualistic split between body and soul and aims at restoring the human person as a whole. We will come back to it in the next chapter when dealing with evolutionary anthropological hypotheses and empirical data on human nature.

Let us remember that what occurred to Paul on the road to Damascus shattered the young Pharisee's proud zeal for the law. So the change in his life first of all meant the recognition of abysmal guilt. He who had acted in good faith when, in his view, only fulfilling the demands of the 'law' of his religion was in fact the true blasphemer. But now, 'even though I was formerly a blasphemer, a persecutor, and a man of violence . . . I received mercy because I had acted ignorantly in unbelief, and the grace of our Lord overflowed for me with the faith and love that are in Jesus Christ' (1 Tim. 1: 13–14).

The terrifying discovery was the realization that something in one's own religion might be used in a completely wrong way, thus leading to evil. The 'law' itself was not sin; 'by no means!' (Rom. 7: 7), but its usage was. Religion becomes a matter of ignorance or knowledge ('acted ignorantly'); but how to gain true knowledge? In his Letter to the Romans Paul exemplifies to the reader in chapter 7 that what he calls 'sin' is an inexorable independent and alien power: 'sin' had been 'seizing an opportunity'; it 'deceived' him and 'killed' him (Rom. 7: 11). There seems to be something at work that we have already noticed in connection with Cain, sin as something 'lurking at the door' (Gen. 4: 7). It exercises its power through even the 'holy' ('So the law is holy, and the commandment is holy and just and good', Rom. 7: 12). By demonic powers which human beings seem to have no command of, the Mosaic 'law' (as any moral law) reveals its ambiguous character in its usage: people become alienated from their own self, sin as self-alienation.

In other words, taking up earlier distinctions, one might also speak of 'original guilt' (*Urschuld*, Mokrosch 2002), tantamount to the older theological term 'original sin', beside 'personal' and 'collective' guilt. The theological terminology can be related to phenomena expressing what can be called 'structural' evil such as aggravated responsibility, that is, individual moral unaccountability because of anonymous economic and monetary processes with the power of ruthless 'globalized' competition and so forth.

With it the issue of human freedom is at stake and needs a fresh, forthright and, in particular, realistic approach. Even though human beings definitely do have a free will in basic respects compared with animals, as the next chapter will show, they have to struggle with limitations caused by their evolutionary genetic legacy, as will be explained and illustrated below too. As in the First Letter to Timothy Paul calls himself 'a man of violence' (in the time before Damascus), so too, in principle, are humans. A book on aggression and violence, on the one hand, and reconciliation and peace, on the other hand, has to unravel why the propensity to violence and war is a central human trait. The anthropology of the Bible and the anthropological discoveries of evolutionary research converge to provide us with a realistic image of the human species. It helps to figure out new roads to moral and religious maturity in straightforward terms.

In pointing to his own life history in his letters Paul exemplifies the structural character of evil as something not simply to be overcome by pious intentions and moral efforts. Nor will one's own 'decision' do; the term is misleading because of its possible associations with anthropological illusions (a point directed against the Bultmann School). Strictly speaking, it is even wrong to say that Paul had 'converted' as if having achieved his renewal by himself. He called it pure gift (cf. the elements of 'justification' above).

Moral and Religious Maturity – a Summarizing Reflection in between

At the end of our biblical analyses as the main theological source for exploring foundations for an education for justice and peace in a world suffering from injustice, violence and war, we can give a preliminary answer regarding the development of personal spirituality. This book is not about politics, although we do have politics in mind, and we will need, for instance, to discuss indoctrination through political ideologies in the next chapters. It is about a lifelong process of learning on the part of individuals and groups. Its focus is peace and the impediments to its realization. The opportunities to learn encompass the whole of one's own life, starting in childhood and adolescence, hence our continuing attention to these stages of life in previous chapters. Moral and religious education, and the shaping of adult spiritual life, are not restricted to individual life journeys; transformative cultural processes, including necessary changes in institutions, have to be attended to too. However, in theology and education it is the individual who is addressed first. So what are the characteristics of an 'adult' moral and religious individual maturity, in so far as we can envisage it at this point?

Once and for all, the times are gone in which, particularly in the nineteenth century and the beginning of the twentieth century, 'soothing' philosophical, educational and similar theological concepts prevailed, shaping the general consciousness. Even after the Second World War it still seemed possible to continue with growing optimism because of new flourishing economies, rapid technological progress, spreading prosperity, at least in the First World, and the overarching feeling of owning unbroken moral strength. Hitler had been defeated, good had triumphed. Although confronted with impending nuclear threats in the time of the Cold War, western nations felt secure and superior. Until the beginning of the new millennium, during a period of more than fifty years of peace in Europe and North America, the general moral obsession was harmony linked to an air of mastery. Perhaps harmony is too positive a word, but it may serve as an indicator. One felt as if one had nothing to reproach oneself for.

There were the Korean War and the war in Vietnam, of course; there were Cambodia, Angola and indeed Rwanda and Burundi, the latter names linked to atrocious genocides, but none of them happened nearby. Suppression and exploitation, poverty and misery, suffering and dying prompted humanitarian action, but didn't shatter general self-certainty. Still today we make the huge error of assuming that we are living in the best of all worlds, thinking that all our faults can be remedied, all weakness overcome. Humanity seems to live, so to speak, in the prime of life, the overall idolized symbols being 'money' (Hull 2000; see also the contributions in Biehl *et al.* 2001) and 'development'.

During the last decades an endless wave of publications has illuminated life as 'development', shaking off the feeling of dread. The term is used in economics and technology, but is also applied to human personality and self-development. Mostly one forgets that its origin is the perception of organic processes in nature. Change or development that is organic happens gradually and naturally rather than suddenly. The idea of organic development doesn't allow interruptions and disjunctions in life. The titles of multitudes of publications mirror the imagery of organic concepts, for instance by referring to the 'seasons' of life, to spiritual 'growth', 'passages' and 'transitions', altogether emphasizing 'continuities' rather than discontinuities, drawing on a psychology apt to explain, promote and encourage life, in spite of ups and downs, as a more or less undisturbed 'journey', coping in advance with 'predictable' crises (Sheehy 1974) with little interest in the 'unpredictable', politically (see 11 September 2001) and privately. In this context 'maturity' has come to the fore as the fitting category for the goal of development. A representative volume reporting the results of an international symposium chose as its title 'Toward Moral and Religious Maturity' (Brusselmans *et al.* 1980).

'Maturity', a classical word from the realm of nature, is used in this book too, but in pursuing 'new' approaches. After all that has been dealt with in previous chapters, we must set ourselves very seriously to finding new answers. By contrasting the descriptions of human nature in the biblical tradition with the witnesses to the nature of the God of the Bible we have chosen a method apt to reveal a much more realistic image of the human species than is presupposed in current discussions in religious education. The biblical texts and biographies such as Paul's document the opposite to smooth continuities. They honestly confess, and tellingly deliver, damning evidence and ample illustration of human failure. 'Maturity' is not displayed by what can be obtained by one's own efforts on a road with predictable crises. Paul, whom we take as a paradigmatical figure, became a morally and religiously mature person when weighed down by the knowledge of his real moral constitution in an ontological sense. In our attempts to trace the reasons for envy, murder, retaliation and injustice from the beginning of the Bible in the Old Testament (Cain and Abel, Lamech), the new view of 'maturity' as advocated here rests on the inconvenient, but factual, enormity of sin.

It is on this biblical basis of old, experiential memory and wisdom that we have tried to collect a first tranche of evidence. In the following we will proceed to explore human nature from the perspectives of recent evolutionary research (in connection with data from social psychology) as another source of evidence. In the light of both, we have to devise ways towards peace that promise at least a certain justice and a certain peace on this globe. Becoming mature is identical to gaining clarity in order to achieve the possible. We have to avoid overworked slogans that cover anything. We have also to leave aside moral and religious rhetoric devoid of empirical testing. The following chapters will link the preceding mostly hermeneutical efforts (already interwoven, however, with empirical data) to empirically based hypotheses from another and quite new field of growing importance that up to now has been completely neglected in the debate on moral and religious education and in practical spiritual search.

IV
PATHS TO PEACE AND HUMAN NATURE

From Killing to Murder – Aggression, Violence and Warfare in Evolutionary Perspective

War as a Historical 'Constant' – John Amos Comenius' Christian Vision of Peace

The God of the Bible is a God of peace and justice. Again and again he appointed prophets to communicate his holy intention to all people openly in public, particularly to those in power, 'in the People's gate, by which the kings of Judah enter and by which they go out' (Jer. 17: 19). The prophetic proclamations and actions ('breaking the jug', Jer. 19: 10 etc.) were risky (Jeremiah was 'struck' and 'put in the stocks'; Jer. 20: 2; see also 26: 24; 32: 2); 'doves' and 'falcons' already existed in Old Testament times. As the frequency of warfare among 'primitive' tribes and modern nations persuasively shows, humans have a propensity for war. According to Charles Burke (1975) there have been only 268 years of peace during the last 3400 years, periods of peace comprising barely 8 per cent of the whole of recorded history. Propensity to war is a 'constant' (Shaw and Wong 1989: 3), and the facts point to causes that are deeply rooted in human nature.

Except for the time of early Christianity the churches have been steadily involved in warfare and rather weak in launching effective programmes for national and international peace, although 'pax et iustitia', peace and justice, were core values in the Middle Ages. Exceptions are rare. In the seventeenth century John Amos Comenius (1592–1670), the last bishop of the Reformed Church of Bohemia, was a courageous fighter for peace. With the stature and authority of an Old Testament prophet, amidst the Thirty Years' War he bore witness to Christian peace ethics, peace politics, and peace education in a way no theologian had done before. In crossing Europe as a renowned refugee he recurrently appealed to political leaders. During the peace negotiations at Breda in the Netherlands he personally intervened, presenting his *Angelus Pacis* (*The Angel of Peace*, 1667), a text meant to help end the war between England and the Netherlands over supremacy at sea.

> The cost of not being content with one's lot, is manifest from this war of yours. For if you had not begun it, your private funds and public treasuries would not have been so depleted; the majority of your subjects would not have been brought to such straits, nor would so many thousands of brave men have perished . . . nor would so much Christian blood have been mingled with sea water; so many ships have been burnt; so many regions, towns, islands etc., have been lost.
>
> (Comenius 1964: 132)

'What excuse can there be' for warfare among Christian nations when they cause

> such upheaval merely for things pertaining to this life, and when they afflict with such
> unrest, distress and harm not only themselves but also the neighbouring kingdoms and even
> the whole world? . . . Of course, neither are those Christians who pretend to fight for God
> and religion, able to justify their deeds because they perform acts not commanded by God,
> forbidden by Christ and barren of result.
>
> (Comenius 1964: 137).

Three hundred years before the foundation of the United Nations and related international agencies, in the sixth book of his *General Consultation on the Reform of Human Affairs* (*De rerum humanarum emendatione consultatio catholica*; Comenius 1966), the *Panorthosia*, Comenius was already suggesting international institutions of this kind which were to strive for the abolition of wars and conflicts between nations and religions. He submitted proposals for (1) an International 'Council of Enlightenment' to provide the necessary wisdom through general education for all (cf. today Unesco), (2) a 'World Consistory' to promote agreements between the churches (see the World Council of Churches (WCC)), and (3) a 'Court of Peace' (cf. today the court in The Hague), all of them forerunners of much later developments.

Comenius was thinking in terms of universal renewal based on his belief in the evolution of the Kingdom of God. In the following I should like to link his eschatological evolutionary perspective to modern research on natural and cultural evolution. In our time the common interest in curtailing the human propensity for aggression, violence and warfare is great, but the discussion fluctuates between pessimism and optimism. The former is nourished by the darkening prospect of possible self-annihilation through nuclear and biological weapons and through ecological catastrophes, the latter is fostered by the glitter of technological progress, although the high-gloss façade of globalization reveals its cracks and fissures. Humankind has not sufficiently learnt the lesson of how to cope with its potentials for mutual self-destruction.

Humanity's propensity for warfare has been described as 'an irreversible instinct, necrophilia, a pathological degeneration of basic human impulses, a spin-off of original sin, or a cancer in the vast body politic' (Shaw and Wong 1989: 2, with reference to Alcock 1972; Jolly 1978). What can we do if the following observation is true? 'We don't know why we have got into this situation, we don't know how to get out of it, and we have not found the humility to fully admit we don't know. In desperation, we simply try to manage our enmity from day to day' (Powers 1984: 55, as quoted in Shaw and Wong 1989: 2). Yet we are not helpless; we have the ability to discover something different that will deliver scientific explanations as well as practical educational responses and possible rational political reactions to the problem. Historical efforts 'to overcome violence' – this being the promising title given to the decade 2000–2010 by the WCC – have to be self-critically complemented by empirical research on human nature. Therefore, the theological focus on God and the biblical vision of peace in the preceding chapters will be interrelated to evolutionary anthropology, social psychology and global ethics in this and the following two chapters. The intention is

- to prove the striking converging compatibility of biblical and evolutionary anthropology; both are disclosing a realistic view of the natural and historical legacy of our species
- to test the biblical visions of reconciliation and peace, ethical biblical key concepts such as the Ten Commandments, 'neighbour's love', 'love of enemies' and secular concepts such as the role of human rights and the concept of a 'global ethic', against the background of explanations of in-group amity and out-group enmity (ethnocentrism)
- to describe and compare opportunities and limits of inter-religious, inter-cultural, and anti-racial education as the most urgent aspects of peace education in multi-faith societies and global conflicts.

Causes of Aggression and Violence – Four 'Stories'

Education for peace is education directed towards taming aggression as a multi-faceted and multi-functional phenomenon – for example, an outburst of anger may be well justified and may support the re-establishment of social relations, while aggression that harms or violates others and destroys community is regarded as negative. A definition that allows for this ambiguity runs as follows: 'Aggression is specified as confrontation between two persons (or social units)' (Mummendey 1984: 75).

In a negative sense, violence can be defined as behaviour intended to harm others by physical and mechanical force with the aim of hurting them directly or indirectly by depriving them of their home, family, territory, individual or collective property and natural resources. The term 'structural violence' (John Galtung) refers to repressive organizations, hierarchical rule, injustice, a general social climate which stifles freedom of opinion, the impact of indoctrinating ideologies and so forth. In all these descriptions 'peace' is negatively described as the absence of violence, oppression, war, destruction. But this negative point of departure does, in fact, offer a productive approach.

First, it is the lack and not the abundance of peace in the world that calls attention to our topic. Second, the issue of violence allows us to draw on considerable research in the social sciences. Third, to begin with the barriers to peace avoids naïve optimism. Fourth, focusing on the negative will lead to 'negative duties' which, compared with 'positive duties', can 'unconditionally be universalized' (Döbert 1997: 81). 'At any rate negative duties such as not to steal, to lie, to cheat or to kill are more strict than the positive ones with the overall appeal "Do good!"' (ibid.). We can insist unconditionally on something that ought not to be done, one can claim it at any time. This is impossible in the case of positive appeals to do good. Goodness is without boundaries, while limits against evil can be set more distinctly. It goes without saying that peace definitely also needs positive descriptions of substantial content in the form of religious visions and divine promises (see the preceding chapter) or as moral ideals and programmes (see Chapter 11). For further explanation we start with well-known facts.

In a schoolyard a pupil is surrounded, then struck with heavy blows, thrown down and brutally kicked; in a park a foreigner is chased by local people, with the same result; two neighbouring nations live in constant hostility with recurrent violent campaigns – why? We are used to looking for explanations on three levels of analysis. But in line with the data available, one can tell more than just three 'stories'; there is a neglected fourth story (Euler 1997: 191). On the first three levels current research has accumulated a huge number of insights which it would be negligent not to utilize.

1 The Story of the Event

A first interest will be directed towards pinpointing the event itself. Who hit whom? How did the bullying start and why? What can be (or could have been) done by immediate intervention or, with a view to the future, by prevention? (On bully–victim issues in schools see the internationally esteemed study by Olweus 1993.) The same interest in facts guides the investigation in cases of ethnic, national, racial or religious clashes, perhaps in the hope of limiting the attack, quarrel or transgression.

This first perspective is that of police or experts trained in reconstructing phases of conflicts, for instance the way a row broke out and escalated. The factors looked for are those that have an observable impact on the violent act itself. On this level, proposals are concerned with stopping the violent *behaviour*, mostly by raising the threshold of aggression (counter-conditioning).

2 Life History

The focus now moves to concern for the persons involved, mainly the offender, unfortunately often neglecting the victim. A prime target is their biographical background, including the close environmental influence of family, neighbourhood, peer group and school career (Böttger 1998). Life history is a compound of many factors such as genetic legacy, socialization, education and biographical events. It is important to know whether traumatic experiences in early childhood, social deprivation or peer group pressure might have contributed to deviation or delinquency. Of interest are psychological hypotheses, for instance whether the offender themselves might have been a victim in the past.

Accumulating and utilizing knowledge in this direction is the domain of psychotherapists (Schulte-Markwort 1994) and social workers. Their proposals will mostly combine re-socialization strategies and therapeutic steps in order to influence traits of the *personality*.

3 The Story of the Specific Culture and Society

A third, broader approach relates to the story of the specific culture, society and nation. Cultural values and norms are entrenched in people. Publicly approved attitudes and patterns of behaviour are learnt by imitation. Shaping of the 'habitus' (Pierre Bourdieu) of individuals, groups and social classes mostly takes place through the 'milieu', often via subconscious channels. Societies can differ in their degree of manifest or hidden violent structures; Sparta was notoriously more warlike than Athens. In modern times nineteenth-century Europe was to develop manifold forms of aggression that have recently been painstakingly described by Peter Gay under the heading of *The Cultivation of Hatred* (1993).

Amongst nations a general climate of sustained mistrust and hostility can suddenly be sharpened by an actual provocation resulting in open conflict. Another growing challenge today is the internal tensions in societies which if not solved raise the prospect of open social strife. To a considerable extent they are occasioned by structural unemployment in conjunction with migration and a general disintegration as a consequence of modernization. In today's turbulent world many people feel alone, without orientation and personally futile, in particular when under employment-threatening conditions. All these factors can mobilize 'instincts' against aliens: 'Don't let foreigners steal your job!' 'Don't rely on others!' If in destabilized situations general solidarity weakens, individual morality will easily erode too. Any spread of general 'anomy' (R. K. Merton) can rekindle and nourish potentials and lead to open struggle. Remedies focus on political stability, democratic participation, equal rights and, most of all, economic security, on factors of *society as a whole*. They are, indeed, very important safeguards for inner social peace, but they do not avoid out-group enmity.

4 The Story of Human Evolution

Human beings belong to nature, an easily forgotten fact, although the biological background is always present in our thinking and acting. In a way, the fourth story to be told is 'the first and basic one' (Euler 1997: 191). Sociologists tend still to avoid the evolutionary perspective of sociobiology for fear of a deterministic view that might relativize the impact of the social environment, their own professional domain. Educators will share similar objections as they understandably want to seize social chances which seem to be restricted if the genes are seen to control not only our physical characteristics and growth, but also our mental, social and moral development. Are these reservations justified?

The Co-evolution of Genes, Mind and Culture

As to evolutionary epistemology, a sociobiological misunderstanding can convincingly be refuted by philosophical protagonists of General Evolutionary Theory in conjunction with Systems Theory (Treml 2000, drawing on Niklas Luhmann). It is proven that the human mind is a most complex and self-organizing (autopoietic) entity. From the angle of philosophy of biology, Eve-Marie Engels describes the process of human knowledge as taking place in an interplay of mind and environment, vividly rejecting the idea of mere 'adaptation' as inadequate (Engels 1989). According to the philosopher Lorenz Krüger, humans have developed a '*free* relationship to reality' (Krüger 1988: 84, as quoted in Engels 1989: 164) which enables them to imagine '*counterfactual* possibilities' such as 'alternative theoretical designs of actions and events with the prospect of anticipating possible consequences and results' (Krüger 1988: 85, as quoted in Engels 1989: 165). The self-destructive dangers *for* humankind *through* humankind do not lie in 'misadaptations of our cognitive apparatus', but, 'on the contrary, in the extremely great flexibility of our cognitive outfit, with the simultaneous rise of our readiness to risks and the reduction of restraints to destroy our own self and the life of our descendants' (Engels 1989: 147).

A similar misunderstanding can easily distort the role of evolutionary ethics. Will sociobiological insights weaken our responsibility as educators in schools and as citizens in politics? This can happen if deterministic axioms prevail, as is the case in some sociobiological theories which we will not follow. In Germany the more recent development of a General Evolutionary Theory is more adequate for both theology and education in that it avoids a one-sided 'naturalistic' understanding of human 'nature' (see in more detail Nipkow 2002). Unlike the whole prehuman realm which completely lacks moral categories and, hence, lacks any notion of moral responsibility, human beings are able to reflect on themselves and on what they are doing. They have developed an understanding that allows behaviour to be called either good or evil. To speak of 'moral analogies' because mammals care for their offspring, as the famous ethologist Konrad Lorenz proposed (1954), is misleading; animals are amoral beings. Amongst humans 'evil' has two elements, the first, indeed, being the legacy of the prehuman phylogenetic past just mentioned, 'so-called evil' as a deeply rooted amorality (see also Lorenz 1963). The second component, however, that alone allows us to speak of 'real evil' and 'real good' (Vogel 1989: 14: 'das wirkliche Böse' and 'das wirkliche Gute') emerged as a result of the specific process of hominization that was to bring forth a moral consciousness.

> Only by virtue of this second component does the first ['so-called' good and evil] obtain amongst humans – as it were afterwards– a moral dimension at all, a dimension which is absent in the whole prehuman field of organisms. It is by virtue of this second stage only that 'so-called evil' in humans could become 'real evil', a feature that raises human beings in a unique way above the realm of all other organisms as do language and culture, reason and the sense for 'the good and the beautiful'.
>
> (Vogel 1989: 14)

The difference can be illustrated by the distinction between killing and murder. Human evolution is a development 'from killing to murder'. Animals will kill without moral consciousness while humans know the difference (or ought to know); and it is exactly this consciousness that provides the great positive educational and political challenge.

Evolutionary data do not paralyse us, but they do disclose the innate propensity both to kind behaviour and to violence, including murder against conspecifics (cf. Chapter 3 on Cain and Abel) in the extreme collective annihilation of others by genocide. The evolutionary approach delivers a differentiating and realistic theoretical framework for human attempts and failures. By revealing the roots of the dark side of human nature it warns against any naïve educational and political optimism.

The first three 'stories' deal with 'proximate causes', whereas a more comprehensive theory will also have to pay attention to 'ultimate causes' (Shaw and Wong 1989: 11–12). By identifying the latter we are able to advance a new, more fundamental and coherent understanding of humanity's propensity for violence and warfare. Although necessary, it is not sufficient to study biographical background factors, environmental social influences and historical cultural legacies, let alone be satisfied with the analysis of surface phenomena concerning the violent act itself. Our educational responses need revision too; we cannot expect success from moral appeals or 'value clarification' alone, much less from authoritarian political interventions or coercive legal responses. They will perhaps control outer behaviour, but they will never reach its inner roots. Fundamental questions remain unresolved.

What *ultimate utilities* have humans sought to maximize when engaging in warfare? Why do individuals ultimately band together, often along ethnic lines, in groups when waging war? What ever-larger evolutionary process favored alliances of groups for competition/ warfare? What is the role of the brain, cognition, and conscious reflection in all of this?

(Shaw and Wong 1989: 11)

Genes, mind and culture are intertwined in a co-evolution (Lumsden and Wilson 1981, Boyd and Richerson 1985), resulting in genetic social predispositions that offer possibilities for cultural techniques to tap into, not in a deterministic, but in a probalistic sense. There is a possible match, not an unavoidable one, between cultural institutions, ideologies and techniques keying into innate universal preadaptations for both good and evil purposes. As already mentioned above, the human 'mind', although in itself a product of evolution too, is constantly actively at work in terms of self-organization. This 'freedom' is not absolute: during the ages humankind's cultural responsive structures (traditions and ideas supporting peaceful relationships as well as the evolution of weapons effectuating hostile demarcations) co-evolved in conjunction with the general central tendencies of our natural legacy. It is this interrelationship which transforms human 'nature' into human 'culture' and avoids naturalistic reductions. The transformation generates relatively free space for responsible and irresponsible action that has to be highlighted as the next step. We have to compare the cultural challenges of today with the results of cultural learning in the early history of humankind.

Are Former Functional Adaptations Maladaptive Today?

Evolutionary considerations aim at a functional understanding; they enlarge the pool of explanations and are misunderstood if taken as normative prescriptions (Treml 2000). The background against which a functional 'value' of cultural achievements is measured relates to two basic purposes of all living, survival and reproduction. With regard to these the 'variations' offered to the next generations can be differently used by 'selection'; one form of behaviour may prove more successful than another one, the word 'success' meaning adaptive utility for the above purposes. Success will usually be manifest by 'stabilization', in social relations as habitualized responses such as rituals (for instance concerning the recurrent distinction between friend and foe), legal rules and moral norms (for fostering cohesion of one's own group), thought patterns (binary coding of 'us and 'others), and emotional patterns of reaction (spontaneous recognition by 'recognition markers' of who belongs to us or with whom one can cooperate or not). We will come back to this in more detail later.

An evolutionary test about successful possible development cannot be decided beforehand, only by looking back afterwards. This opens doors for self-responsible reflection on the best social, political, moral and religious paths to follow in the future. The human cognitive apparatus (the mind) and consequent behaviour are not bound to an inflexible genetic leash. But strong central tendencies (Lumsden and Wilson 1981) with a weight of their own do have, indeed, the chance to develop too.

Thus, we face a mixture of several forms of learning. Ninety-nine per cent of humankind's development, which covers about 1 to 2 million years since Homo habilis (at Olduvai), took place very slowly; the proper charting of human evolution is still controversial (for a rough survey see Campbell 1985). Long periods of time were necessary for genetically induced 'selections' and 'stabilizations'. The resulting predispositions have built up a legacy that must be taken seriously. We may call it the 'learning of the genes' (Scheunpflug 2001: 45). Seen sociologically, it was bound to life in rather small groups. With increasing speed since the development of urban settlements, towns and hierachically structured (stratified) societies (from about 6000 BC), the evolution of cultural adaptations to more complex surroundings was to propel the 'learning of the brains' (p. 47) which in turn accelerated this process by a re-entry into the pool of cultural 'variation' as a new offer for 'selection' and 'stabilization'. Not only are modern societies of today entities of the highest internal complexity, they are also confronted with environments of extreme external complexity. Everybody is aware of the interdependencies and the accelerated speed of technological development within a 'globalized' 'world society' (*Weltgesellschaft*; N. Luhmann), which leaves us with the open question of whether at all, and if so how, in particular from a moral perspective (in the form of a global ethic), 'learning of societies' takes place (Treml 2000; Scheunpflug 2001: 57).

Apparently, some of the formerly adaptive predispositions and attuned cultural responses, such as solving problems of competition by war, are maladaptive today. Surely the human mind has coped with its own propensity for aggression and violence with a remarkable degree of success. But at the same time it has become perfectionist in devising ever more effective means of mutual destruction. Humans became the most cooperative beings in the world and simultaneously were to develop as the most aggressive animals, not just killing, but murdering.

Communal Life between Cooperation and Competition – the Two Sides of Social Groups

In prehuman evolution for some species living in groups evolved as an adaptive advantage for it improved cooperation and defence. Compared with living in solitary isolation the evolution of social forms of life offered the following advantageous aspects (Voland 2000: 29–50), accompanied, however, by disadvantages and, in the long run, by lethal costs.

Diminishing Predatory Pressure

It is evident that the larger a group the more effective common defence will be possible, for a shared attention minimizes predation risk statistically. As risks are not equally distributed – a position at the margin of the herd is more exposed to attacks – competition and social fighting will arise for the more central and hence more protected places, the phenomenon of 'selfish herd' (Hamilton 1971). Everybody is at the same time the protector and the rival of his or her fellows.

Improved Protection Against Infanticide by Males

Amongst many species of mammals (nonhuman primates, lions) males try to kill the offspring of females in order for the females to be more quickly ready again for conception. From the perspective of females, male aggression and sexual coercion are coped with in a twofold way, by maternal grouping against males and by looking for a male 'bodyguard'. In both cases reproduction interests play a role which leads to specific forms of sociality.

More Efficient Food Acquisition

This advantage of communal life needs no commentary. An open question is the cause–effect relation; did cooperative hunting evolve when group life already existed, or did cooperative social structures develop because natural selection rewarded them?

More Successful Defence of Limited Resources

For the topic of this study this aspect is crucial. Again the positive function of groups is evident, but the fact of life in groups explains also the adaptive function of aggressive tendencies amongst group members themselves because of intra-group competition. According to the focus on 'individual selection' in more recent discussions, both social bonding and 'kin altruism' or 'nepotistic altruism' on the one hand, and individual interests on the other hand are jointly genetically 'at work'. One basic precondition for successful survival and reproduction was social cohesion by bonding and mutual cooperation within one's own group; success in intergroup competition and contest was to depend on within-group cooperation in a pragmatic dimension. In addition, in an emotional dimension, early bonding, which had become necessary in species with a long period of caring after giving birth to offspring (as is the case with humans), essentially contributed to the evolution of affective, 'affiliative' relationships. Affiliation, bonding and cooperation became one side of the coin, connected, however, not only to intergroup, but also to intragroup competition and contest as the reverse side.

Human beings show a great flexibility in developing alternatives of behaviour which enable them to find a well-taxed optimal balance between binding and separating tendencies (Voland 2000: 64). But still today communal life casts its long-lasting shadows as side-effects. Conflicting individual interests influence group life and create social tensions. To gain 'social supremacy' as one of the central tendencies of the past 'seems to have maintained its early biological function' (Voland 2000: 88). The result was that in human history 'an evolutionary arms race arose' (Richerson and Boyd 1998: 91). 'The last ten thousand years have witnessed the repeated emergence of ever more powerful societies, but so far no sign of any perfect equilibrium adaptation' (p. 92) with respect to humankind as a whole – regardless of how individuals may have found their personal equilibrium and individual social, moral and religious maturity.

In-group Amity and Out-group Enmity – Two Codes of Morals

> Me against my brother; me and my brother against our cousins; me, my brother and my cousins against our non-relatives; me, my brother, cousins and friends against our enemies in the village; all of these and the whole village against the next village.
>
> (Barash 1979: 140)

In daily interaction, people tend to discriminate in two directions: first, according to gender between female and male as an area of highly exciting private interest – although not without considerable difficulties too (see the next section); second, with a very much greater impact on social life, locally, regionally, nationally and globally, a subtle distinction is made along the line of 'us' and the 'others'. A third form of coding refers to 'near' and 'distant'. The last two forms of categorizing are more or less interrelated, since the we-group consists of what we experience nearby, in family, kinship, neighbourhood, club, local congregation and ethnic affiliation, an important 'recognition marker' being common language or dialect. Solidarity weakens with growing distances while the readiness for mutual help increases with growing nearness.

Perceptual differentiations and social classifications revolve around two focal points, social relationships (communal life) and affairs of property or resources, that is around who one *is* and what one *possesses* (cf. the preceding section):

- Who belongs to me or us and against whom do we have to protect ourselves?
- What belongs to me or us and what do we have to defend against whom?

'It is not simply *that* we classify that is so important, but (1) *what* we classify and (2) *how* we act on our classifications through cognition and related emotions' (Shaw and Wong 1989: 81–2, drawing on Bock and Klinger 1986). Binary classifications are widespread and easy to learn, such as kin/non-kin or friend/foe. We are also not surprised how emotive we are about our cognitive categorizing. Emotions seem to reinforce our cognitive discriminations while rational arguments justify or even sanctify our emotional reactions.

Where does classifying begin and where can it lead? The Arab proverb quoted at the beginning of this section starts with 'I' and presupposes the ability of differentiation between close kin (brother), more distant relatives (cousins), local people (the own village) and strangers (the other village). Differences are felt and socially established within one and the same village. The coding of 'near', therefore belonging to 'us', versus not 'belonging' becomes manifest between newcomers as 'outsiders' and 'established' native inhabitants (Elias and Scotson 1965). It seems as if 'boundary maintenance' in any form constantly needs new nourishment. In my home, a village with more than 3000 inhabitants on the outskirts of Tübingen, derogatory judgemental reactions increased alongside further political differences when some newcomers favoured 'green' values against 'conservative' ones defended by the majority of the established villagers with little understanding of ecological issues.

One way to study barriers to mutual understanding and peaceful conviviality is to observe 'primitive' societies (with respect to the concept and characteristics of war, see van der Dennen 1995). 'When in doubt about ultimate causes, go to the primitives' (Iain Prattis, anthropologist, as quoted in Shaw and Wong 1989: 23). D. Barash reports that when the Tiv in Nigeria want to extend their territory, without exception they select for their attack the neighbouring group that they think contains their *most distant* relatives (Barash 1979: 132; 1981: 153, in the German edition).

Again we meet the category 'near/distant' in connection with 'kin/non-kin' or 'us/others'. The sociobiology of ethnocentrism still delivers many data of this kind today. In recent years, genocide in Rwanda (between Hutu and Tutsi), war in the former Yugoslavia (between Serbs, Croatians, Bosnians, Albanians) and war in Afghanistan between Pashtuns and the northern tribes make causative ethnic factors highly probable. We feel as if history has rolled back into the tribalism of the stone age. But with respect to the role of ethnocentrism one should avoid a mono-causal explanation. Ethnocentrism is a potent force pointing to a universal 'central tendency', as defined above, that is as a product of the 'learning of the genes', but not without other factors in the field of the 'learning of the mind'. It displays its most destructive power when combined with xenophobia, fear of strangers in several forms, the deepest fear in the field of social relations. In this broader concept not only ethnic but also general cultural factors are included, contributing to a complexity of strangeness generated by ethnic demarcations *and* different ideologies, value systems and economic and religious factors (Serbs as Orthodox Christians, Croatians as Catholics, Albanians in Bosnia and Kosovo as Muslims).

In multi-ethnic states many factors jointly come to bear on the social climate as a whole. In European countries tensions are exercabated by right-wing provocations. What begins in small villages and primitive tribes can be pursued in changed forms on a larger scale (but with a similar core), resulting in never-ending regional military conflicts and open racism.

Why did famous codes of morality such as the Ten Commandments not have a broader impact in history? The reason is rather simple. They evolved as instruments for peaceful in-group cohesion, not for use outside. The normative prescriptions not to murder, to steal, to lie and to intrude upon sexual relationships and familial bonds were meant as safeguards for internal social strength, order, security and reliability. In small societies (clan, tribe, small populations) killing would directly have endangered the very existence of the community and at least weakened the strength necessary for resisting competing others. Stealing property – mostly held collectively at that – would have damaged society's resources. Lying would have been lethal for mutual trust. Sexual disorder would have propelled sexual male competition and added to general disorder. It was never wrong and blameworthy, however, to kill enemies, plunder their settlements, practise blood revenge and steal the women and slaves of other societies. There is no question that in the course of human history much has been achieved in abolishing slavery, the theft of women and (with exceptions still today) blood revenge. Means once functional for survival and reproduction of one's own group became dysfunctional in later history, for instance slavery in the traditional form in modern industrial societies (while on the other hand new divisions arose in the form of the division of labour). However, one characteristic limit of those old commandments could not easily be improved upon, their non-validity for out-groups. Double moral standards are still alive, as the British philosopher John L. Mackie states with uneasiness for our time: 'It is perfectly possible for people to combine the finest moral sensitivity in relation to their fellows with extreme inhumanity towards . . . human beings whom they see in some way alien to themselves and their associates' (1992: 282). How can forms of morality such as the Ten Commandments or 'love of neighbour', which, indeed, meant people living nearby, be expanded? From a moral perspective this is the most urgent task facing our world (see Chapters 10 and 11).

The Role of Gender

If from evolutionary perspectives reproduction is crucial, we may assume also that male competition and female choice belong to the central innate tendencies we are dealing with. Again, functional descriptions and explanations concerning the logic of selection and reproduction cannot and must not replace moral distinctions and normative educational responses, but the latter should be given in the full context of proximate and ultimate preconditions. Obviously genetic learning has produced *pre*-adaptations which are 'whispering' within our nature (Barash 1979), or in other words, although war as a matter for mostly males (a sad truth throughout history) is not in our genes, primary (genetic) antagonistic dispositions are fostered by cultural and societal ideologies which appeal to masculine traits that 'attune' to gender specific 'whisperings' within males.

Everyday experience teaches that competition accompanies the choice of partners amongst human beings. The habit of presenting specific features as 'recognition markers' that attract the other gender and promise increase of fitness is widespread, influencing different reproduction strategies (for cross-cultural sex differences in human mate preferences tested in 37 cultures see Buss 1989; 1999). We also meet double moral standards as another indicator of 'deep structures' at work. Cultural history delivers abundant data for different moral codes concerning gender that have led to almost two different 'worlds' with a clear supremacy of male power. Why?

The invention of 'bi-sexuality' in evolution made females produce a small number of germs (ovum), males an incredibly greater amount of sperm. Females had to develop reproduction strategies to support their own scarce valuable potentiality and balance the investments in the process which were much higher than for males (energy consuming pregnancy, long period of lactation, risky nurture and breeding). On the other hand, males were to become keen on securing their reproductive success by possibly meeting many women and successfully diminishing the uncertainty of their paternity. There is also ample proof from historical studies that the hypotheses concerning the different strategies and moral codes are valid (as to the relationships between economic and parental strategies found in longitudinal historical studies, see Voland and Dunbar 1995; for sexually selected neglect of one's own offspring, see Voland and Stephan 2000).

With respect to the role of aggression and violence amongst mammals and humans, the overall 'mega-theory' predicts that violence will appear most frequently in that period of life 'when reproduction is linked to competition. This points particularly to the beginning of the time of reproduction, the younger years . . . moreover, mainly to males . . . The sub-theory about sexual selection would explain why the rate of violence and the risks are higher with males than with females' (Vogel 2000: 113). Both theories can be supported empirically.

According to the careful standard investigation on homicide conducted by Martin Daly and Margo Wilson (1988) in several metropolises in the USA and Canada, which included rich ethnological literature and historical studies, homicide on the basis of sexual competition among males is nearly forty times more likely than is the intra-sexual rate of killing amongst females in competition for males. Moreover, male offenders are, indeed, younger, the period of highest density of killing being the ages between 20 and 34, the time of highest competition among males.

Another fact concerns infanticide amongst humans, resulting from conflicts about parental investments. The data refer to the killing of unborn children (abortion) and born children, of primary stepchildren and even of infants who are genetically related ('filicide') (Vogel 2000: 115–17). A study found that in 1976 the chances of a child in the USA being severely maltreated were about a hundred times higher when living with a stepfather or a stepmother (Vogel 2000: 116; similarly Daly and Wilson 1988).

In history filicide is a very old custom that is still practised in many societies, and indeed in some of them is not regarded as a criminal act. The innate emotional tendencies and cognitive reproduction strategies have been formed over long periods of time, presumably when there were indicators of (a) deformities, (b) external handicaps (poverty, overload), (c) doubt regarding paternity, and (d) the lower value of girls. Worldwide female infanticide is much more frequent.

From a moral point of view, many parents have developed a deplorable 'right' to decide about their children, including a 'claim of return' in the case of physical and mental defects (that is to let the foetus die). Modern procedures of artificial reproduction complement and improve the old biological reproduction strategies while at the same time making them, as it were, less expensive with respect to investments (Vogel 2000: 129). After the invention of 'sex without reproduction' – a specific human invention – now 'reproduction without sex' has become possible (pp. 129–30).

A controversial point in the ongoing debate, with some objections to a one-sided sociobiological interpretation, refers to the question of whether men or women are to be regarded as the chief perpetrators of warfaring propensities. R. P. Shaw and Y. Wong argue that the propensity is equally prevalent, and that the 'greater visibility of males in warfaring can be attributed to division of labor' (1989: 179). They draw, first, on Margret Mead's observations that women play a crucial role as defenders of reproduction (ibid.), second, on the growing proportion of female soldiers in the United States (p. 180). Although conceding the historical facts about the so-called 'male supremacist complex' as based on extensive ethnographic evidence, they also question the viability of the explanatory core concerning differences in reproduction strategies, as pointed out above (p. 181).

With this caveat we leave the presentation and discussion of background factors from the perspective of the sociobiology of aggression, violence and warfare, and turn now to a consideration of psychological mechanisms and cultural methods, at the same time recalling the assumption of a mutual, co-evolutive interrelationship. This is essential (a) for any attempt to devise educational, cultural, political and, last but not least, theological responses to the propensity for aggression, violence and war, and (b) for weighing the necessity and possibilities for moral reflection and religious belief systems.

Chapter 10

Paths to Peace – a Multidimensional Approach

What is that which lies, kills, steals within us? I don't want to think about it.
(Georg Büchner, German dramatist in a letter to his fiancée Minna Jaegle, *c.* 1834)

The sum of the matter is that the times are out of joint, and that teachers cannot escape, even if they would, some responsibility for a share in putting them right.
(John Dewey, 1935, referring to *Hamlet*, I. 188–90 in Dewey 1987: 340)

The Meaning of an 'Integrating' Approach

The stage for the following discussion is set by the tension between what is 'whispering within' (Barash 1979/1981), the innate 'ultimate' tendencies of human nature, on the one hand, and moral responsibility, on the other. 'Tendencies', even if they are as central and pervasive as those towards aggression, violence and war, cannot be used as normative guidelines. Deducing norms from facts is blamed as a 'naturalistic fallacy'. But to neglect facts when weighing what *should* be done against what *can* be done is irresponsible too. Moral and religious maturity is characterized by integrating attention to facts and sensitivity to values – a first meaning of the word 'integrating'.

I am speaking of ways to peace, not only of education for peace, in order to indicate that the situation today necessitates a broad approach that can integrate several aspects in theory and practice such as social, cultural, political, moral, religious and educational factors. This approach needs interdisciplinary inquiry to connect the social sciences, cultural theory, evolutionary theory, ethics, theology and philosophy of education – a second meaning of the word 'integrating'.

Within this integrative frame I am absolutely certain of the key role of education in a broad sense. If compared with that of animals, human learning (that is the specific forms of how humans learn, young animals learn of course in their way too) can be regarded as the most effective invention in the evolution of the human species. Unlike what happens in all other species, human learning has become successful as the instrument of adaptation and cultural transmission to subsequent generations. The development of the genes takes an extremely long time and we may assume that since the appearance of Cro-Magnon man, who lived in Europe 45 000 years ago, not much has happened genetically, that's why we call him 'modern man' (Homo sapiens sapiens). Cultural evolution is generally more rapid than genetic evolution. The learning of the mind occurs much more quickly, mainly due to language as the 'ladder' for leaving the evolutionary 'niche' which other beings are bound to during their whole existence. Specific leaps of 'cultural evolution' were prompted by the invention of writing, later of printing, and in our times of computer-based communication. Today education can utilize all these means.

In the preceding chapters our remarks on education were restricted to religious education from Christian perspectives drawing mainly from biblical sources. Now the circle has to be extended to general perspectives, thereby particularly pursuing and deepening, as a third aspect, our specific integrative interest in anthropology, that is the integration of biblical anthropology concerning 'God and human nature' (see particularly the specific focus in Chapter 8 about Paul and the role of 'guilt' and 'sin') and secular knowledge on 'human nature' gained by evolutionary hypotheses and data.

From an analytical point of view, 'education' can be categorized in three directions,

- primarily meaning '*intentional*' education in the classical form of methodically planned 'direct' (or 'explicit') teaching
- second, pointing to '*functional*' education that comprises all forms of non-planned factors of 'socialization'
- third and most recently, a type of '*extensional*' or 'indirect' education has been suggested (Treml 2000: 74–81). It refers to 'intended' processes of learning that will work in a 'functional' way.

My fourth interest is to integrate these three educational forms above; for intentional teaching alone will not be sufficient to cope with our issue. While 'functional' (or 'implicit') education happens as a side-effect of other activities (for instance infants or older children learning in a household just by watching how the roles between mother and father are distributed as a non-discussed sharing), 'extensional' education takes place when, for instance, parents deliberately ('intentionally') convince their child to spend a year abroad for the opportunity to learn 'functionally' in a completely new environment. For the purpose of 'intercultural education' the knowledge of cultural differences becomes more and more important. It opens up paths to cultural and religious understanding as can be exemplified below by shared experiences between young Israelis and young indigenous Arabs in the state of Israel – one main stage of conflict and struggle for peace in our time. 'Extensional' education tries to combine the effectivity of intentional education, which stems from its condensing space and time, with the effect of a 'complete environment' (J. W. Goethe) and its radiating functional impact (Treml 2000: 80)

Eventually, fifth, the word 'integrating' has practical consequences for the churches (as well as for other living faith traditions). One of the most urgent tasks for the future seems to me to be to provide for concerted efforts in local congregations as well as in church schools, in working with children and young people as well as with adults, in helping individuals in their spiritual journey and at the same time equipping the churches to become a voice heard in public. In its shocking pervasiveness the propensity for aggression, violence and warfare requires encompassing and integrating efforts to promote reconciliation and peace.

Love and Affiliation as Evolutionary Roots of Peaceful Community

In the evolution of vertebrate social behaviour the development of nurturant individualized broodcare seems to have constituted 'a turning point' (Eibl-Eibelsfeldt

1998: 25). As the natural history of behavioural patterns clearly shows, human patterns are characterized by two strong features (not one alone): (1) aggressive demarcation against others and (2) affiliative interaction, hate and love (Eibl-Eibelsfeldt 1971). Agonistic behaviours are the older vertebrate heritage and control dominance-submissive sociality (Eibl-Eibesfeldt 1998: 33). The reptilian brain still forms a structure in the human brain as large as a fist (Bailey 1987), but although the old dominance–submission mechanisms continue to operate in humans, they are not the only 'innate' (genetic-based) central tendency. From the earliest stages of phylogenesis (and likewise in ontogenesis, that is individual development) caring and loving dispositions play a basic role; 'familial dispositions are the basis of humankind's prosociality' (Eibl-Eibelsfeldt 1998: 21). Are we allowed to assume that we can draw on this fact as a main source for promoting social life in terms of mutual understanding and peace? It is, indeed, from this early social context that our appreciation of 'belonging' comes into being, the capacity to connect to others nearby and even to attach to larger society, in short, our readiness for affiliation as such. On this elementary basis our notions of communal life have been culturally formed as a community that qualitatively differs from mere assemblies or gatherings.

However, people can also tend to overemphasize 'community' (in German *Gemeinschaft*) with very ambiguous results, as was to happen in German history. In the last three decades of the nineteenth century, after Germany had defeated France in the war of 1870/1871 with the effect of unifying Germany and the foundation of the (second) German Reich, proclaimed in 1871 in Versailles, the rise of ever stronger collective national and ultra-patriotic feelings shaped the consciousness of the vast majority of the German population. When Germany was in turn defeated by France in the First World War, German nationalism became the soil for nourishing thoughts of revenge which led to the humiliating occupation of France in 1940. Feelings of bonding can be misused.

Throughout life, two modes are experienced by the infant in relation to caring parents, in particular to the mother – giving and receiving. The early learning of getting something is different from other forms of exchange such as negotiating or cooperating, although they will also have to play a rather important role in domesticating violence and securing peace (see the end of this chapter). The individualized mother–child bonds are very strong since they are nourished by affective expressions. Caressing, embracing, kissing (derived from kiss-feeding), and baby talk in a voice raised by one octave are deeply embedded in maternal behaviour (Eibl-Eibesfeldt 1998: 25–6).

The Swiss educator Johann Heinrich Pestalozzi also saw the child's belief in God as being firmly rooted in maternal care. In his view, the feelings of 'love', 'trust', 'gratitude' and 'obedience' that are the basic outcomes of a caring mother–child relationship will be transferred to God from the moment when the name of 'God' is positively and repeatedly mentioned by the mother (Pestalozzi 1991[1799]: 227–8). 'God is the God of *my mother*, he is the God of *my heart*, he is the God of *her heart*; I don't know any other God, the God of my *brain* is a *chimera*' (p. 237).

Religious life is often based on the idea of a close, family-like community, as is vividly mirrored in Christianity in metaphors describing the church as 'familia Dei' ('God's family') or 'mother', in calling the pope 'The Holy Father', in speaking of church members as 'sisters' and 'brethren' or as 'children', which makes them become 'siblings'. If the emotional patterns of early bonding can be extended and applied to larger entities of social life (regions, nations, continents), kind and peaceful relations among humans can be established, even if others do not belong to one's own family. In the same way as Pestalozzi spoke of 'the voice of the heart', the American philosopher Michael Walzer argues optimistically that within humans the 'heart' is speaking a 'universal' language of 'humanity' which connects us emotionally to other people, be it from quite different countries, such as 'French or Norwegians, Chinese or Indians', from different religions such as 'Catholics or Muslims', or from political camps: 'liberals or socialists' (Walzer 1999: 42). To what extent is this optimism justified?

Extending Altruism beyond 'Kin Altruism' – a Crucial Challenge

Fortunately, human beings are not only egoists. Sociobiology has discovered not only the crucial role of life in groups per se as an evolutionary advantage (see above), but also altruism as a mighty social power. From a phylogenetic point of view, we do not care only for ourselves, but also for other people, with, however, a primary concern for family and kin of one's own, hence the term 'kin altruism'. Is this enough? In the view of most people, morality accomplishes its function when one surpasses nearby interests and emotional inclinations to one's fellows. Moral philosophers would regard an individual to have developed a moral self if moral obligations are felt towards others too, in particular strangers, even more, to all human beings whosoever. It is this general philosophical assumption that underlies concepts of 'universalist ethics' (I. Kant) and, if put in geographical terms, 'global ethics'. It is only through the growth of a global moral responsibility, as many see it, that the struggle against poverty can be won, worldwide mutual understanding achieved, 'inter-cultural education' and 'inter-religious education' promoted, and in all of it 'education for justice and peace' effectively set to work.

Our nearest relatives are parents, other siblings and our own children with whom each of us shares half of our genetic make-up. The relation to grandparents and grandchildren, uncles and aunts, nieces and nephews is a quarter, to cousins and great-grandchildren an eighth of a shared genetic heritage. 'A reasonable upper limit of relevant kinship in sociobiological perspective seems to lie perhaps with a 32nd share' (Vollmer 2001: 18). Why these figures? We want to explain the truth of the Arab saying quoted at the beginning of the last chapter. Proverbs from other cultural backgrounds could easily be added. It seems to be a universal trait that 'kinship' powerfully orients our prime moral obligations. 'Peaceful' living together is much more frequently to be expected and more easily to be educationally achieved in family and family-like communities. This limitation, however, if it were to lead to the building of insurmountable barriers between groups, would never allow us to cope with violence in society at large, in particular multi-ethnic and multi-faith societies, let alone really worldwide (not to forget aggression and violence even in the family and between close relatives). How can the priority of 'love of neighbour' which in its origin was meant literally, meaning those living next to oneself as family and neighbours, be explained? How can the circle of feelings of fellowship and moral responsibility be extended from local to global interrelations so that altruism becomes an 'extended altruism'? Eventually, how can a non-limited understanding of 'love of neighbour' (and of the Ten Commandments or of other moral rules in other religions) be implemented effectively? The discussion of these challenging questions will be the agenda of the following sections.

The Limitations of Altruism

To begin with the explanation of the limitation of altruism, the seminal work of William D. Hamilton (1964) introduced the concept of 'inclusive fitness' as the now leading explanatory model of altrustistic behaviour replacing (or better integrating) the 'individual-related' Darwinian stance ('Darwinian fitness') as well as 'group selection theory' (GTS) (cf. also Wilson 1975).

> GTS maintains that a group whose members willingly deny their own self-interest, or place themselves at risk for the benefit of the group, are less likely to become extinct than rival groups whose members consistently put their own selfish interest first . . . The problem with GTS is that it bypasses the competitive process at the heart of natural selection; it transcends and subordinates individual interests to the good of the group. Evolutionary biologists have shown that this simply does not fit the facts . . . and they have been instrumental, along with most zoologists, in discrediting group selection theory . . . By adopting GTS, sociologists overemphasize true altruism while economists overemphasize self-interest. Both miss the point.
>
> (Shaw and Wong 1989: 25)

In the German debate on this issue, the idea of 'group selection' has been attacked because it easily lends itself to supporting a nationalist and racist ideology. During the Third Reich, the ideas of 'the benefit of the group', at that time 'Führer, Volk und Vaterland' ('Leader, People and Fatherland'), were to systematically oppress the individual by reinforcing his/her blind submission to the collective, with dubious support on biological grounds. Biology-based ideologies led to boosting national supremacy in racist categories, with horrible results. What follows for our purposes?

Avoiding the misuse just mentioned, modern evolutionary research points to an explanation of why individuals would jeopardize their life to help other individuals. The explanation reconciles the obvious dichotomy of self-interest and altruism. Hamilton's findings launched a discussion that was to result in the hypothesis that neither the group nor the individual but rather the genes operate as the basis of selection, (a) directed to enhancing personal reproduction and personal survival (the individual component or so-called 'Darwinian fitness'), but also (b) directed to the enhanced reproduction and survival of close relatives who share the same genes by common descent (the kinship component). 'Inclusive fitness' means the sum of both. The processes at work must not be misunderstood as if a 'selfish gene' (Dawkins 1976) is intentionally operating like humans – a misleading metaphor. We are dealing with a theoretical construct, the validity of which depends on its explanatory scope.

Until recently, the concept of group selection has had a cool reception, although it was not discarded altogether as a possibility. Richerson and Boyd (1998) argue that it is group selection that takes place in the case of warfare – our topic. Eibl-Eibesfeldt (1998: 34) does not see any 'real difference since the outcome remains the same. The routes of selection are of course intrinsically interesting but the biological result is differential survival of the members of competing groups according to loss and victory'.

From Local to Global Responsible Fellowship

The first radial extension beyond family and kinship was (and in a way still leads to) clan and tribe as probably the typical form of human sociality in the stone age.

Another well-known form of a broader affiliative inclination (and often also institutional affiliation on local sub-levels) means fellow-countrymen and -women with whom one feels akin by dialect, customs, clothing (traditional costumes), festival traditions and shared fate (*Schicksalsgemeinschaft*).

The next circle consists of people or nation as the social entity marked by race, language, national religious tradition, government. A common feeling of belonging together is still based on many 'natural' similarities, but more and more it requires efforts of its own. Beneath the level of standard speech even language usually differs widely (see the role of dialects), thus generating feelings of mutual obligation that rank higher than overarching national ones. Thus national ideologies have to serve in forming a national self. In moral terms a successful ethic becomes ethnocentric or develops a national character, indicating ethno-national strength, but also often a lack of radical openness.

Today countries are forming regional unions such as the European Union; the ethical equivalent of which would be a eurocentric ethic if the interests are restricted to the region. Looking at types of civilization or culture, there are good historical grounds to distinguish between western culture, Asian culture and the culture of Islam. Authors differ in trying to overcome the barriers between these cultures for the sake of global understanding, tolerance and reconciliation, or in questioning such an idea as illusionary, even more, recommending the robust (and militant) strengthening of (western) cultural identity as the ultimate form of grouping and necessary precondition of inner and outer power.

From this perspective, a 'clash of civilizations' (Huntington 1993) seems to be unavoidable. It forgets, however, that moral philosophy and international law have developed an ethic of human rights in order to encourage global efforts to bridge cultural diversity. The specific profile of a human rights ethic is controversial; even quite a few moderate Muslims deny the moral validity and utility of the shape human rights have taken in the western world. In all cultures terrorists despise them; nevertheless they embody the core of humanity from classical times on, for they respect the individual person in his/her freedom and dignity (see in more detail Chapter 11).

As this circle is still anthropocentric, a biocentric ethics would meet the truly elementary global common goods and express the form of broadest moral responsibility (Albert Schweitzer, Hans Jonas). For the sake of subsequent generations, the present generation should take this perspective seriously. We will come back to it.

The Problem of Realization

The last horizons of the expanding circle resonate with our deepest hopes, but how can we advance and reach those goals without falling prey to illusions? What can realistically be expected and educationally supported, if people normally will gravitate to near, not remote obligations, to the familiar, not the strange, to dodging responsibility that has no links to their own daily troubles? What if people respond ostrich-like with their heads in the sand? Step by step the next sections will check the opportunities and also the limits. Biblical visions of peace as well as those taken from other spiritual traditions (Chapter 11) have to be confronted with the many factors that shape the condition of our thoughts, emotions and actions.

'Sacrificial Altruism' for What Purpose? The Clarification of Moral and Religious Criteria

The more we climb up the ladder to higher forms of ethics, the more doubts arise as to how moral and religious aspirations towards justice and peace in the world can realistically be achieved. The Austrian anthropologist Franz Wuketits remarks (1995: 19),

> In reality a moral cosmopolitanism does not exist, concepts such as 'humankind' are artificial constructs that from an evolutionary angle do not anchor in human nature. The idea of a globe as our home let alone a universe where we feel at home, is an abstraction which by a living being that has lived for millions of years on relatively small territories can be thought of, but not really felt.

Therefore, the question is: 'Are there cultural evolutionary processes that can support the evolution of norms and sentiments that permit people to live in large cooperative groups, even in the teeth of small-scale loyalties based on kinship and reciprocity?' (Richerson and Boyd 1998: 81). Human beings are, indeed, unique in the scale and quality of their use of learning from others and their environment as a mode of adaptation. It started with the step from bands to tribes and led to powerful nations. 'While kinship, reciprocity, and dominance organize higher primate troops into units as large as hunter-gatherer *bands*, there is in the nonhuman species no social unit corresponding to the ethno-linguistic *tribe*' (Richerson and Boyd 1998: 91). That means, all social units larger than bands, that is tribes, nations, states, complex societies, world religions, international alliances and, together with them, forms of ethics beyond kinship altruism such as nation-oriented, state-related or universal moral concepts, have been and are still being generated by 'cultural evolution', not directly by genetic evolution. To Peter J. Richerson and Robert Boyd it is 'striking in humans how a rather abstract, large, impersonal, marked group (Protestant, Irish, Serb, Jew, German, etc.) can attract great emotional salience and motivate desperate deeds of great risk to participants' (p. 90). This is true, but the authors seem to underestimate the moral ambiguity of their observation.

First, the word 'cultural evolution' is regarded as prestigious, something to be admired because it is imported and influential, in short because it embodies moral progress. On the one hand, we will indeed describe as 'cultured' a person who is capable of appreciating and participating in an elegant manner in an array of artistic, intellectual and moral issues. On the other hand, 'a central function of cultural patterning is to reduce the inherent biological diversity among people' (Tiger 1998: 101). It is precisely this great intrinsic biological variability among people that necessitates some unifying capacity in order not only to coordinate the socio-economic, political and military behaviour of citizens, but in many respects also to impose upon them rigid uniformity by coercive or indoctrinating means. 'For example, in what is perhaps the most sharply sculpted of cultures – military groups – a stringent dominance hierarchy, constant repetitive drill, and a set of narrowly defined procedures are necessary' (p. 102). Culture allows for the display of variety and at the same time restricts it by producing mass phenomena.

Second, the moral quality of larger social units is not self-evident. Is nationalism or patriotism something valuable beyond any moral doubts? A mere functional analysis fails to identify the ethical issue at stake. According to Lionel Tiger cultural acquisition devices have evolved as the basis for the readiness with which people acquire and attempt to maintain the special character of their particular group. These devices function as mechanisms for relatively quick and reliable inculcation of social values which can serve different purposes in varying ways, also in questionable ones. This can be illustrated by 'sacrificial altruism' as an expression of 'kinship altruism'.

Everybody knows of sacrificial altruism shown by parents who defend their children by risking their own lives. Another example is the soldier who is ready to be killed in action for the sake of his nation. An extreme form, however, is people who as 'walking bombs' deliberately murder innocent citizens for the benefit, as they believe, of their own socially and politically oppressed people and on behalf of their religious faith as a means of serving their God. In this case self-sacrifice is highly controversial and will evoke very different reactions; what one group will call a heroic deed will be called terror by another.

War too has lost its former sublimity. Soldiers killed in action are honoured equally by their warring nations. The example of heroic self-sacrifice is refracted through the windows of totally divergent standpoints or darkened by the irritating fact that there must be something wrong when both warring parties glorify their dead on the same grounds. Moral legitimations seem to become arbitrary. What is good for the one is wrong for the other – mutual killing for a sham truth? Consequently, elucidating and evaluating moral criteria is the primary task in public debate and public education.

A further step of analysis would have to be devoted to the psychological mechanisms that can explain why each side in a conflict believes itself to be on the side of good whereas the others are regarded as bad. We postpone this analysis to the next section. With respect to the issue of moral legitimation, the fact that we have least doubts about the legitimacy of a mother or a father risking and giving their life for their child indicates the direction in which we should seek an answer to the problem of criteria.

Our moral feeling tells us (1) that in the case of parents helping their child sacrificial altruism serves the life of the weak and defenceless. Moreover, if (2) one's own death is meant as vicarious exchange for the life of the weak, that is if it is not dependent on and connected with harm done to others, we will also approve much more easily. Admittedly, we have to consider the objection of what to do if the offender is encouraged to continue the aggression. The possibility of exploiting non-aggressive and non-retaliative sacrifice must be taken seriously; but it does not discard as wrong or useless the two moral criteria mentioned.

In putting the two aspects together we are reminded of the structure of Jesus' sacrificial death as also (1) on behalf of the weak and defenceless and (2) a form of non-violence. This structure of moral behaviour is complemented by the inner strength to forgive the offender (see Chapter 7). As the overall value and paramount ethical criterion, the idea of 'preserving life' shows up in terms of Christian faith, 'God as the friend of life'. This last perspective forbids warfare in the name of God; war is never his intention.

Observations and case studies show that there are many people whose near relatives (their own children) have been murdered who suffer from immense inner difficulties in understanding the logic just outlined. They cannot forget and nobody is entitled to expect them to. Can they forgive? After a time some are able to do so, as they have confessed. They 'gave' the murderer a new chance of life in analogy to the logic of how they themselves would have been 'giving' their own life for the life of their child.

The two other cases of 'sacrificial altruism' ought to be carefully assessed according to the same overarching moral guideline of how to minimize death and preserve life. A terrorist looks for a maximum of persons killed by his or her atrocity. Military interventions to stop terrorism should in a reverse way minimize the number of persons killed or harmed. The asymmetry of despising life must be answered by the asymmetry of preserving life.

Traditional national warfare is no longer a viable means of solving conflicts, for two reasons. The age of a mere exchange of death toll should have come to a definite end. In the face of a more or less similar amount of death, it draws its dubious legitimation from a life-despising and unreasonable calculation at that, not from reasonable, let alone moral grounds. Second, the mere means of mutual destruction as such have increased in a way that makes no sense of warfare of this kind.

In the next section we will see that national warfare has also become obsolete through learning from history. Furthermore, it is ruled out by the growing role of international strategies of conflict solving based on the organization of the United Nations (pp. 152–3). The Nobel Peace Prize awarded to UN General Secretary Kofi Annan in December 2001 honours the fact that global institutions are politically and morally regarded as the new mediating instrument between nations (for the function of mediating 'intercession' see Chapter 7 and further illustrations below).

To summarize, the basic step of all public efforts to promote peace, including education for peace, is the clarification of moral and religious criteria, with history and memory as indispensable sources.

Beyond Nationalist Ideologies – Learning from History

In past centuries no explicit public peace education existed in Europe, let alone in categories of global peace. The general guideline was the young generation's preparation for national pride, self-confidence and participation in 'just' national wars.

Allow me to illustrate this through two autobiographical testimonies, the first my own story. Being born in the year 1928, I had to undergo a pre-military education from an early age. Immediately after 1933 when the Nazis took over, they started a systematic nationalist and racist indoctrination which exploited the natural enthusiasm of youngsters for risky warlike adventures. Less than a fortnight after turning 15, on 1 January 1944, I was called up to an anti-aircraft unit on the home front. In March 1945 a group of us was sent home; but still completely dazzled by the spirit of militant patriotism (not racist Nazism, because of resistance to this point in my family), I planned to voluntarily join one of the retreating German units.

Hitler's war was a crime, not a 'just' war, but the long history of inurement to 'just' national wars, and the specific reminder of the 'unjust' Peace of Versailles at the end of the First World War, had prepared a ground that could easily be exploited. From the very beginning of the new regime in March 1933, any public discussion of moral criteria different from national ones was stifled; advocates of democracy and global peace were persecuted. The conservative German elites believed in Hitler as a safeguard against international Communism and as a guarantee of national renewal. The ideology of 'national socialism' was to develop out of the ideology of 'nationalism'. Without the nationalist historical horizon the new 'völkische Weltanschauung' (national ideology) would never have gained its broad backing in the German population. Within this national context the so-called 'just war' (*bellum iustum*) was philosophically justified by a national 'right to war' (*ius ad bellum*).

The second testimony is that of Annette C. Baier, from New Zealand, who at a conference in 1988 impressively described how she had learnt these national lessons in their irresistible truth, as it seemed to her, in her country, until she realized their historical arbitrariness.

> Most of us have had the luxury of learning these lessons as members of fairly well recognized groups with recognized territories and authority structures, groups whose rights to defend their official values from perceived attack, or to express their expansionist colonial values, have been taken for granted. As a New Zealander I, for example, learned early that it had been all right for the British troops protecting my colonial ancestors to kill Maoris who resisted British rule, that their killing was in a different moral category from the 'barbaric' assaults of Maori tribesmen on white settlements, let alone from their occasional ritual eating of an uninvited missionary or intruding British official. I later learned that it was all right for my uncles and older schoolfellows to set sail around the world to Europe, in order to kill Germans and Italians; or to kill their Japanese Pacific neighbors, since we were at war with these peoples and God was on our side. Still later, once peace was made, I learned that it was retrospectively all right for at least some of those German, Italian and Japanese to have killed my fellow countrymen, since they were soldiers whose job was to kill, and they may have been nonculpably ignorant of the fact that God was not on their side. As I went on to study history, it became clear that the answer to the question of who it is who makes someone a soldier, or other member of a military force, rather than a mere murderer or barbaric warrior, the question who gives out the licences to kill, could not simply be 'authorities of a nation-state'. For I learned that that was a relatively recent and for a long time a largely European phenomenon.
>
> (Baier 1991: 40–41)

We are living in a historical period of transition. National legitimations are questioned by a growing transnational moral consciousness. Convictions which had been taken for granted lose their false appearance of eternal moral legitimacy. Philosophical moral arguments reveal their character as later rationalizations. But who then authorizes the balancing of war and peace, if it is no longer the nation-state *alone?* In Europe, with a European Union expanding step by step, that 'largely European phenomenon' of stubborn nationalism is going to be replaced by an integrated European peace diplomacy which in addition seeks to become embedded in the even broader legitimation of the United Nations as a global institution. The former frame of reference is about to change from a frame of mutual demarcation to one of mutually inviting openness, from nation-related to international-oriented education. The core with respect to individual formation is a revision of identity-building, identity by meeting the otherness of others (see in more detail pp. 168–70).

'Family Semantics'? Respecting Common Rules, Law and Human Rights

In line with international agencies as peace-making instruments, we have to test whether the expanding circle of mutual obligation and solidarity is allowed to stop at a level before that of a human rights ethics and the weight given to it in the constitutions of democratic countries.

An effective device working as an 'identification mechanism' (Shaw and Wong 1989, chap. 5) is language, in applying family vocabulary to genetically non-related others. If one tribe has conquered the territory of a neighbouring one, what is to be done after that? Social cohesion between the different tribes is achieved if the conquerors succeed in adopting the defeated tribe as 'brothers' and 'sisters', as if both belonged to one and the same 'kinship', so that 'kin altruism' will work within a widened circle.

After David had become the head of the 'House of Judah', he not only succeeded in integrating the most competitive tribe, the Benjaminites, who had provided the first king in the history of Israel, Saul. He also successfully managed to unify all the other tribes as *his* 'kinship': 'Then all the tribes of Israel came to David at Hebron, and said, "Look, we are your bone and flesh"' (2 Sam. 5: 1). Whatever the real genetic relatedness may have been, the genetic fiction uses the familial bonds which among family members are 'whispering' within them (David Barash), in order to form a larger family-like social unit: 'We belong together for we are brothers and sisters.' Today, in societies comprising millions of citizens with multi-ethnic composition, the direct identification mechanisms (reminding of common descent) are no longer very useful or are obsolete. Nevertheless, speaking of 'brothers' and 'sisters' is widespread.

With respect to the former socialist German Democratic Republic (East Germany), in the Federal Republic of Germany (West Germany) talking of 'our brothers and sisters' was meant to affirm the fellowship between the populations in both parts. Many centuries earlier some Swiss cantons formed a federation which was sealed by the famous oath on the Ruetli mountain, 'Let us be a unique nation of brethren, never separating in predicaments and danger.' In French history, in a 'Chant of Soldiers', 'fair France bids her children arise, soldiers around us are arming, on, on, 'tis our mother who cries' (as quoted in Shaw and Wong 1989: 91). 'France is clearly not a "mother", but by breathing life into these abstract entities, reification makes them part of our family heritage and well-being' (p. 96).

The language of kinship bonding, on the one hand, and the innate predispositions for becoming bound and mutually obliged, on the other hand, meet and match, the first, as it were, by 'keying in' the given 'locks' or channelled 'traces' as the second factor of innate predispositions. The expanding circle works by psychological identification mechanisms which build up a fictive lineage system of common descent. Thus, family feelings are induced even in large societies of factual anonymity.

However, what if this process of inclusion aimed at strengthening in-group cohesion stops at the level of ethnic or national unification? It will necessarily exclude those who will not become 'genetically adopted' (for the phrase 'genetic adoption' see Mohr 1997: 20). By placing many new members within the new larger in-group, many more may be left outside the circle, marking them as not 'akin', not 'belonging to'. This dangerous consequence can only be overcome by expanding the circle to categories of universal inclusion. The next wider circle, of a universal nature with corresponding universalist ethical principles, is necessarily humankind as a whole.

Education for peace is not allowed to stop halfway. Ethnic or national fictions by 'quasi-blood' relations (Eibl-Eibesfeldt 1998: 43) are basically deficient for both moral and pragmatical reasons.

Sharing the Same Human Dignity

Human beings share the same human dignity regardless of kinship, be it real or fictive (moral argument of philosophical ethics). Nor does the biblical perspective allow anything else (Christian ethics). 'So God created humankind in his image, in the image of God he created them; male and female he created them' (Gen. 1: 27). The universal perspective is renewed and accomplished by God's revelation in Jesus; death and resurrection are directed towards universal salvation (cf. Chapter 8 on Paul).

'Humanity' as the idea of broadest scope requiring unlimited shared responsibility may be a vision that in evolutionary perspective is not, indeed, anchored in our genes, but it is a necessary vision to concentrate upon – in philosophical vocabulary a necessary 'regulative idea'. The same is true of the idea of 'peace'; both ideas belong together and must not be separated. In terms of morality, 'humanity', 'peace' and 'humankind' are inseparable aspects of one and the same vision.

Shared Rules and Human Rights

Inclusion–exclusion demarcations which stop halfway will also easily cause resentment; they are considered to be basically unjust, and are rejected because they rely on irrational criteria (fictive kinship). A sound foundation on which to start education for peace is certainly by strengthening social cohesion in the family and applying family semantics and feelings of belonging to the larger 'family' in the classroom community, the school community or the local Christian congregation. At the same time, however, we have to proceed to another frame of reference, for children do need knowledge about how to settle family quarrels, stop classroom bullying, negotiate escalating conflicts in school, neighbourhood and society. These conflicts, as the reverse side of the coin, cannot be settled in terms of family metaphors alone, they need shared rules that are based on rational agreements alongside the ideas of justice, fairness and equality. Equality is defined as sharing the same status, rights and opportunities for all members of a society or group regardless of ethnic, racial, national, cultural or religious affiliation.

In many schools from the elementary and primary level onward, teachers introduce children to the meaning of rules, in particular as a means of solving quarrels, or at least taming aggression. Against the background of our analysis, a naïve trust in 'family-like' cohesion fails to perceive the fact that aggression and violence begin within the inner circle of family life itself: 'Me against my brother, my brother and me against our cousins etc.', whereas the following statement of a girl in primary school illustrates the positive impact of rule education on daily life as part of regulating violence as one precondition of peace among others in larger society (even among siblings): 'When I am quarrelling with my sister, we first agree not to hit or pull hairs or scratch' (Faust-Siehl *et al.* 1995: 164).

As children grow older this approach will lead to knowing about basic rights (such as in the German constitution), and to respecting human rights as their foundation. The plain lesson to be learned is about the role of law established for the benefit of all alike.

Already among children it is easily understood that law needs the support of a public lifestyle. It matters, for example, how politicians behave in solving their conflicts and settling their disagreements. In short, peace education is to be linked with 'civic education' in schools and 'functional education' in public life.

Taking Care of Nature and Common Cultural Goods

The problem of extending the circle of emotional bonds and obligations which are rooted in the 'we-group' identification between mother and child and other family members has led to the following interim balance. In larger societies attempts to promote social cohesion within a much broader framework owe their possible effectiveness to the way they hook into the species' typical dispositions that once evolved in phylogenesis to elicit bonding and that are repeated in the early emotional relationships in ontogenesis. To draw on them is necessary but not sufficient. They can, but do not have to, help to contribute to overcoming the human propensity for aggression, violence and war, and to promote reconciliation and peace. Appealing to family-like bonds and duties can also exclude others. Therefore it was necessary to proceed to the wider circle of basic rights for all which points to basic values for all around the central idea of 'human dignity' (*dignitas hominis*), including 'dignity of life' (*dignitas vitae*), the right of everybody to live a worthy, dignified life.

Recollecting the 'expanding circle' roughly outlined above, the widest circle to be identified is not the universal anthropocentric, but a universal biocentric one, in moral categories, respect for life as such. Historically the issue has been little debated; today we simply cannot afford to neglect it, since for the first time our species has the power to destroy its own natural foundations (not only to exploit certain resources). Again, as in the preceding sections, we will try to interrelate the analyses of this part to the contributions to peace displayed in Part II, thus integrating tradition and present issues.

In the Hebrew Scriptures, for Christians the Old Testament, and here in the second account of creation in Genesis 2, historically the older one, we read, 'The Lord God took the man and put him in the garden of Eden to till it and keep it' (Gen. 2: 15). This mandate balances the earlier mandate in Chapter 1 of the Book of Genesis where humans are honoured to have 'dominion' over all living species (Gen. 1: 26). In modern theology care for our globe as a 'garden' is emphasized more than ever before in history. In the seventeenth century, exceptionally, John Amos Comenius urged his contemporaries to exercise an utmost careful 'dominion' on earth. His general guideline was to avoid violence wherever possible: 'Omnia sponte fluant, absit violentia rebus' ('Everything may flow spontaneously; may violence be absent to things'). With this maxim for life Comenius applied the idea of peace to nature. But what did he mean?

In his outstanding main educational work, *Pampaedia*, the central fourth part of his *Consultatio catholica* (*General Consultation on the Reform of Human Affairs*), which consists of seven parts, Comenius argues that not only is humankind 'to be renewed by the abundance of the world', but conversely humans have to serve the world of things (goods) too. For

> it is also the interest of the things themselves, in their situation of being [helplessly] submitted to human dominion, to be governed by wise people, even more, by people full of wisdom. Humans, whosoever they may be, can become confronted with things, whatsoever they may be. If now they are not able to treat them according to their natural destination, they will fail the appropriate treatment at all. In this case the nature of things will have to suffer from violence; they will moan and lament under the yoke because of being abandoned [exposed] to vanity [nothingness]. Things [goods] are ready to serve, but they can't if they are treated without knowledge.
>
> (Comenius 1966, 2: 28)

True knowledge is responsible knowledge and includes everything under the dominion of humankind. Human beings live in conjunction with all living organisms and with an organic nature in a relationship of mutual service. One origin of this breathtaking view is Comenius' belief in God's creation as cosmos. The Bible tells a story about creation that places everything that exists into a coherent order. Another motivation seems to be gratitude; God who serves people deserves grateful service in return. The final idea behind it presumably refers to the unique position of the human species. Whoever excels others in capacities should take care of the less gifted, the weaker. Human beings are given stewardship over all things on earth, a mandate to preserve life, not destroy it. This, however, is exactly what we have been dealing with in the chapters above on God and humankind, to put it in the words of the Psalms and the prophets, God as 'righteousness and peace', and 'peace through justice' (see the title of Part II).

Thus, education for peace has a lot to do with helping children to perceive how soil, water and air, as well as plants, animals and all the goods we produce need our careful attention. Again we can and ought to start early in childhood. Children are open to the realm of the living. They show spontaneous feelings of care and love towards animals. They can be introduced to the beauty of nature, embracing the small and being moved by the large, mighty and tremendous, the little flower and butterfly and the pouring rain and thunderstorm. They can observe (and should be told) how rapidly species (for instance butterflies) have decreased in number. Texts and pictures from the world of Buddhism and Hinduism can show how religions understand about caring. In modern source books for religious education stories about Francis of Assisi belong to the curriculum in both Catholic and Protestant classes. St Francis regarded all creatures as God's handiwork, referring to them as brothers and sisters. He preached to the birds and spoke of 'brother Wind', 'sister Moon' and 'brother Sun'. In praising God and his creation he indirectly also cast the light of faith upon evolutionary natural history.

In higher classes and adult education ecological peace education can be linked to political analyses, since conditions of peace are undermined by robbing people of their natural resources. In a global perspective – as pursued throughout this book – ecological destruction in poor countries and whole continents such as Africa follows poverty, and at the same time ecological death sharpens poverty. Poverty is a main root of silent despair and violent uproar. Thus, against a background of suffering, to enable people to preserve nature and to overcome poverty are essential presuppositions of peace.

> For the creation waits with eager longing for the revealing of the children of God; for the creation was subjected to futility, not of its own will but by the will of the one who subjected it, in hope that the creation itself will be set free from its bondage to decay and will obtain the freedom of the glory of the children of God.
>
> (Rom. 8: 19–21)

Perceptions, Emotions, Ideologies – Human Indoctrinability and Critique of Ideologies

The existence of formalized legal codes (Codex Hammurabi) imposed by King Hammurabi of Babylon (1728–1686 BC) as well as rules of behaviour such as the Ten Commandments, all of them more or less grounded in commonly shared religious belief systems, did much to reduce humankind's potential for aggression, but not enough. It was the humanistic movement of the Renaissance (Erasmus) and the Enlightenment and the interrelated efforts of those Christians and Christian groups who transformed the value of human dignity, which for Jews and Christians was based upon God creating humankind 'in his image' (Gen. 1: 27), into individual human rights, who tried to empower human reason and strengthen the ideas of tolerance and peace (see Kant's *Perpetual Peace*, 1795). Developing the positive potentials of each individual through education promised a way out by curbing the inclination to attack one's own kind. '*Aufklärung* (Enlightenment) was to instigate "the parting of the human being from his self-inflicted tutelage" (I. Kant)' (Frey 1998: 191).

The question today, however, is whether the powerful new mass communication systems will still support or instead prevent individuals from exercising their freedom. Has self-inflicted tutelage been replaced by a media-inflicted dependence, as experts in communication theory and media psychology ask? Evolutionary psychology goes a step further in questioning an unlimited 'freedom of will' as such. Recollecting the hidden dependence of human efforts to tame aggression on the remaining tough innate tendency to aggression, doubts are more than justified. Even legal means become suspicious. 'The main effect of measures to control the violence of individuals by legal means may, in fact, have been to simply redirect aggression towards those less well protected by the law', ironically suggests Siegfried Frey (p. 190). I do not agree with regard to international and constitutional law, which are grounded in basic and human rights. But even today, after thousands of years of human civilization, new forms of barbaric terror, irrational hostility and ethnic prejudice are still powerfully at work.

At the beginning of this new millennium, human affairs call for a theoretical model that goes behind 'intentional' education (directed to the cognitive refutation of prejudices) to reveal mechanisms at work in 'functional' socialization processes on mostly subconscious levels. We will briefly consider here communication theory's pattern of affect-laden 'perception'.

Modern communication theory and evolutionary epistemology meet in that they both highlight the role of non-verbal signals and the role of the person who interprets them. 'What the sender can produce is a stimulus; its evidence must be *accorded* by the receiver' (Frey 1998: 203). We have to take into account all factors, particularly 'the way that nonverbal behavior enters into the process by which "*understanding, creative understanding*, or *creative misunderstanding is achieved*"' (ibid.). This sounds very positive as long as one forgets the '*dogmatic nature of visual perception*' (p. 204) due to subconsciously filtering perceptual mechanisms. Perception and judging will usually take place within the framework of 'inferential communication'; that is, the meaning and value of an information stems solely 'from what the viewer happens to read into it' (p. 203). The language of gestures, facial movements and the appearance of the body trigger behavioural reactions that 'unfold in such an automatic fashion that ethologists have come to refer to these perceptual filters as "innate releaser mechanisms"' (p. 207). It is highly probable that non-verbal communication producing 'involuntary snap judgments produced by unconscious inference' must have been our ancestors' 'favorite way of making psychological sense out of what was observed in other people' (p. 206).

We need not go into detail to grasp – as a next factor – the fundamental relevance of images in whatever form they reach individuals, groups and larger populations. They operate as 'a prime knowledge system', in particular in shaping the image of our own identity as well as the imagined identity of others (Deutsch 1998: 303). 'Without images, the "other" would be absolute and unfathomable (a stranger); the "self" would be fragmented and vulnerable' (pp. 303–4). Walter Lippmann's early opinion on the role of photographs as 'the most effortless food' (1950 [1922]: 92, as quoted in Frey 1998: 209) is supported by Lionel Tiger's 'ease of learning hypothesis' (1998: 102): just by looking at a person one thinks it possible immediately to form a secure judgement about him or her, either in a positive or a negative sense, 'ease of learning' due to 'ease of indoctrinability' (p. 103). 'Meaning is extracted selectively from only a small portion of what is actual observable. We take those things that stand out and make them fit with what we already know and expect.' Thus people 'concoct an image with an emotional bottom line: positive or negative' (Deutsch 1998: 302).

Data attest that stereotypes are usually charged with a strong affective component; there seems to be a somatic basis for what Frey refers to as our 'gut reactions' to other people (1998: 213).

At the political level, TV-mediated images of political leaders can decide elections. Hence the personal presentation of politicians, verbally and, more importantly, non-verbally, is carefully managed. The advisers' psychological guidelines are (1) to present the leader in such a way that people instantaneously recognize *similarities* with themselves. The political leader should embody something 'we all share'. Next to be conveyed is (2) the feeling of *trustworthiness*, and then (3), *power*, for one wants to be empowered oneself by belonging to the powerful. Political leaders succeed in persuading their followers if they communicate the feeling of security and overall provision. From a psychoanalytical point of view one may assume that a political leader by appealing to the 'inherent archetype of the significant "other" (the parent)', subconsciously evokes memories of one's own being parented in early life (Deutsch 1998: 311).

It goes almost without saying that the processes mentioned above need little or no reflection; they work without logical processing and objective analysis. The reactions are immediate, spontaneous, effortless. Paul Leyhausen, a psychologist who became a close collaborator of Konrad Lorenz, described quite early on the way non-verbal 'impression' is directly translated 'into sentiments and affective states . . . without the participation of reflection, comparisons, reasoning and judgments' (1968: 50, as quoted in Frey 1998: 207–8).

Perceptions – emotions – indoctrination: we are used to speaking of the last when deliberately planned forms of persuasion are applied. At this point it is necessary to make the distinction between 'indoctrination' and '*informal socialisation*, which includes spontaneous *imprinting*' (Salter 1998: 422; my emphasis). What may correctly be called indoctrination should be reserved for 'directed, systematic effort' (ibid.) to inculcate convictions and shape behaviour, aimed at converting a person's whole character, sometimes applying methods of great thoroughness in the form of 'brainwashing'. The gradual development of character traits, attitudes and patterns of behaviour is something different. Kin loyalty develops 'naturally' by 'functional education' (informal socialization).

What matters anthropologically in terms of human evolution is, however, that both forms utilize the innate 'whisperings' within us, in particular the two universal experiences of

- *caring/bonding*, which includes the distinction between dominance and submission (see the difference between the powerful parents and the helpless infant)
- and *us/others* and *in-group/out-group*, an experience connected with the need for internal cohesion and external demarcation (both achieved, if necessary, also by violence).

Both the 'informal, functional' processes of imprinting and the 'intentional' processes of indoctrination are 'tapping into' those innate predispositions that we have called 'central tendencies'. Thus, indoctrination and indoctrinability correspond to each other and – of importance morally – it is this interrelationship that makes human nature exploitable.

In my view, a sharp distinction between imprinting and indoctrination is not easily made if there are strategies by which both types are fused. To some extent our third form of 'extensional' education can clarify the issue. Social environments can more or less 'intentionally' be formed so that they have a 'functional' impact ('extensional' education). This is already the case if a society knows about negative informal socialization influences and fails to resist. Indoctrination is also indirectly fostered if children and young people are not protected against pervasive indoctrinating 'persuasion'.

What the word 'indoctrination' particularly stands for and is condemned for today is the inculcation of values and behavioural patterns without providing for critical assessment and without presenting alternative religious positions. The discussion on this point mostly refers to the nature of doctrine and the compatibility of religious upbringing and the liberal ideal of rational autonomy (Astley and Francis 1994, part 8), rather than emphasizing the general indoctrinating processes in society, as we do here. Neither was what we are dealing with in this book a problem in previous centuries. In western schools methods that involve the closing of the pupil's mind are rejected. Modern concepts of Christian upbringing and education will mostly emphasize openness (Nipkow 1985: 26–30; 1996: 48–50; Laura and Leahy 1994). But in our context, this development is not the problem.

As to our issue of aggression, violence and peace, indoctrination by an 'ideology', the latter understood as a 'noncognitively induced strong conviction' that 'as such implies dogmatism' (Geiger 1998: 412), can become the source of not only narrow-minded, intolerant religious attitudes, but also hostile demarcation, aggression against others and war. Geiger's explorations in 'charismatic authority and legitimacy' help us to understand how and why 'ideological indoctrination often works so effectively in mobilizing organized mass action. Indoctrination may indeed make large-scale collective behavior look legitimate if it is reconfirmed by charismatic interactions or institutional authority ultimately derived from charisma' (p. 419). Irrational personal and ritualized charismatic 'radiation' can still replace sober public discussion. This is possible in politics as well as in religion. In short, the issue transcends the traditional debate on religious education in schools and touches society and politics as a whole.

An illustration from the field of politics is given by James N. Schubert's analysis of the experimentally tested 'Rally round the flag effect' (1998). The principal purpose of the study was to explore the impact of televised political speeches upon public attitudes. One result was that 'television clearly did make a difference' (Schubert 1998: 256), and the author concludes: 'In the future, prime-time nationally televised addresses may be the principal form in which leaders in the United States seek public support for their decisions committing military forces' (pp. 256–7). The rally effect is especially interesting as a case in which people form attitudes in a 'relatively short time', 'often with little prior knowledge and in response to novel stimuli' (p. 261).

The political and psychological techniques applied aim at tapping into existing social and emotional dispositions; they don't need any physical force. It is the noncoercive power of symbols that motivates unselfish behaviour ('sacrificial altruism') and makes it look like an expression of freedom; in reality it is rather a mixture of freedom and emotional persuasion. This discrepancy between overt and covert is the 'ideological' core, the term understood as 'false consciousness'. Another example, now from the field of religion, would be a similar 'rally round the charismatic guru effect'. Both are problematic.

If education is to promote transnational mutual understanding and interfaith dialogue by self-critical reflection, education for peace cannot but help to unmask the strategies and mechanisms that exercise subtle political or religious control over minds. In order to resist this, modern Protestant religious education has developed an approach called 'critique of ideologies' as an indispensable general dimension of religious education in state schools. In its core it comprises three steps: (1) asking what a political or religious ritual such as 'rallying round the flag' or 'rallying round the guru' means (hermeneutical interpretation); (2) explaining why people will follow (explanatory analysis by social and evolutionary psychology); and (3) moral assessment of the underlying political, moral and religious criteria (normative philosophical and theological check).

Such an approach will meet objections from several points of view. First, politically, if the political (and military) case seems to be absolutely clear since the enemy is identified and no reasoning is necessary. In this case critical questioning is likely to be condemned as defeatist, and civilian opinions are brushed aside by military rationale. Fortunately, times have changed insofar as international peace agencies (UN Security Council) and international non-government organizations (INGOs) try to make space for rational and moral considerations. Schools can participate in this discourse in elementary ways. Practically it should start with placing our topic in the curriculum of civic, moral and religious education, organizing interdisciplinary projects about it.

Another objection, more probably coming from certain anxious conservative religious authorities, will remind of the danger of disorientation when laypeople lack clear religious authority. In the 'Legend of the Grand Inquisitor' within his novel *The Brothers Karamazov*, Fyodor Dostoevsky (1821–81) lets the Grand Inquisitor defend his totalitarian religious rule against Jesus himself by the argument of human dependence on such a rule. Today we know that true faith has to come from within one's own soul as an act of free conversion.

Gender Difference in Aggression – Questioning Masculine Ideologies

Against the background of the most intimate forms of aggression, no educational discussion on violence and peace can afford to neglect the significant difference between the genders. In Chapter 9 the most important general data from an evolutionary point of view have already been presented. We are left to briefly reflect on some consequences for moral and religious education.

Learning meets different conditions, among them traces and grooves in the wax table of the mind, which, indeed, is not empty, no tabula rasa. Therefore, unintentional learning by imitation as a powerful form of functional education is highly selective. The differences between the genders that evolved in our evolutionary past belong ultimately to the traces and grooves that evolution has left for cultural influences to key into. No wonder that military ideals and pseudo-military customs exert their influence mainly on males – it is a case of artificial keys matching the natural locks.

History contributes in a major way to a country's general value system. Nations that had to fight against constant aggressors or other nations that had to conquer their territory in long-lasting struggles show perhaps a higher degree of militant defensiveness still today. One must not blame history as such, the question is how to handle the historical legacies. Today it is necessary to consider long-term after-effects for the future since times and constellations have changed.

As already mentioned, Peter Gay, German emigrant and retired Sterling professor of history at Yale, has described the very 'cultivation' of a military behavioural habitus in relation to a codex of masculine values almost all over Europe in the nineteenth century (Gay 1993). Masculinity became an ideal and remained nevertheless at the same time a trauma. Gay's opening chapter ironically describes in detail the custom of fighting non-lethal duels with rather heavy swords among German student corps, a 'milder' form of the fatal duels to be found among the European aristocracy. These playgrounds for one's own propensity for aggression were justified by the values of bravery and honour. The nineteenth century, the author concludes, was to become an age of equally aggressive destruction and aggressive nation-building, an ambivalent 'progress', which in retrospect helped to release the energies that were to contribute to the mass killings of the First World War, and more, in the next century.

Recent research (Zulehner and Volz 1998) on so-called 'new males' signals a change in the image of maculine ideals. While 57 per cent of the 'traditional' 'masculinity-oriented' males show a 'strong' preference that others lose their job first if unemployment rises, another large proportion of 40 per cent have a 'relatively strong' wish for this, and only 3 per cent show a 'weak' tendency to such egoistic motives; the picture is reversed when we consider 'new' males. Here only 7 per cent share a 'strong' tendency that the fate of unemployment may hit others first, while 61 per cent have almost no interest at all. Parallel reactions could be observed when another colleague was preferred in employment.

The most conspicuous difference showed up in 'the inclination to violence'. Among the 'traditional' group 10 per cent were ranked with a 'strong' tendency, 54 per cent with a 'middle', 36 per cent with a 'weak' inclination, while with the 'new' males only 9 per cent showed a 'middle' and 91 per cent a 'weak' tendency.

We can leave it open whether the 'masculine' genes which have been activated and selected in endless periods of learning in adaptation to the male role of hunter and warrior have contributed to the more robust physical stature and condition of males. At any rate nature seems to have justified males' energies – and society needed and rewarded them. What is needed today?

Either/Or Thought Patterns – Resistance to Cognitive Simplifications

The 'ease of learning hypothesis' (Lionel Tiger) necessitates at least a brief look at thought patterns. How and why did human cognitive structures develop in the history of the species? The answer can tentatively be given when one considers that probably neither upright walking nor the use of tools became the decisive motor of the evolution of the intellect; it was rather social interaction. The greatest difficulty imposed on humans by their environment was how to negotiate with other humans. The challenge of coping with a multitude of other human beings forcefully propelled the development of the brain; humans developed, so to speak, a 'social brain'. To come to terms with other humans who possessed the same cognitive abilities such as finding out about the other's intentions, perspective taking, making alliances, negotiating compromises or deciding on struggle, required enormous efforts. As a crucial means language evolved, the most complex instrument of communication. In all this genes, mind and cultural evolution worked together. The flexibility of human learning became the major evolutionary advantage of the hominides over other primates. Evolutionary psychology, a rather young branch in the field, a sort of 'missing link' in evolutionary research, profited much from the seminal work of Leda Cosmides and John E. Tooby (Barkow *et al.* 1992) who found many empirical hints in support of the close interrelationship of social and cognitive evolution. Primates also apply their cognitive apparatus in order to use their conspecifics as social instruments to achieve a purpose such as forming alliances in contests or competition, cooperation and manoeuvres of deception.

The basic social requirement was securing survival and providing for reproduction with the consequence of distinguishing between in-group and out-group. Hence one may assume that the distinction between 'us' and 'others' channelled the well-known mode of binary thinking (the word 'binary' refers to a system of numbers 'using only the two digits 0 and 1; it is used especially in computing). The human mind co-evolved with human sociality. If so, cognitive coding participates in the propensity for demarcation, separation and war, and it is probably not only our affective outfit that so often makes compromise and reconciliation difficult even today. As a 'deep structure', the inclination to 'either/or' thinking is also an eloquent example of the 'ease of learning hypothesis' for it is, indeed, so much easier to categorize according to a simplifying binary logic than to look for more complex explanations that reflect the capacity of 'post-formal' operations.

While Jean Piaget investigated cognitive development up to the age of 14/15, arriving at the level of 'formal operations', it was his fellows who went 'beyond' this by exploring late adolescent and adult cognitive development (Commons *et al.* 1984). Starting in adolescence the development of abstractions can lead to thinking in a triadic structure, the main forms being dialectical thinking (in philosophy G. W. Hegel, K. Marx), paradoxical thinking (S. Kierkegaard) and complementary thought patterns (cf. Reich 2002). In politics (and, of course, in daily life) attempts to solve conflicts will hit upon severe difficulties if those in power are locked into inflexible and unreformable 'either/or' patterns. The same is true of conflicts in church life where, in the light of J. W. Fowler's theory of faith development (1981), different formal 'structures' of 'stages' (not only controversies about religious content) may form the hidden deep-structural core of heated disagreement.

There is no doubt about Fowler's frank opinion on 'synthetic-conventional faith' (stage 3). On the one hand, these 'kind of persons we have been describing often constitute the most consistent corps of committed workers and servers in the church' (1987: 88). On the other hand, Christians described as being in this stage are regarded as narrow-minded in the scope of their social awareness and sense of political responsibility compared with what they should be as members of an open, critical public and as members of a so-called 'public church' (Fowler 1991: 147–97). A 'public church' means communities of faith who offer their witness 'in publicly visible and publicly intelligible ways', in a 'principled openness and commitment to the common good'. This is made manifest 'in the presence and activities of its members – as persons and as a corpora', through 'witness, service, advocacy, lobbying, and, if needed, protest' (p. 160). By contrast, members who have developed a 'synthetic-conventional faith' sometimes show an 'anti-intellectual' and 'defensively convential' frame of mind (Fowler 1987: 88). A famous field of diverging structures of mind is the struggle about the true understanding of the Bible in the tension between modern exegesis and literal interpretation. Against these conflicts Fowler suggests 'a stage level of aspiration' (1987: 97) which has to guide and inform church leadership, pastoral care and adult education. Such a level of aspiration, which for Fowler is 'conjunctive faith' (stage 5) can serve as a normative invitation. People at this stage have 'the capacity to understand and relate to Christians of each of the other stages' (1987: 94). They establish a mental and emotional climate of mutual tolerance, ecumenical Christian learning and interfaith reconciliation, 'living the paradoxical character of public Christian faith in a pluralistic world' (Fowler 1991: 195). They 'can relate nondefensively to persons and groups of other or no religious background in the larger public because of an openness born of identity and conviction' (Fowler 1991: 156; see also Nipkow 2003). Thus, they more or less illustrate cognitive patterns beyond binary structure.

Religious fanaticism exemplifies how a binary logic can be radicalized when leading to cognitive ideological oversimplifications between 'God' and 'satanic' powers, 'good' and 'evil', 'elected' and 'damned'. When aligning with terrorism the results are disastrous. With regard to the most radical devaluation of other people (genocide) Erik H. Erikson (1966) has spoken of 'pseudospeciation'. He described how humans are capable of defining members of hostile or foreign groups as members of other species; 'they could be subject to predation rather than aggression' (cf. Tiger 1998: 105). In German history an example is the definition of Russian Communists under Stalin as 'sub-humans' (*Untermenschen*). Another example is speaking of a hostile political leader as an 'non-person'.

Mere complaints will not get us anywhere; nor will military actions alone. If people's reactions were simply to adhere to the same cognitive pattern of 'either/or', incapable of triadic patterns looking for a 'third way' (political compromise or, between different faiths, 'reconciled diversity'), then the binary ideology of the enemy would have won. Moreover, from their leaders the masses would functionally learn the moral legitimacy and dubious effectivity of an archaic logic that in the case of blind retaliation falsely appears as an unavoidable law on earth. A type of reaction that developed as a necessary adaptation to archaic situations of survival has become a ridiculous maladaptation for complex conflict analysis and resolution today.

How to Overcome Deep Structural Barriers – Sharing Life and Common Learning

For cogent reasons we need to explore concerted ways in politics and education that reach the minds to be changed, now understood as a change of cognitive 'structures'. Cognitive-structural theories of moral development (Lawrence Kohlberg, Fritz Oser) argue that because of the 'deep structural' character of 'religious reasoning' changes cannot be expected from being exposed to better information only. Fritz Oser's studies on religious judging (or 'reasoning') (in drawing on Kohlberg's studies on 'justice reasoning') were theoretically based on the distinction between religious 'knowledge' accumulated by religious information and religious 'deep structures' resulting from developmental learning (Oser and Gmünder 1984: 42). While on the level of informational 'content learning' pupils are able quite easily to gain new knowledge, this does not result in a change in religious judging. Their responses echo wonderful kind and pious views on a forgiving God, but when confronted, for instance, with a story from daily life about a rich man who had forgotten God when he was doing well and asked God for help when falling ill, the children were eager to see God mercilessly revenging himself and exercising rigid punishment (p. 43). Even adult believers of admirable spirituality can welcome plain reciprocal retaliation – the triumph of binary logic over spiritual self-understanding and another example of ideology as self-betraying consciousness.

In the state of Israel, projects where Israeli and Palestinian children successfully live together in a village and attend the same school seem to generate structural attitudinal change. Located near the road from Tel Aviv to Jerusalem, in Neve Shalom/ Wahat al Salam, a bi-lingual kindergarten and a bi-lingual primary school are attended by both Jewish and Palestinian pupils. The school also attracts parents from other places who are not afraid of bueaucratic obstacles and sanctions to sending their children to the school against the will of the Israeli authorities.

A special 'School for Peace' (SfP) has been added to promote the spirit of peace among older students. They are offered three-day courses, one utilizing role-play with the participants being given the task, as representatives of their respective governments, of negotiating about settlements, refugees, Jerusalem and non-violence. Meetings of Palestinian and Jewish women have started too, or are in process.

The founder of the village and school, Bruno Hussar, a Jew who after his studies became a Christian and later a priest, but also remained a Jew (Sieben 1998: 395), chose the name Neve Shalom from Isa. 32: 17–18:

> The effect of righteousness will be peace,
> and the result of righteousness,
> quietness and trust forever.
> My people will abide in a peaceful
> habitation [green] [= neve shalom],
> in secure dwellings, and in quiet
> resting places.

Hussar emphasized the interrelatedness of peace and justice. Without the latter peace will easily be perverted to mere lip-service. It is easy to pretend to favour peace, it is inconvenient and sometimes painful to do something for peace by just sharing. Sharing is the key to justice, and justice the precondition for peaceful living together.

Today the legacy of history is apparent. Small groups of Zionist Jews from Russia, Poland and Romania immigrated to Palestine to settle in the earlier home of their ancestors. They needed land and bought it from landowners who mostly lived outside the country and had leased the land to tenants. These Palestinians had cultivated the land for many generations. This was the point when the conflict began. The Jewish historian Ruben Moskowitz (Jerusalem) asks what might have happened if both sides had developed more mutual understanding of the suffering of each other, the Palestinians for the frustration and despair of the Jewish immigrants, these for the misery of those who were now going to lose their land and become refugees. Some of the Zionists had been ready for compromise, others not. The Arab leadership and some of the Zionists remain implacable (Moskowitz 2001).

The newsletters of the Peace Education Standing Commission of the World Conference on Religion and Peace (WCRP), an international non-governmental organization, regularly report about initiatives on the same line of sharing life and learning by 'living together in the Holy Land' (Schoneveld 2001), thereby commenting also on the role of religion.

> Although the Israeli–Palestinian (or Arab–Jewish) conflict is not a religious, but a political, ethnic and territorial conflict, religion nevertheless plays a crucial role in it. Both parties use religious arguments to justify and strengthen their claims. In addition, religious elements play often implicitly and unconsciously a major role in the identities of the conflicting parties.
>
> (Schoneveld 2001: 24)

The idea underlying a project initiated by the Dutch theologian Jacobus Schoneveld is to test educational curriculum material developed by an Israeli and a Palestinian organization in the classrooms of Israeli and Palestinian high schools in order to promote mutual understanding of the other's religion. From 1967 to 1980 Schoneveld was advisor in Jerusalem for the Netherlands Reformed Church, from 1980 to 1996 general secretary of the International Council of Christians and Jews at Martin Buber House, Heppenheim, Germany; in 1997 he returned to Jerusalem to help develop the project as research fellow of the Harry S. Truman Research Institute for the Advancement of Peace of the Hebrew University and as scholar-in-residence of the Tantur Ecumenical Institute for Theological Studies in Jerusalem. The project has now entered its third year and is continuing under the very difficult circumstances of the year 2002.

In terms of learning theory the approach hopes for effects resulting from cognitive informational learning. As far as one can see, it favours what in other experiments has been called 'cross-cutting' (Krupka 2002: 165–6) This strategy 'looks for common features and differences that run across existing intercultural lines of conflict. Thus, barriers of communication are ruled out and broken off' (p. 271). An example often used is to draw on Abraham and derive Judaism, Christianity and Islam as 'Abrahamite religions' from the same origin as 'a symbol of hope' (Kuschel 1995).

Even if the effect of this approach may be limited, the symbolic learning effect of the very fact of Israelis and Palestinians cooperating may weigh more. Living together in mixed groups will probably prove the most promising method of education for peace, as Neve Shalom/Wahat al Salam shows. When thinking about promoting structural moral change, L. Kohlberg complemented classroom discussions on dilemmas by reforming the school as a whole, calling it '*Just* Community School'. 'Just reasoning' at a post-conventional level at stages 5 and 6 is, however, neither a quasi 'natural' developmental goal nor does the term fully cover the meaning of justice as social justice, whose achievement in the world is hindered by strong powers of self-interest. Structural-cognitive theories are more or less limited to *forms* of reasoning, they fail sufficiently to take account of the *substantive* global issues.

Additional reasons why a more comprehensive approach that embeds teaching *about* peace and justice in contexts of concrete sharing *of* peaceful life deserves attention are given by data presented in the following important section.

The Face of the 'Other' – Evocation of Humanity through Face-to-face Encounters

Ways to overcome, or at least mitigate, the human inclination to violence and war have been described above from several points of view. But whether we considered the task of clarifying moral criteria, of learning from history, of obeying rules, respecting law and supporting human rights, of caring for nature, of critically assessing ideologies, including masculine supremacy, or of overcoming dangerous cognitive either/or patterns, most of them have one handicap in common. With the exception of the importance of sharing life (see the preceding section), the question left unaddressed was how to reach an individual's heart in order to motivate action in such a way that xenophobia and out-group enmity are effectively transformed into conviviality towards others, especially strangers. Sharing life and common learning is the first answer at a deeper level. It is directed to a holistic experience which involves the whole person and, at the same time, evokes awareness of social interrelation. In the following we shall pursue this promising approach in more detail, although it is not without risks because of the physical nearness involved. We shall try to specify it, illustrate it by examples and particularly explore its anthropological foundation, mainly by drawing on the social philosophy of Emmanuel Lévinas, which will remind us of important findings in the chapters above on biblical anthropology.

Points of Departure in Infancy – Mother–Child Bonding

To begin with a perspective of biological anthropology, after a child is born, it experiences warm caring and social nearness. These memories are kept in mind throughout life, even if only unconsciously; they seem to remain the source of longing for much of all later community. Individual mother–child bonding creates a relationship of *trust*; it also holds true, however, that a stranger is met with *distrust*.

> The first manifestation of distrust of strangers appears early in life and is well-known as the phenomenon of 'stranger awareness' or 'fear of strangers'. Every healthy baby demonstrates during its first months of life a basic trust: any approaching human being will be greeted with a smile. From approximately the age of six months onwards, the baby then distinguishes between persons it knows and strangers, the latter releasing now ambivalent responses. The baby may smile at a stranger, but usually after a few seconds it will turn toward its mother and hide its face. It will fluctuate between approach and withdrawal responses or show superpositions of these two behaviours.
>
> (Eibl-Eibesfeldt 1998: 27–8)

The phenomenon is universal and does not depend on prior bad experience with strangers. It persists throughout life as an awareness of strangers, though not necessarily as xenophobia (to be defined as a morbid dislike of foreigners) or hostility to foreigners. Both trust and distrust can be used for positive and negative purposes. 'By "familiarization" with others, behavior shifts along a continuum from mistrust to trust' (Eibl-Eibesfeldt 1998: 31). In this sense, as already mentioned, physical nearness is ambivalent, simultaneously risk and promise.

Human contact is connected with looking at each other, primarily perceiving the other's face. A baby first realizes dimly the mother's face. In the Bible, references to God's face or countenance are numerous, in particular playing a role in blessings by indicating a most intimate relationship as a source of consolation and peace. We are approaching the core of peace of the soul – the holy centre of the issue of peace as community with God: 'The LORD bless you and keep you; the LORD make his face to shine upon you, and be gracious to you; the LORD lift up his countenance upon you, and give you peace' (Num. 6, 24–6). At the end of all days when there will be 'a new heaven and a new earth' (Rev. 21: 1), God's servants 'will see his face' (Rev. 22: 4).

The face is the most vulnerable part of the human body. Normally humans shrink from directly hitting someone's face. In Germany hitting a pupil is forbidden in schools. In 'primitive' societies eye-to-eye contact is sometimes regarded as the beginning of personal exchange and will stop further aggression. On the Molucca Islands headhunting could only be exercised from behind the back. If the face of the adversary had been seen, the act of killing would have been murder. In this case the two parties would have 'exchanged' something, be it only the mutual look at their faces (cf. Barash 1979: 156–7; 1981: 179, in the German edition). If hostages have been captured, the negotiations and decisions taken in order to free them are mostly prolonged so that the kidnappers might learn about their hostages as individual people by face-to-face contact. Physiognomy, that is the cast of facial features, embodies a person's individuality in a striking uniqueness and vulnerability.

Perspectives from Social Philosophy and Anthropology – Emmanuel Lévinas

Not only biological factors in earliest childhood point to the basic role of social interrelation in human life, including its religious impact, it is also a specific approach in modern social philosophy and anthropology that throws light upon our issue. In his writings about human sociality, the Jewish philosopher Emmanuel Lévinas focuses on the human 'face' as the centre of 'encounter' and 'dialogue', thereby drawing on Martin Buber, the Jewish philosopher of dialogue, who introduced into the debate the word 'Begegnung' (encounter). It is noteworthy that in the twentieth century it was Jewish philosophers rooted in the Hebrew Bible, the Old Testament, who created 'dialogical' thought patterns. One of the most important contributions from the biblical heritage worldwide in the field of social philosophy lies, indeed, in this emphasis on 'dialogical' relationships. In a comparable way, as 'post-formal' cognitive patterns of thinking (thinking in complementarity and triadic dialectic patterns) (see pp. 163–4) leave behind 'binary' coding at the epistemological level, so too does a true 'dialogue' at the social level. Some ideas taken from Lévinas may illustrate this. Surprisingly enough they also deal explicitly with the issue of peace. Lévinas' views allow us to connect important factors of our sociological and evolutionary analysis in Chapters 9 and 10 with several points displayed in the preceding theological chapters.

We have to go beyond a flat understanding of 'face' and 'dialogue'. The two terms revolve around human responsibility, a term which is deliberately featured in the title of this chapter. In Lévinas' view the very first point of departure in philosophical anthropology is not the 'I' but the 'Thou' in the 'relation' of 'I and Thou' (Buber 1937) or, as Lévinas would say, it is the 'Other' ('l'Autre') and his 'challenging' me to act responsibly in the 'face' of his needs. Instead of starting with the 'self' and reflecting its development towards mental, moral and spiritual maturity, understood as more or less one's own perfection only, Lévinas' concept of true humanity rests upon the location of the individual 'outside (exterior) of oneself' as his essay on 'l'extériorité' (1987) displays.

In another book, entitled in German *Außer sich* (*Outside Oneself*) (1991), with more explicit reference to biblical language and tradition, Lévinas speaks of the 'neighbour' or 'brother' who waits for me, their 'face' 'demanding' my 'response'; 'responsibility' as a word denoting the readiness and ability to respond to what 'I' owe to 'Others' (p. 62).

In Lévinas' view I cannot simply select the 'Other' as I may want to, according to my favourite expectations and preferences. The 'Others' happen to meet me or I happen to come across them, very often against my will, hence, I am asked whether I can 'stand' the other's strangeness. Nothing other than this 'visitation' (*Heimsuchung*) (1992: 50) in the biblical sense of the word characterizes true 'plurality' as 'difference' that challenges me. Plurality is regarded not just as a many-coloured variation that kindly invites people to personal enrichment, but as an inconvenience. From this perspective describing the 'multifaith approach' in religious education as mutual enrichment would be insufficient. For illustration Lévinas mentions Cain and Abel and confesses that although Abel is my brother, he remains for me a different person, a stranger, so that I feel within myself the refusal 'to be my brother's keeper' (Gen. 4: 9) (cf. Chapter 3 above). Nevertheless, the other person as brother does remain the ultimate meaning of life, the meaning of the meaning, whom my life should be devoted to because of God having created me: my life is a gift which requires my life as a gift for others (cf. Chapter 7 above). Lévinas warns against being misunderstood. He does not deny the role of 'self' (1987: 443), for it is my 'self' (after having become 'my' identity) that alone will be able to 'respond to the urgent order [demand] of a face' (1987: 444, quotes translated from the German edition).

Two features of Lévinas' approach are remarkable in the context of this chapter and of this whole book. First, Lévinas approaches the same ambivalence of trust and distrust, affiliation and rejection, love and hate, community and war, as has been described above as an evolutionary legacy. Furthermore, his indepth philosophical explorations reveal also the same deep resistance of humans to what he calls the 'Otherness' of the 'Other'. That means that the light shed in his studies on the difficulties in the realm of social human relations and the light that evolutionary psychology casts on human nature and the intricacy of ways to peace converge. Lévinas' concept is highly appropriate for clarifying basic anthropological presuppositions of intercultural education as a major part of education for peace. Moreover, the whole of moral education and true moral maturity is highlighted if maturity is understood, together with Lévinas and other Jewish authors as well as Christian theologians, as a life with responsibility in a plural world.

Second, Lévinas supports a biblical understanding of 'sacrificial altruism' that surpasses, and corrects, the (mis)understanding of the term in evolutionary ethics. Sociobiologists are sometimes inclined to ridicule the selfless love of Christians, as does Edward O. Wilson in his remarks on Mother Theresa (1993: 147). He tries to explain her behaviour by referring to her religious self-interest in connection with her obedience to the Roman Catholic church, underlying a motivation drawn from her service to Christ and the knowledge of 'the immortality of her church' (ibid.). Wilson seems to be unable to understand the logic of love as something beyond egoistic calculation (see Chapter 7).

Lévinas speaks of 'goodness' and 'justice', with the latter reminding us of God's nature (see God's 'righteousness' and 'justice' in Chapter 4). 'The relationship to the face takes place as goodness' (1987: 438), the word 'face' standing for the other individual as a person and as God's creature. 'Goodness' is not seen as a value as in Platonic philosophy, a value belonging to the realm of eternal ideas. It is nothing fixed; it 'occurs' in a 'process', in an 'encounter' or in 'dialogue'. This view contradicts the mainstream of European moral theory as far as it is rooted in Greek philosophy. The chapters above on biblical patterns of thinking were meant to lay a similar foundation. Or in other words, with Lévinas, it is not an eternal 'being' (être), but something 'beyond being or different from being' that 'happens' ('autrement qu'être ou au-delà de l'essence'; Lévinas 1992/1974). Biblical Hebrew thinking meets with Christian thinking when Eberhard Jüngel, a systematical theologian at Tübingen university, entitles a book of his *God's Being is in Becoming* (2001). According to Lévinas the 'First Philosophy' is not 'ontology' but 'ethics' (that which happens in 'asking/demanding' and 'responding/responsibly acting' between 'faces'); otherwise philosophy would be the 'oppression of pluralism' (1987: 320), for human diversity rests on pluralizing interactions.

Human beings should be open to the coming of the 'Other', be it the familiar 'neighbour' or the unfamiliar 'foreigner' or *the* 'Other', God. 'War does not follow per se from the empirical fact of the diversity of beings who restrict each other' (1987: 321). It occurs only if one refuses to understand one's own self essentially from the perspective of the other. If 'ego' is merely defined by 'ego', war will be implicitly or manifestedly an everlasting pending presence.

What is peace in Lévinas' eyes? It cannot be achieved by imposing a totalitarian 'whole' on humankind, for instance a world-state that cuts off diversity and favours a closed system without windows to transcendence. We need a pluralism that acknowledges plurality and individuality; this is expressed in my 'going' to those people different from me. 'Peace is the unity of diversity (plurality) and not the mere addition of elements that plurality consists of. Hence peace is not identical with the end of battles . . . Peace must be my peace, peace in a relationship which starts from an I going to the Other' (1987: 445); the ethics of peace is achieved and accomplished 'in service and hospitality' (p. 435).

Concrete Suffering and Compassion

Seen from some distance, Buber's and Lévinas' approach is an interpretation of universal anthropological facts in terms of 'personalist philosophy', which to a certain extent neglects the possible systematic oppression and elimination of the personal. To give just one example: human compassion is weakened if direct personal contacts are systematically replaced by anonymous ones. This transformation takes place in many institutions and spheres of life such as administration, the economy, technology, finance and the army. The most cynical example is modern technical warfare, with its systematic prevention of combatants observing actual dying. In wartime, the media also avoid presenting pictures of dying. The ugliness of suffering is replaced by the cleanness of high-tech destruction. The death of non-combatants on the other side is labelled 'collateral' damage.

Reports from the Vietnam war by the Italian reporter Oriana Fallaci, who accompanied a bomber crew, speak for themselves.

> The third time I had put up with the thing and was only eager not to miss the moment when Andy would uncouple the bomb . . . The fourth, the fifth, the sixth time I had become accustomed to it. Now I could observe the spectacle from a certain distance, and this spectacle consisted of little figures who fled from their bunkers and sandbag barricades, waving their arms in order to free themselves from the flames, and one suffocated in the flames. I would lie if I were saying that I had felt guilt or mercy.
>
> (quoted in Wickler 1991: 154)

When observing the abominable terror of 11 September 2001 on television with my wife, I felt an odd *abstract* shock. I became conscious of it when I compared the collapse of the towers with the white piece of cloth someone had been waving from a window in one of the upper floors; only then did I realize the terrible fear of a *concrete* individual. I told this to a friend. He had felt the same. His little son, Simon, was also terrified by the person waving for help, but after a while Simon imitated the collapse of the towers with his bricks.

Research data from the field of social psychology on the affective precondition of helping another child who was sad because her toys had been damaged clearly support the assumption that face-to-face contacts foster compassion and an ensuing readiness to help. If a child could directly participate in the sadness of another child, watching her tears, these direct 'emotional signals' were influential in evoking 'empathetic reactions' (Halisch 1988: 96).

In a recent empirical project on learning compassion, which was stimulated by the Catholic theologian Johann Baptist Metz and his theological interpretation of Jesus' actions as primarily intending to respond to human 'suffering', not sin (sin in Jesus' eyes being rather 'the refusal to participate in the suffering of others'; Metz 2000: 11), pupils took part in practical courses working in hospitals, institutions for the disabled and a home for the elderly (Kuld and Gönnheimer 2000). The practical work was accompanied by periods of instruction, for emotional encounters without reflection will not deepen knowledge about the factors contributing to human suffering. Tests before and after the experiment showed a remarkable increase in compassionate feelings and in the pupils' capacity to evaluate the issue. Interestingly, in the beginning, compared with the girls, the boys were less ready to take part in the project; afterwards, the boys had approached the same level of positive attitude and had enlarged their competence in emotionally relating to others (Kuld and Gönnheimer 2000: 91). This greater need in learning corresponds with the data presented in the section above on gender differences.

To sum up, as far as peace presupposes feelings of compassion and readiness to help, as opposed to insensitivity to suffering and a lack of that readiness, evoking compassion, promoting empathy and training for mutual perspective taking (Robert Selman) as looking at each other from another's perspective are most important steps in interpersonal relations. The productive point is for children and young people to come in close contact with people in need, 'looking' at each other.

Literature Evoking Compassion

School subjects with a significant proportion of narratives in their curriculum, such as religious education, languages, literature and history, are called upon to develop human sensitivity and altruistic motivations. In one of his most mature plays, *The Caucasian Chalk Circle* (1946; see Brecht 1963), Bertolt Brecht (1898–1956), the German poet and playwright who wrote against war and the exploitation of the poor, describes the situation of a maid, named Gruscha. All of a sudden she is left with a baby whom the mother, the executed Governor's wife, has left behind while trying to save her own life, not caring any longer for the life of the little one (nor did all the others). Gruscha wants to get rid of the baby too; it is the son of the Governor, the heir, 'the noble child', and therefore a very dangerous burden. Thus she lays him down, and discards him. But against her will she returns and bends over the child,

> Just for one more look, just to sit with it
> For a moment or two till someone should come

Its mother, perhaps, or someone else –
For a long time she sat with the child,
Evening came, night came, dawn came.
Too long she sat, too long she watched
The soft breathing, the little fists,
Till towards morning the temptation grew too strong.
She rose, she leaned over, she sighed, she lifted the child,
She carried it off.

(Brecht 1963, 3, the end)

The 'singer' comments, 'Terrible is the temptation to be good' (ibid.). The compelling language of the child's face ('too long she watched') overwhelms Gruscha's resistance in tempting her to care for the little one, leading to danger, even involving risk to her own life. Improbable selfless love becomes probable – by virtue of the voice of the face which speaks to the ears of the heart. It can happen, but in contrast consider the well-known 'bystander' phenomenon (Latané and Darley 1970) where as rising numbers of onlookers gather at an accident the readiness to help decreases.

Brecht's message is focused in the following statement of the musicians: 'In the bloodiest times there are still good people.' At some points of the play Brecht's belief in humanity as simple kindness is associated with hints at the Christian virtue of respect for life. On one occasion Gruscha addresses Michael, the Governor's son, with the words:

Michael, you cause a lot of trouble.
I came by you as the pear-tree comes by the sparrows.
And because a Christian bends down and picks up a crust of bread
so it won't go to waste.

(Scene 4)

At another time, indirectly, the Psalms are remembered,

I had to tear myself to pieces
For what was not mine,
But alien.
Someone must be the helper.
Because the little tree needs its water.
The little lamb loses its way,
When the herdsman is asleep.
And the bleating remains unheard.

(Scene 4, the end)

In Psalm 121: 3–4, we read,

He who keeps you will not slumber.
He who keeps Israel
Will neither slumber nor sleep.

As a former teacher of religious education as well as of German and English literature, I myself had the opportunity of happily learning how these different fields jointly interpret each other. They are ways to evoke, at least to some modest degree, compassion, thoughts of peace, joy in caring and emotions of kindness. The theologians should discover the deep human content in world literature, and teachers of literature and the arts should become sensitive to the spiritual content in their curriculum, not least the impact of biblical experiences (Kuschel 1998).

In a study (N = 991), L. Montada, A. Schneider and B. Reichle (1988) have explored the correlations between readiness to help and emotions with regard to predicaments of (a) unemployed German workers, (b) poor people living abroad, and (c) Turkish immigrants living in Germany as foreign workers. The data proved the hypothesis that 'emotions are important predictors of pro-social behaviour' (p. 147). In particular compassion showed up as a powerful component. Incidentally negative effects did not arise against the indigeneous unemployed, but did significantly against Turkish immigrants (p. 149).

Everywhere ethnic and cultural differences prove to be a major field of discrimination, in full accord with the basic assumptions of this chapter. Consequences for education point to the need to provide for face-to face contacts between different groups and, even more important, for shared experiences around common tasks and projects. Thus, the result of the preceding section can be fully supported from several new angles, the key role being played by interpersonal sharing, as was also clearly apparent with regard to the initiatives described above, designed to challenge the Jewish–Arab conflict through non-violent means.

Mediating in Conflicts and Confrontation with One's Own Guilt

From the field of politics we know about the role of face-to-face contact in solving conflicts. The examples are numerous, the phrase 'the spirit of Camp David' having become a classic saying. We remember also the function of mediators from neutral countries in negotiating between hostile camps. The character of these sometimes desperate efforts manifests the extraordinary confidence and hope that is placed in this strategy of personal face-to face encounter. In several countries programmes for training pupils to act as mediators in quarrels at their own school have been practised for some years, although only sporadically.

Another form of using direct eye-to-eye contact is in the re-socialization of young delinquents when, in a specific phase of the programme, the 'hot chair phase', the offender is forced to stand up while other young people sit and stare at him, confronting him with his crime. The salient point is for the offender to realize the suffering of the victim by being shown photos of the victim. The double confrontation, both with the victim and with the others sitting around him, draws again on the compelling force of concrete human 'nearness'.

From a psychoanalytical point of view the offender has to become aware of his motives and learn that his damaged self-confidence, that in many cases was at the root of the violent act as a proof of strength, needs no externalized aggression, that is, turning the pressure of self-aggression against the outside. Lost self-confidence, emotional weakness and self-aggression (or whatever else may play a role too), by no means excuse the violent act itself. Hence, the offender has (1) to see and share the sufferings of the victim, (2) to realize his or her own guilt, (3) to overcome the resistance to apologize, and (4) instead to become open to forgiveness.

From a theological point of view, Chapter 8 on the life story of the apostle Paul illustrated the necessity of inner conversion which is being experienced as new freedom. It enables the offender to ask for forgiveness and – at the same time – helps the victim (or relatives of the victim) to forgive the offender and no longer cherish thoughts of revenge and retaliation. It is a mutual process which is usually painful for both sides. The churches' specific role in the field of aggression, violence and war is to explain guilt and forgiveness as necessary preconditions for reconciliation. These categories are largely forgotten in public life. The general reason why seems to be to avoid an impression of weakness. Politicians and businessmen want to be 'tough' as do all young boys. How many of us are convinced, young and old, that only tough economic policies will succeed? Another revealing catchphrase among children and youngsters today is 'cool', which, however, is often used to hide 'warm' feelings which males are ashamed of (cf. pp. 161–2 on masculine ideologies). Gruscha, the maid, wasn't.

'Reciprocal Altruism', the 'Golden Rule', and Mutual Self-interest – Education for Peace by Cooperation

What, however, if the values of love and compassion are destroyed by an education for hate and retaliation? What if face-to-face encounters between politicians as the only non-violent means remaining to keep peace talks alive are in vain? What if one forgets that the winner–loser logic aimed at total submission of one side will not succeed in establishing firm and enduring peace?

Under certain circumstances, there is a realistic pragmatic chance to achieve at least a readiness for cooperation based on mutual self-interest. Evolutionary ethics deals with it under the heading of 'reciprocal altruism" (Trivers 1971). The necessary circumstances are (1) a common dependence on natural resources that have to be shared because of sheer geographical location (for instance water supplies), and (2) long-term territorial proximity or, to put it in other words, if the conflict cannot be resolved by 'ethnic cleansing'. The problem can arise in one and the same town if a complete separation of competing groups is not possible and a road that leads to the school of one portion of the population crosses the territory of the other group (Northern Ireland). The problem can spread in whole areas such as the Balkans where the idea of neatly separating Serbs, Croatians, Bosnians, Albanians and Macedonians meets with many difficulties. At the time of writing the situation is fragile in the Middle East. At any rate, ethnic cleansing, in revealing an interest in complete separation, would manifest the complete political and moral failure to achieve a peaceful multi-ethnic society and sadly illustrate the dreadful legacy of the negative pole of social evolution, uncompromising in-group amity versus out-group enmity. What kind of cooperation would perhaps be able to stop this separation? We start with a well-known fact.

'Conspicuous examples of co-operation (although almost never of ultimate self-sacrifice) also occur where relatedness is low or absent' (Axelrod 1984: 90). Altruistic and cooperative behaviour is possible without family bonds, kinship and personal or physical nearness. We are not dependent on merely mobilizing the affectionate ties of family affiliation and kinship altruism in a doubtful attempt to extend them to universal brotherhood and sisterhood (see pp. 153–4) or to draw only and mainly on human face-to-face potential although it remains one major source of hope (see the preceding section). All these approaches may provide some promise of supporting reconciliation and peace in micro communication, in situations of private interaction or in a school class and, in some cases, also between parties in bigger conflicts. Yet for the macro level of worldwide struggle they are still weak. In the ongoing debate on concepts of global ethics with which we shall conclude the discussion in the next and final chapter, the chief means to prevent or at least to mitigate and control conflicts involve international rules based on international treaties following the reasonable argumentation that people need one another for their mutual benefit and profit. As to law, its history is mainly centred in the logic of 'reciprocity'. This principle deserves careful attention.

We had good reason to start the educational proposals of this chapter with, alongside the role of value clarification, education for law-abiding behaviour as the common framework for social cohesion, instead of trusting too much in 'family semantics'. Constitutional rights in democratic countries ought to honour and protect everybody without precluding groups of minor 'fictive kinship' such as foreigners who are only tolerated but not really accepted as members of the national 'community' and 'family'. 'Constitutional patriotism' is a term indicating a more sober, but also a more realistic core of commonly shared obligations. Humans are not used to loving each other beyond the confines of a small circle. Education for peace as education for creating bonds of love is presumptuous. A quite different task is to acknowledge the same rights for everyone. What matters in society and worldwide is not just sympathy with those we happen to become acquainted with, but respect for the many we will never come to know personally.

The category of 'acknowledgement' (or 'recognition') has obtained great attention in the recent philosophical debates on political and cultural concepts (Jürgen Habermas, Axel Honneth) and on intercultural and inter-religious education. In this context I have developed a 'hermeneutics of mutual acknowledgement in truthfulness' (Nipkow 1998, vol. 2).

The issue is reflected also in the debate between 'communitarians' and 'liberals', between those emphasizing 'values', in particular those strengthening their own community, and the advocates of universal individual 'rights' (cf. the debate between, and about, J. Rawls, R. Rorty, M. Walzer, Ch. Taylor). There are arguments for both positions; in this sense I started with liberal rights as human rights for all, but tried to substantially fill in this framework by drawing particularly on experiences that promote a community that includes the stranger as the inconvenient 'Other' in his 'Otherness' (E. Lévinas).

How can acknowledgement be realized without force? Unlike Kant, who stressed the inner moral struggle to obey the moral law, I do not despise utilitarian and pragmatic considerations which lead us to trade and economic exchange, which in history followed the principle of reciprocity. The most famous expression of it is the Golden Rule as a guideline in all cultures and religions. It invests its hope in everyone's own reasonable self-interest.

Confucius (*c.* 551–489 BCE): 'What you yourself do not want, do not do to another person!' (Sayings 15. 23)

Rabbi Hillel (60 BCE to 10 CE): 'Do not do to others, what you do not want them to do to you!' (Shabbat 31a)

Jesus of Nazareth: 'Whatever you want people to do to you, do also to them' (Matt. 7: 12; Luke 6: 31)

Islam: 'None of you is a believer as long as he does not wish his brother what he wishes himself!' (Forty Hadith of an-Nawawi, 13)

Jainism: 'Human beings should be indifferent to worldly things and treat all creatures in the world as they would want to be treated themselves'. (Sutrakritanga I, 11. 33)

Buddhism: 'A state which is not pleasant or enjoyable for me will also not be so for him; and how can I impose on another a state which is not pleasant or enjoyable for me?' (Samyutta Nikaya V, 353.35–354.2)

Hinduism: 'One should not behave towards others in a way which is unpleasant for oneself, that is the essence of morality.' (Mahabharata XIII 114, 8)

(all quotes from Küng and Kuschel 1993: 71–2)

Reciprocal altruism has nothing to do with self-sacrifice as the extreme characteristic feature of a 'strong' altruism with the emotional mother–child and kinship relation as its paradigm. Its basis is mainly a rational one of calculating advantages and disadvantages, profits and costs. But: 'Under what conditions will cooperation emerge in a world of egoists without central authority?' What if everyone wants to maximize his or her own profit? With this question Robert Axelrod starts his seminal study on *The Evolution of Cooperation* (1984: 3). How can cooperation ever develop in situations where each individual has an incentive to be selfish? The answer is simple: because of the problem that springs up 'when the pursuit of self-interest by each leads to a poor outcome for all' (p. 7).

Axelrod's study uses as a model the so-called Prisoner's Dilemma game, where the chief components of the situation just indicated are present. There are two players, each of them having 'two choices, namely cooperate or defect. Each must make the choice without knowing what the other will do. No matter what the other does, defection yields a higher payoff than cooperation. The dilemma is that if both defect, both do worse than if both had cooperated' (pp. 7–8). In this case the 'punishment' for mutual defection is high for both. If only one party defects the reward is highest for the defector, with no win at all for the victim. In the case of mutual cooperation there is the same reward for both (p. 8).

The fascinating question is which strategy out of many concerning the relation of cooperative and defecting steps will objectively render the greatest success for both sides. A further special assumption underlying the whole is, as already mentioned above, that the competing and mistrusting parties, individuals or nations, will have to deal with one another for a longer time (p. 20). The factor of time is important, for if the conflict-laden contact is short, one side might dare to damage the other without fear of revenge because they will soon be out of reach: 'if you are unlikely to meet the other person again, or if you care little about future payoffs, then you might as well defect now and not worry about the consequences for the future' (p. 15).

The abstract formulation of the problem of cooperation as a Prisoner's Dilemma on the line of Game Theory puts aside many vital features that make interaction unique, as Axelrod well knows (p. 19). Nevertheless, the outcomes deserve attention. A computer tournament, with two rounds, was organized involving computer specialists and enthusiasts as contestants coming from different academic fields and several countries. The two-stage arrangement allowed the contestants to learn from the results of the first round of the tournament. An interesting interaction occurred between people who drew one lesson from the first round and people who drew another.

Evolutionary biology proved to be a useful way to think about the issue at stake in view of future generations (p. 49). Educators are interested in interactional strategies in education and politics which ensure, if possible, long range results. It was the strategy called TIT FOR TAT that proved to be by far the most productive in both tournaments, and the more so the longer the time span considered (p. 53).

- First, TIT FOR TAT is a *clear and kind* rule for it always starts with a cooperative step as its own first action. Axelrod calls it a 'nice strategy'. It invites people to cooperate and to behave in the same reciprocal manner.
- Second, it is *retaliatory* in that it immediately answers a bad, defecting reaction of the other side with the same reciprocal defection. Thus the idea of taking advantage of the kindness of TIT FOR TAT is quickly frustrated. 'TIT FOR TAT benefits from its own nonexploitability' (p. 53).
- Third, this strategy is *forgiving*; if B apologizes and comes back to continue cooperating on equal terms, A will also continue with his/her own cooperativeness.

'What accounts for TIT FOR TAT's robust success is its combination of being nice, retaliatory, forgiving, and clear' (Axelrod, p. 54).

What about its chances of changing an atmosphere of hostile mistrust into one of trust? The answer is of great educational importance as it throws light on the chances of small cooperative groups in a non-cooperative environment.

> A world of 'meanies' can resist invasion by anyone using any other strategy – provided that the newcomers arrive one at a time. The problem, of course, is that a single newcomer in such a mean world has no one who will reciprocate any cooperation. If the newcomers arrive in small clusters, however, they will have a chance to get cooperation started.
>
> (p. 63)

Isolated individuals are powerless, groups are not, even if small. A world of non-cooperative egoists is vulnerable if it must see that in the long run ruthless economic suppression, asymmetrical political demands and military supremacy do not pay.

A last point is the role of cues, which indicate how the other will probably act or react, and whether the reciprocal cooperation will remain stable. Interestingly enough Axelrod touches on 'the recognition of individual faces' as a central instrument for learning about each other (p. 102). It recalls the data and reflections above: 'the ability to recognize the other player is invaluable in extending the range of stable cooperation' (ibid.). Our argumentation in favour of face-to-face contacts is corroborated in spite of the reservations mentioned at the beginning of this section.

As to educational consequences, cooperation deserves to be a paramount topic in schools, practically and theoretically. Although a rational approach, it can and should be assisted by promoting certain attitudes – a classical field of any moral education and religious formation. One is, 'Don't be envious!' (p. 110). In terms of game theory: don't behave as in a chess tournament where only one person can win and the other must lose – a zero-sum interaction. 'But most of life is *not* zero-sum' (ibid.). If the other is better off for the moment, think of the long run. Then 'the other's success is virtually a prerequisite of your doing well for yourself' (p. 112). The next rule for behaviour is 'Don't be the first to defect' (p. 113), but do invite kindness. Is it too far-fetched to say that one can notice a parallel to the Christian faith in God's preceding love for humankind ('gratia praeveniens', prevenient grace) and the core of the 'justification of the sinner' 'by grace only'?

TIT FOR TAT always retaliates symmetrically. In the light of this very reasonable trait any asymmetric retaliation will manifest its irrational character. Moreover, excessive and continuing asymmetric counteractions will be experienced as unjust. They will be felt as humiliation, and most probably will provoke revenge resulting in a never-ending spiral of violence.

We have, of course, also to admit the limits of strategies of cooperation, including the successful TIT FOR TAT. Richard D. Alexander (1987) suggested that Axelrod's result could be extended to very large societies through what he called 'indirect reciprocity': 'If one of us helps you, you may help some third person who in turn helps the other of us. Rather than being restricted to pairwise interactions, perhaps reciprocity can encourage cooperation among large, diffuse networks of reciprocators' (Richerson and Boyd 1998: 75, summing up Alexander's suggestion). However, P. Richerson and R. Boyd doubt whether the results really do generalize to large groups: 'As group size increases, it rapidly gets very hard for reciprocity to increase when rare in a population dominated by unconditional defection' (pp. 75–6). It seems to be still harder or impossible to take up reciprocal negotiations between whole nations if the language of armaments is being spoken.

Reviewing this chapter, the different ways to peace which have been described and discussed in the sections above are parts of a coherent whole. From the strong moral assessment we began with (concerning moral criteria) down to the pragmatic strategy of cooperation discussed as a last resort, from the level of international agencies down to the level of direct face-to-face contacts, whether considering the indoctrinating impact of ideologies or taking into account the stubbornness of peace-preventing prejudices and either/or patterns of thinking, in society and in church, we need the integration of several methodologies and the cooperation of several disciplines. The overall focus of this study has been to combine the wisdom of the Bible, as a unique theological source of how human beings have learnt about themselves in order to act responsibly and hopefully in facing God, with the hypotheses and data of evolutionary research with respect to human nature. The main crossroads of both are anthropology and ethics in a global horizon. The global perspective with which we started in the first chapter will be the concluding one in our last chapter.

V
GLOBAL PEACE
AND RELIGIONS

Chapter 11

Peace and Spirituality – in the Light of Different Faiths

Sign of Hope – a Growing Global Moral Awareness

If even highly plausible 'rational choice theories' such as Axelrod's cooperative strategy, based on rational mutual self-interest, can fail and thus reason be defeated, how can we expect that a religious vision of peace will not be frustrated too? One hopeful sign of a change of mind is the gradual transition from the age of nation states to an age of transnational problem-solving in a 'global civil society' with a slowly growing global moral awareness. The very fact of numerous international institutions at work, and a continual sequence of international conferences appealing to a global public, indicates the emergence of a global society as a network of interdependent continents, regions and countries. The agenda of these agencies is spurred by 'planetary turbulence'; civilization has entered its 'planetary phase' (Tellus Institute 2001: 3). The issues are:

- the scarcity of world resources (global freshwater supplies; timber extraction and oil drilling from public land, use of non-renewable resources)
- worldwide threats to human welfare and the environment (changes to the global climate; world armament and disarmament, nuclear, biological and chemical weapons)
- worldwide exchanges (economic globalization, world trade and finances; global transfer of new technologies; scientific exchange)
- the circumstances of people all over the world (population pressure; extreme poverty; refugees; labour and unemployment; the role of women in development, the worldwide status of children; housing, health)
- patterns of global expenditure (for instance military vs. social expenditure)
- global governance (United Nations policy, global security, international non-governmental organizations)
- global ethics (human rights, new values and lifestyles concerning affluency and consumerism; world religions) (cf. Kennedy *et al.* 2002).

The overall situation stretches between two contradictory possibilities, since the legacy of the industrial era is contradictory.

We inherit the capacity to eradicate the scourge of human deprivation, but the world remains mired in poverty and inequality. We have the scientific knowledge and command the technological wizardry to harmonize economics with ecology, but lack the institutions and political will. We are offered the historical opportunity to build a culture of peace, social renewal and self-realization, but lack the necessary breadth and depth of vision. Our global condition is rife with both opportunity and predicament.

(Tellus Institute 2001: 5)

Where does religion enter the political and scientific agenda? Mostly it doesn't at all; the analysis just quoted mentions it marginally. If religion is taken notice of, it is mainly in the context of the battle against religious fanaticism and of maintaining public tolerance; religion does not count in terms of private spirituality and individual religious development. Interestingly, though, therefore, experts in the study of psychological development occasionally approach the realm of public affairs from their side. What in James W. Fowler's impressive developmental investigations began by studying the spiritual journey of individuals was to lead to reframing his stage theory in terms of how to serve a 'public church' in response to general public issues (1991). Thus, when speaking of 'moral and religious maturity' in light of the worrying challenges of today, the word 'maturity' in the sub-title of this book will obtain a more complex meaning too.

Spiritual Maturity and Ethical Globalization – a New Approach

In the panic-stricken days after 11 September 2001, when the world was confronted with a new form of terrorism, and where large parts of our globe, or even almost whole continents (Africa), are suffering from poverty, starvation, Aids and pollution, the issue of religion can't be restricted to how individuals in affluent western countries are to develop spiritually for their own personal sake; we have also to ask whether a forthcoming world society will master the challenges facing us through a sense of shared global responsibility for the sake of all. How can believers and religious institutions contribute beyond their own self-interest?

In order to take this ethical perspective into due account, the focus of the preceding chapters has not only been, in anthropological terms, the evolving 'self', but primarily the interrelation between 'self' and 'others' (E. Lévinas). Living in a social context is prior to the single individual, since personal fulfilment depends on humanizing social conditions, and individual autonomy needs freedom which politicians have to provide for. Correspondingly, in sociological terms, our analysis tried to encompass not only individual face-to-face encounters, but also the impact of collective restraints and ideologies that exploit evolutionary predispositions to indoctrination. What are the barriers to, and the opportunities for, a shared responsibility amongst nations and religions viewed against the background of the so-called 'global commons', the common good for all?

People are becoming afraid of globalization; anti-globalization protesters at international conferences are only the tip of the iceberg. Developing countries and marginalized regions complain of being left out; it seems to them that only a few rich and highly technologically equipped nations benefit from globalization. Yet even in affluent societies people's anxieties are growing. Who will lose their job next? Can politicians still control what is going on? Are national parliaments becoming weakened by multinational economic power?

New international non-governmental agencies and initiatives to mitigate side-effects are a good thing, many may think, but how can they reach people in their daily needs? What is at stake is the quality of life at the grassroots. Globalization without humanity erodes the moral substance of societies and will undermine the social preconditions of a market-driven globalization itself. That is why economic globalization is to be complemented by an 'ethical globalization' (Robinson 2002). People should experience globalization as a positive power in their lives and as an opportunity for all the world's populations. The existing and widening divide between rich and poor, globalization winners and losers, reflects a shaming social injustice; a lack of global justice, however, poses major risks to global peace.

In our preceding analysis, from biblical as well as evolutionary anthropological perspectives, we were encouraged to pay high attention to individual face-to-face encounters. There is justification in trusting in the power of people looking into one another's eyes as a nucleus of reconciliation and new community. Where people meet, hearts can be converted. At the same time, our moral and religious attention was extended beyond the traditional scope of 'love of neighbour' – in the literal sense of the word neighbourhood – to approach the global neighbourhood of the remote, the unfamiliar, the strange, the frighteningly unknown, the hostile ('love of enemy'). Nobody can afford to live in self-complacent isolationism. Human atrocities and misery are still too great, while international efforts are still too weak, although it ought to have been long since clear that 'what happens in the world matters to all of us' (Comenius, *Unum necessarium*, 1668/1964: 144).

In reconceptualizing the notion of maturity it would be a mistake to take the general and the particular, the social and the individual, public responsibility and private accomplishment as opposites to be played off against each other. They need to be held together, for it is each individual human being that counts and is to be honoured in his or her incomparable peculiarity, dignity, beauty and vulnerability. Human rights are always individual rights. But, it is never one's own dignity and vulnerability alone, but always the other's too that is to be respected.

In this study the enlarged geographical focus has been taken account of in the composition of its parts, beginning with global perspectives in the first chapter and concluding with them in this last. The enlarged interrelational social focus has been taken account of by considering the nature of human sociality, both from biblical perspectives concerning the basic relationship between humans in the light of belief in God (Chapters 2–8), and from evolutionary and socio-psychological perspectives referring to groups and societies living in a collective climate either of amicable affiliation or hostile demarcation, of constructive cooperation or ruthless competition, of mutual care or mutual destruction, of love or hate (Chapters 9 and 10). When daring to speak of 'new' approaches to moral and religious maturity, it is this twofold broader range of attention relating to space as well as sociality that is meant to serve as a necessary frame of reference. 'Maturity' is to be conceived of as lying at the crossroads of these coordinates.

Maturity as a Widened Self

The first crossroads is, as already mentioned, the overall basic tension between the general and the particular, the community and the individual, the near and the far, the familiar and the unfamiliar, our own anxieties and the despair of millions worldwide. Maturity is the attribute of a 'widened' self characterized by two basic abilities, to participate in what is different from one's own, be it nation, people, preferences, values, religion and so on, and to face up to confrontations and conflict instead of avoiding them.

Maturity as Autonomy

Peace in the world incorporates peace of mind. This doesn't contradict what has just been said. Whatever we are supposed to contribute to the welfare of the general, the public, the global, to peace between peoples and religions, it has to start with the individual, the individual's growing gifts and competences to feel, think and act, and to end with each individual's maturity as autonomy. Unlike other spheres of life such as science and the economy where the 'general' is aimed at, in the interconnected areas of education, culture and spiritual growth the point of departure as well as the goal of the life journey is the individual person, as a child, a youngster, an adult, each of them in his or her different circumstances and transitions to new horizons.

Being Aware of Ambiguities

What does 'peace of mind' mean? The phrase is to be protected against misunderstandings which will immediately become clear when we are recollecting the situation that has prompted our whole enterprise. The restlessness of the world around us leaves us with restless hearts and minds. The wickedness of human behaviour outside confronts us with our own destructive potentialities inside. Peace of mind does not mean tranquillizing the soul. It means to be able to live in full awareness of the ontological and moral ambiguity of oneself.

Accepting Imperfection

One's own nature has to be accepted in light of what Carl Gustav Jung has called the 'shadow'; it is that which darkens self-esteem and feelings of grandiosity. It is what undermines peace outside us because of lack of peace inside, because of fleeing both one's own self and the surrounding world as they are. Things are falling apart. In psychoanalytical parlance, it is the intolerable within us that we are projecting on to others and not tolerating in them because we cling to a false ideal of perfection and a fixed notion of identity.

Given that we wish to be physically sound, whatever reminds us of possible disability is separated off, shunned, looked at with dislike or disgust – or mere pity.

Given that we are afraid of losing our own ethnic, cultural and religious identity, the strangeness and otherness of other races, cultures and religions is avoided or, worse, held in contempt.

Maturity means befriending personal and universal imperfection (cf. pp. 209–12).

Resisting Illusions

Maturity means becoming able to accept the fallibility of all life and to resist illusions. The reason why we started paradigmatically with a story of biblical injustice in the

Book of Genesis, and step by step traced the desperate cries for justice and peace in the Book of Psalms, was because those early Old Testament narratives 'have few peers in the history of provocative texts on the human condition' (Dershowitz 2000: 20). In speaking of envy, murder, guilt and sin, they confront us with uncomfortable phenomena. We are irresistibly forced by these tales to become aware of what we don't want to listen to. A similar provocative, hurtful effect springs from evolutionary hypotheses on human nature which reveal the deep-rooted inherent propensities for xenophobia, racism, aggression and violence of which we are ashamed.

Reasonable Scepticism, Hopeful Trust, Absolute Vision

Yet maturity is not resignation. Unlike reasonable scepticism, fatalism can never be a trait of a mature person. Realizing the factual does not mean approval. The reason for proceeding beyond the Book of Genesis and tracing the great story about God in his ways of responding to human nature down to the renewal of his promises in Jesus of Nazareth, Jesus' sharing life with others and telling about God's kingdom as something already beginning with him, the wandering Jewish rabbi – a monstrosity to the ears of the pious, the educated, and the mighty which was to lead to his execution – was to counterbalance scepticism with hopeful trust in what is more than just necessary: the absolute vision.

What would our human affairs look like if the vision of divine justice and shalom didn't exist? As believers we are used to speaking of 'the leap of faith', which is theologically correct language coined by the Danish theologian Sören Kierkegaard in the nineteenth century. But for good reasons it is also permissible to speak of the reason of faith too (see *The Reason of Religion*, Rössler 1976). Religion is a matter one can reasonably argue about and passionately advocate. Humankind's frenzy calls for an extraordinary alternative.

A Disciplined Frame of Mind

Although empirical analysis is a basic requisite of any realistic educational programme, stopping there would have been to stop halfway. Empirical research can never have the last word, at best the last but one. Even though evolutionary explanations are directed to digging up 'ultimate' factors behind the 'proximate' (see Chapters 9 and 10), they can't replace normative consideration of human purposes. But, more than ever before in history, a mature outlook on general public affairs and actions will include being informed about normative claims, about empirical preconditions and about the relations between both as characteristics of an empirically and intellectually disciplined frame of mind.

Spiritual Maturity

The kind of maturity envisaged can be called 'spiritual maturity', since it (a) integrates moral and religious maturity, (b) indicates the origin of the inspiring and encouraging power of religious vision as a gift of the Spirit, and (c) does not get lost in naïve views, but is marked by modest expectations thanks to the clarifying filters of empirical assessments.

Spirituality in the Plural

Spirituality exists in the plural. The term 'spirituality' stems from Catholic monastic traditions in the sixteenth century, when the Jesuits under Ignatius of Loyola developed ascetic practices in order to control and shape mind and soul. Still today, Catholic religious education mostly refers to 'spirituality' from the classical perspective of prayer and meditation, in recent decades also mingling with influences from mystic traditions and Asian Buddhist practices (mostly Za-Zen) (Simon 2002).

In the meantime, the semantic horizon of the term has been broadened considerably. It is used everywhere and risks losing any definite connotation. It is connected with living faith traditions and esoteric forms of quest for meaning, with syncretistic New Age paths of religious experience as well as exciting transcendent experiences in 'popular culture' and the arts (Crane 2001). There is even the tendency to replace the very term 'religion' itself by the term 'spirituality' to avoid any exclusiveness and to embrace whatever people might direct their longings to. There are perhaps criteria that should be taken into account lest 'spiritual maturity' become a vague affair that can mean everything and says nothing.

Human Quality and Universality

It is the firm conviction of this book that moral values based on religion and spirituality can support good social order and even world peace provided that religious and spiritual attitudes are not narrow-minded. 'Religion', 'faith' and 'spirituality' do not promise something good and healthy per se. But what distinguishes the one or the other form of spirituality, the positive and negative ones? Is it (a) possible and (b) permissible to introduce normative questions? I definitely affirm both possibility and legitimacy. As morality concerns values and norms it logically calls for an analytic as well as a normative approach.

Amy Gutman (1995) has discussed the different normative answers to conflicts in multicultural societies. She criticizes a 'cultural relativism', a 'political relativism', a 'comprehensive universalism' and argues convincingly for a 'deliberative universalism'. In view of aggression and war on the tragic road our species has taken 'from (mere) killing to (deliberate) murder' (Vogel 1989), it would be absurd to bracket normative reflections and judgements in moral and religious affairs, even on subjects which seem to be 'holy' but hardly deserve this attribute. In the last century, Anglo-Saxon analytical philosophy in particular tried to tackle moral issues exclusively in descriptive and analytic terms, not altogether without success. But to analyse the language of morality leaves the substance of morality, religious and non-religious, open, including those issues which cannot remotely be left without critical commentary as they concern positions that fostered racism, tolerated totalitarianism and mass murder, violated human rights, caused social injustice or blessed terrorism. All of this needs a normative response by the world community. I note that for many years in some conceptions of religious education 'valuing' has been taboo, and the term 'spirituality' has been used with exclusively positive connotations, even though it doesn't of itself clearly and unmistakably explicate either its normative moral criteria or its normative range. Let me briefly discuss both points.

As to its moral implications, spirituality will necessarily fail to contribute to general public peace if it rests upon a divisive structure of thought that rigidly distinguishes between believers and non-believers and consequently fosters absolutist attitudes. Religions are allowed to cultivate such within their own walls, as long as they don't cause public harm. However, one might assume the absolutisms in a religious 'micro-society' can cause public harm on a macroscale in the long run.

With regard to the normative range or generalizability of spiritual practices and ethical views, religions differ widely. We can roughly list, first, the beliefs perhaps of a tribe, the members of which may derive their religious identity from a totem as their common ancestor, hence naturally implying a very narrow normative range of obligation.

Second, in modern times the very opposite, people with highly individualized forms of spiritual search, will not claim any universalization either, due to the very nature of such a spirituality in its subjectivity and normative neutrality. 'You may choose that way, I'll choose this. It's all the same.' One might, of course, declare precisely this spiritual individualism as the new overall programme that is most apt to contribute to justice and peace worldwide, but it is difficult to discover which traits may have a moral and spiritual impact that is of relevance to the general public and liable to be sufficiently effective to receive public attention.

A third group are sectarian-like religious communities which often voluntarily retire from general social life and common responsibilities.

This leaves the so-called world religions. Do they satisfy the two criteria of possessing a convincing human potentiality and at the same time universability? No simple answer is possible. Judaism, Christianity and Islam didn't develop historically as static, unchanging monolithic entities. Each of these religions incorporates liberal traditions, conservative movements and radical wings. This is evident even in Islam although the Qur'an is regarded as God's final answer to the discord between Christians and Jews as well as to the dogmatic quarrels among Christian theologians, all of which is in any case regarded as sinful aberration. In spite of this self-understanding of the Qur'anic relevation as spreading ultimate clarity on God's plan, showing the end of all dissension and launching the restoration of the one human community (which already at the beginning of creation had originally existed, Sura 10. 19) – a restoration which for the future implies the claim of the realization of universal peace – history testifies early dissension among the Muslim community (umma) too, with the schism between Sunnites and Shi'ites, not to mention the harsh clashes within present Islam between liberal (Euro-) Muslims and Islamic fundamentalists.

The great Asian religions also manifest plural forms, as for example the different Buddhist schools show (see the varying emphases of Theravada, Mahayana and Vajrayana Buddhism). Plurality is even more evident in the immense variety of rites and techniques for spiritual growth and mental control to be found in Hinduism.

Religious plurality must not by any means become a barrier to enhancing the opportunity of a future era of reconciliation within religious diversity as one factor on the stony road towards peace. In his pioneering exploration of our issue, the Catholic theologian Hans Küng categorically stated more than ten years ago, 'No peace among peoples without peace among religions' (1991). In the meantime, national and international conferences on dialogue between different faith traditions provide encouraging results of shared good will. However, while there are enough wonderful declarations, 'we need something more prosaic: implementation, implementation, implementation' as Mary Robinson, the former UN High Commissioner for Human Rights, recently stated (Robinson 2002).

Where to Find Answers to Radical, Unbridgeable Diversity

Economic globalization needs ethical globalization in key areas, with the banning of war and the means of providing for peace as the most elementary prerequisites, since except in the case of war as an absolute ultima ratio (see pp. 193–4) the devastating harm done to people through warfare annihilates or paralyses every other kind of human welfare. Furthermore, harming people who are not guilty cannot ethically be justified. The principle of personal accountability forbids the punishment of innocents – 'punishment and reward, if they are to be just, must be individualized'; this is what Judaism learnt in history (Dershowitz 2000: 234). Modern wars with their extreme military destructive force, even if intended to be 'technologically precise', fail to obey this moral imperative. Additionally, we are observing a backlash against human rights by a sad return of military action taken as a swift means to solve problems originating in deep-rooted historical experiences with long-term consequences which require long-term compromises for the future. Reconcilation between peoples will not be realized through a mindless escalation of mutual violence or military force.

The present types of global ethics are prompted by the unrivalled experiences of the First and Second World Wars and the atrocities of genocides, such as the Holocaust. What happened then took place in terrible forgetfulness of all moral progress in recent history. Theories of global ethics today attempt to put a final stop to this. Geographically they relate to the 'globe', and normatively they claim the applicability of a moral obligation that is universal; hence their labelling as 'universalist' ethics.

The fundamental function of an ethics of human rights (see the 1948 Declaration) and the related role of basic rights in written liberal constitutions is the moral obligation to respect each human being as an autonomous individual in her or his freedom to enjoy 'unalienable' 'rights'.

Starting from the same idea of individual freedom, trends such as an ethics of discourse (Karl-Otto Apel, Jürgen Habermas) strengthen the liberal camp by pinning their hopes on non-hegemonic communication and symmetrical consensus-building among equal subjects.

A notable more recent trend concerns the concept of a 'Global Ethic' (*Weltethos*), which is rapidly winning worldwide attention. Complementary to, but in a certain degree of tension with, universal 'rights', it emphasizes 'irrevocable' universal 'directives'. The original concept (Küng 1990) was adopted in 1993 in Chicago by a 'Parliament of the World's Religions' (in Küng and Kuschel 1993).

A third type of universalist ethics is rooted in faith traditions where the belief system encompasses all people. According to their religious self-understanding, in Christianity as well as in Islam the doctrines of universal salvation imply universal welfare. The normative basis of their ethical concepts is of a transmoral religious or spiritual nature, the character of their moral directives being a matter of duties. Protestant ethics are programmatically founded on 'freedom' (see Martin Luther's famous 'Die Freiheit eines Christenmenschen', 1520). What is meant here is spiritual 'freedom *by* faith', not to be confused with the modern ethico-political idea of 'freedom *of* religion' as a paramount human right. Nevertheless, support for individual freedom and autonomy did and still does flow from the Reformation understanding of spiritual freedom, a fact that remains of secular public and cultural relevance.

Since we are dealing with moral issues in connection with religion, it also makes sense to discuss an attempt that strives to promote mutual understanding between the religions through the concept of a so-called 'pluralist theology'. This tries to do justice to pluralism by identifying points of coincidence leading to ultimate unity, thus advancing toward a 'universal theology of religions' in the singular (Swidler 1987). It is an approach that has an ethical impact indirectly, though with some advocates such as Paul F. Knitter the impact may also be a direct one, since Knitter links his philosophy of religion with liberation theology.

All 'universalizing' concepts mentioned deserve to be examined with greater care and in more detail. This, however, transcends the focus of the present study, and has already been attempted elsewhere (Nipkow 1994; 1998, vol. 2, chap. 12). It is perhaps permissible to be somewhat selective from the point of view of the specific issues of the preceding chapters, in particular the last on evolutionary ethics. Do the concepts of human rights, discourse ethics, a global ethic and of 'universal theology' pay due attention to the central question of how to effectively overcome the legacy of deep-rooted in-group/out-group patterns of thought? Do they include considerations of the constitution of human nature? Let us begin with the theological concept of a 'universal theology of religion'.

A 'Universal Theology of Religion' and the Neglected Socio-political Reality

Our analyses must not result in any relativizing and harmonizing glossing over of existing political, cultural and religious differences as sources of conflicts. We cannot afford to deny concrete facts. Theoretical generalizations, however, theological ones included, easily lose touch with the ugly concreteness of practice. In their understandable efforts to bridge gaps and proclaim worldwide reconciliation, visionary religious programmes advance dreams which mostly cannot stand up to the test of reality. Thus, moral and religious education programmes attain the status of mere good will. The churches' loss of public credibility will increase with their lack of expertise in respect of socio-political issues.

In addition, western theology is distrusted through fear of philosophical and theological 'constructs' imposed on indigenous cultural traditions and religions. 'The time is gone when the oikumene could be the mare nostrum . . . when we could speak of Christianity on the one hand and all the other religions lumped together', as Raimundo Panikkar, the well-known theologian in the field of dialogue between western and Asian spirituality who was brought up at the crossroads of Catholic Christianity and Hinduism, stated some years ago (1987: 121). In Pannikar's view, we are forbidden to perpetuate former colonialism by inventing a rationalistic religious *'lingua universalis*, which amounts to reductionism, to say the least' (p. 124) – an 'Ecumenical Esperanto' (Swidler 1987: 20).

Pluralism in its ultimate sense is not the tolerance of a diversity of systems under a larger umbrella; it does not allow for any superstructure. It is not a supersystem . . . The problem of pluralism arises when we are confronted with mutually irreconcilable world-views or ultimate systems of thought and life. Pluralism has to do with final, unbridgeable human attitudes.

(Panikkar 1987: 125)

In explicitly criticizing the rationalistic western bias of 'pluralist theologians' who are developing a 'universal theology of religion' Panikkar continues:

It is easy to be pluralistic if the others abandon their claim to absoluteness, primacy, universality, and the like: 'We pluralists have alotted each system its niche; we then are truly universal.' This, I submit, is not pluralism. This is another system, perhaps a better one, but it would make pluralism unnecessary. We have a situation of pluralism only when we are confronted with mutually exclusive and respectively contradictory ultimate systems. We cannot, by definition, logically overcome a pluralistic situation without breaking the very principle of noncontradiction and denying our own set of codes: intellectual, moral, esthetic, and so forth.

(p. 125)

In my view, John Hick's distinction between 'the Real in itself' and the Real 'as humanly experienced' (Hick 1989: 236) ('The Real' pointing to the Ultimate Reality, the Divine), which is to explain all religious diversity according to 'Kant's epistemological model' (p. 240), represents a classical example of a rationalistic meta-religious superstructure, betraying its origin by explicitly leaning on Enlightenment western philosophy.

I do not see how the construct of an ultimate common denominator of this kind of thought pattern allows believers to identify with and rediscover the specificity of their concrete spiritual life. Nor can by its very nature an approach from the angle of philosophy of religion sufficiently take into account how religions are culturally, socially and politically embedded in the specific conditions and conflicts of their environment, which they mostly are a part of or closely involved with.

'A Global Ethic' and 'Global Responsibilities' Between Promise and Misuse

Can the interest in overcoming violence (see the present World Council of Churches' decade 'to overcome violence') and promoting peace find orientation in Hans Küng's concept of a global ethic? It is much nearer to the point, since the global moral situation is its explicit focus, in the dramatic opening words of the Declaration:

The world is in agony . . . Peace eludes us . . . the planet is being destroyed . . . neighbours live in fear . . . women and men are estranged from each other . . . children die! . . . *But this agony need not be.*

(Küng and Kuschel 1993: 13)

In discussing this programme we necessarily have to include an appreciation of human rights ethics because Küng's initiative refers to it. Although I feel sympathetic to the intentions of the approach (I was involved in its educational implementation in about sixty schools), four reservations may be mentioned as a sort of a caveat. With them as background the importance of the approach can more appropriately be highlighted. They concern (a) the tendency to (an unavoidable) moral and religious minimalism, (b) impediments caused by human nature in the process of implementation, (c) conflicts that will inevitably originate from controversial interpretations, and (d) political misuse of the focus on global 'directives', that is 'responsibilities' and duties.

The Unanswered Question of Different Interpretations and Consequences

The methodology which had to be applied in Chicago in order to find a consensus had necessarily to reduce differences. To give a prime example, because of the Buddhists' objection the word 'God' had to be deleted throughout (Küng and Kuschel 1993: 61–5). Although a central statement of the introduction to the Chicago Declaration runs as follows, 'a global ethic does not reduce the religions to an ethical minimalism but represents the *minimum of what the religions of the world already have in common now in the ethical sphere*' (Küng and Kuschel 1993: 8), the Declaration does exactly this, it summarizes a 'minimum' although, with regard to its moral impact, this minimum covers fundamental fields of moral behaviour. There is no doubt that the attempt to at least define a minimal moral consensus is of high value. But it evidently also leaves a lot of problems open, in particular the concrete interpretation of the four 'irrevocable directives' (p. 24):

- 'You shall not kill!' 'Have respect for life!' (p. 25) – 'commitment to a culture of non-violence and respect for life' (p. 24)
- 'You shall not steal!' 'Deal honestly and fairly!' (p. 27) – 'commitment to a culture of solidarity and a just economic order' (p. 26)
- 'You shall not lie!' 'Speak and act truthfully!' (p. 30) – 'commitment to a culture of tolerance and a life of truthfulness' (p. 29)
- 'You shall not commit sexual immorality!' 'Respect and love one another!' (p. 32) – 'commitment to a culture of equal rights and partnership between men and women' (p. 32).

Mutual Moral Self-obligation and Human Nature

Before turning to the second caveat, concerning the neglected condition of human nature, the strengths of the Declaration should be outlined. First, it is an admirable and important step of symbolic power that representatives of the world's religions have launched a process of mutual moral self-obligation. Second, it is notable to state one's resoluteness to strive for consensus and one's readiness to engage in corresponding actions and not leave matters merely with a symbolic event. Third, as the most outstanding new focus, Küng's concept of a 'global ethic' is directed on 'ethic' as in the meaning of 'ethos' (not 'ethics', which means the doctrine or the system, see Küng and Kuschel 1993: 60). Thus it aims at the weak point of any concept that is one-sidedly concerned with only abstract moral theories or programmes.

The key idea of promoting an 'ethos' is to want to utilize shared and lived morality. The English word 'ethos' means the characteristic moral spirit of a community, people or system. It is the spirit of a group or a 'form of life' (Ludwig Wittgenstein) that moves people to do what they should do. Küng's concept seeks the motivational basis for moral behaviour and acting. When Mary Robinson in her Tübingen lecture (2002) impatiently urged 'implementation' of human rights in concrete situations, she identified the same problem. Proclaiming access of all people to all rights requires politicians who feel compellingly obliged to grant them. Signing a charter of human rights is one thing, putting it into effect another.

What we are calling the political will on the level of politics is repeated in public life on many other levels too: do people seriously 'will' the good, and not for themselves alone, but for others? In the history of practical philosophy (philosophical ethics), it was Kant who emphasized the 'will' as the crucial driving force in the individual. The widespread modern term is 'commitment'; the fact of coming across it in innumerable documents is a telling proof of what the arena of today requires. It is not just any commitment; according to Kant it ought to embrace the true moral spirit or way of thinking (*Gesinnung*), which leads us back to 'ethos'.

It is in accordance with the line of interest in an 'ethos' that the Chicago Declaration dares to speak of 'binding values' and 'fundamental moral attitudes' (Küng and Kuschel 1993: 18), the first stressing the character of personally felt obligation, the second a moral 'habitus', that is, habitual moral virtues and enduring moral dispositions (for the renaissance of this approach see MacIntyre 1981 and communitarian ethics; for its original classical expression, see Aristotle). The Declaration comes very much to the point when it states, referring to the contribution of religions, 'they can provide what obviously cannot be attained by economic plans, political programmes or legal regulations alone: *a change in* the inner orientation, the whole mentality, *the "hearts" of people*, and a conversion from a false path to a new orientation for life. Humankind urgently needs social and ecological reforms, but it needs *spiritual renewal* just as urgently' (Küng and Kuschel 1993: 22).

The agenda of global issues is the setting; spiritual renewal and with it a conversion of minds and hearts is the centre. Interestingly, Kant already pondered the difficult problem inherent in the focus on inner life. He very clearly knew that the movements of a human being's mind are not at our arbitrary disposal. No wonder that the Chicago Declaration speaks of a 'conversion'. The reason for this is the dilemma between freedom on the one hand – a person's autonomy ought to prove itself by acting in no other way than under the idea of freedom (Kant 1785: BA 99, 100) – and the accomplishment of effective change on the other hand. How is it possible, Kant asks, for someone who is naturally a wicked person to make himself become a good one? It transcends all our ideas as Kant is forced to confess (1793: B 50, 51)! His own 'solution' is a sort of escape in envisaging the possibility of a sudden revolution in mind, a sort of rebirth (with explicit reference to John 3: 5: 'being born from above'), so to speak a creation, a change of the heart (B 54, 55).

The parallels are obvious, the old and ever new problem too: how to make a human being become a moral person from within. In the light of the chapters on the evolutionary history of human nature we understand perhaps a little better why this question cannot find ready answers. Nor are we surprised that Kant and the Declaration on a Global Ethic are bothered by the absence of a capacity for moral change, otherwise neither would have been prompted to use metaphors which circumscribe a sort of supranatural event. It is easily said that economic globalization must be accompanied by an 'ethical' one; it is a huge task to achieve this in practice.

To give an illustration with respect to the topic of this book: how can moral 'directives' such as the four of the Chicago Declaration which belong to the Ten Commandments and can be found in other religions too become a forceful moral power in view of the tension between in-group amity and out-group enmity (cf. Chapter 9)? Those directives are widespread worldwide because of the very same social function everywhere in the early history of humankind and still today; they are necessary for the cohesion and survival of one's own group. They have never been applied in the same demanding spirit of moral obligation to out-groups. On the contrary, killing, stealing, lying and sexual violence were considered legitimate means for the purposes of defence as well as preventative attack or provocative aggression. The Declaration does not discuss the problem on this level, nor do the other patterns of universalist ethics mentioned previously such as the ethics of human rights, the discourse ethics or the Christian ethic of 'love of neighbour'. The present study is aimed precisely at this blind spot.

There is a great temptation to think that adopting declarations will do. The enormous efforts undertaken by the Global Ethic Foundation located in Tübingen since 1993 show that more is needed. Much more efficient than the Chicago Declaration itself has become its function as a stimulus for a many-layered process consisting of weighty follow-up studies and publications, top meetings with politicians (UK Prime Minister Tony Blair, UN High Commissioner Mary Robinson, UN General Secretary Kofi Annan and other politicians), public exhibitions, among them in UN Headquarters, competitions in schools in Germany and Switzerland concerning the Declaration and so forth. The most recent document in line with Küng's approach (and with his participation) is *Crossing the Divide: Dialogue among Civilizations* (Picco *et al.* 2001), a publication that UN General Secretary Kofi Annan had asked an international Group of Eminent Persons to produce. The document convincingly outlines a new paradigm incorporating principles among which 'equal footing', a redefinition of the term 'enemy', individual 'responsibility' and 'cooperation' around shared 'issues' feature centrally.

Conflicts and Struggles Still Waiting

It is by these additional steps of implementation (see also Küng 1997; Küng and Kuschel 1998) that we may hope to clarify the different interpretations and controversial practical consequences to which the general semantical character of the 'irrevocable directives' gives rise. The passionate debates at the Chicago conference itself, as well as the long pre-conference discussions, revealed the bulk of disputed questions left still unanswered. This is also true with regard to our specific issue of war and peace, violence and non-violence. In his commentary Küng writes,

> the Declaration deliberately took a middle course which could secure a consensus: between a 'Realpolitik' of force in resolving conflicts and an unrealistic unconditional pacifism which, confronted with violence, expulsion, rape, death and mass murder, unconditionally repudiates the use of force. First of all the Declaration states in principle: 'Such conflicts, however, should be resolved without violence within a framework of justice. This is true for states as well as for individuals.' However, it immediately adds: 'Persons who hold political power must work within the framework of a just order and commit themselves to the most

non-violent, peaceful solutions possible. And they should work for this within an international order of peace which itself has need of protection and defence against perpetrators of violence' (III 1 b); whenever possible non-violently (III 2 d).

(Küng and Kuschel 1993: 68)

This modesty in expectations is along the lines of our own approach, with its mixture of scepticism and hope. The explanations given in the Declaration are attuned to reality, curtailing naïve enthusiasm and avoiding verbose vagaries. Yet thus they also clearly show where the conflicts and struggles are still waiting.

Possible Misuse of the Focus on Obligations

The human rights approach, with its roots in the British (1689) and American (1776) 'Bills of Rights' and, in particular, the French Revolution (Déclaration des Droits de l'Homme et du Citoyen, 1789) has met with much criticism from the supporters of Shari'ah-Islam in the Islamic world and from Chinese authorities. From the Islamic point of view the following central convictions prevent Muslims from joining the western human rights tradition.

First, all Muslims are seen as belonging to a unified universal community (umma) which by its very nature does not provide room for any pattern of opposition. The present umma represents the restored unified humankind of God's creation. According to this original reality in Heaven, all people who are born are understood to be Muslims, with Adam having been the first. Abraham was the next decisive step in that he, 'as God's friend' and true 'Muslim' represented the global Abrahamic community which by further steps of prophetic succession was to become realized in the present umma. The revelation to Moses was complemented (and indeed replaced) by the revelation coming down to Jesus; the revelation to the Christians and before that to the Jews was completed by Mohammed: and each time the earlier revelations were now seen as being preliminary ones. The 'Scripture' that God transmitted (Torah, the Gospel, the Qur'an) possessed the same eternal content in different languages, until expressed with ultimate clarity in the Arabic of the Qur'an.

From this perspective the possibility of a universal alternative to the universal umma is unthinkable. A world community in line with western concepts of human rights or based on any secular ethic is an aberration from the truth. The term 'secularization' has no equivalent in Arabic; it is translated by 'non-religious', with the implication that the Islamic religion is the only true one in God's eyes (the Qur'an also being the only clear reflection of the heavenly original). Any alternative is, strictly speaking, a presumptuous alternative to God and, therefore, atheism. Today, in particular after the Iranian Islamic Revolution, Islam is conceived of as the proper spiritual alternative to what is perceived as the more or less corrupt, materialistic universalism of the western world. Inclusive concepts of a 'global ethic' are faced with the challenge of how to respond to such an inclusivist exclusivism.

Second, in the context just outlined there is no room for the independent individual and the idea of religious 'individualization' in a constitutive ontological sense. That is why so many Muslims have basic difficulties with individual human rights while other Muslims actively support them.

Third, in relation to this overall reality of the universal umma it is unsurprising that Muslims think more in terms of obedience to duties (the concept of faraid) as stressed in the Qur'an, than of possessing basic individual rights in the western political and legal sense of the term. Yet the Islamic tradition also features prominently a premodern concept of human dignity – which, however, is not identical to the idea of human dignity that at the time of the European Enlightenment was to lead to institutionalized individual human rights (cf. Donnelly 1989).

Human rights as Islam perceives them – speaking of 'Arabic-Islamic Human Rights', not of 'general' ones (cf. UN Conference on Human Rights, June 1993, Vienna) – are valid only within the Divine Law of Islam, the shari'ah. It is an open question whether attempts to develop European or North American forms of Islam (cf. important work by, for example, Bassam Tibi 1993 and Abdullahi an-Na'im 1990) will succeed so that a public 'culture of rights' (Lacey 1992) can flourish as a new means for approaching the idea of individual human rights.

Against this background one can assume that Küng's concept of global 'directives' (and the related Universal Declaration of Human Responsibilities by the InterAction Council, a proposal drawing on Küng's global ethic and adopted by a large group of 25 elderly statesmen and many other high-rank personalities in April 1997 in Vienna, see Küng and Schmidt 1998) might more easily be welcomed from the Islamic side. The 'four irrevocable directives' are in a modified way also to be found in the Qur'an, such as not to kill (one's own children, Sura 17. 31, or others whom God has forbidden to kill, 17. 33), not to steal the property of orphans (17. 34), not to follow (or say) things one has no knowledge of (17. 36), not to fall prey to unchaste behaviour (17. 32).

The interest in responsibilities in the shape of duties can be observed more clearly in China where in 1997 in Beijing the first 'Conference on a Global Ethic and Traditional Chinese Ethics' was held (followed by a second in 2001). If anything, in China the emphasis is very much on collective, not individual, rights, with strong appeals to traditional Chinese ethics, Asian values and present duties of citizens (Küng and Schmidt 1998: 125–9). Obviously, though, a focus on universal global responsibilities can be misused, contrary to its explicit intention, by bracketing out their links to human rights.

To summarize: in a way the deficiencies of probably all 'universalist' concepts are evident. Nevertheless they are necessary foundation stones of a peaceful world order. Only through universal human regulations can the worst be avoided, or at least mitigated, in respect of international conflicts, terrorism and war. Historically, the European universalist concept of individual 'rights' is grounded in basic moral 'values' (which communitarian standpoints should take notice of). Against this background its importance is evident in light of many forms of individual oppression, including the appalling violation of human dignity that is represented by torture, and by forms of flagrant discrimination against women. The weakness of modern western universalist concepts lies in their abstract nature, which leads to their specific historical and cultural origins being forgotten and diminishes their chances of being implemented when confronted with alternative cultural and political concepts (Islam) or non-democratic regimes (China).

Spiritual Sources for Reconciliation and Peace – Interfaith Dialogue in Freedom and Mutual Respect

The discussion of integrated ways towards peace in Chapter 10 began with education for law in the spirit of individual human rights and corresponding basic rights in the written constitutions of liberal democracies. 'Religious freedom' is an outstanding substantial part of these rights. On the one hand, it is taken as 'negative freedom of religion' only, in this case meaning the protection of the individual against a state that imposes religion on its citizens. We find this form of religious freedom which more or less regards religion as a matter of the private sphere in countries with a strict separation of state and church or other religious societies as in France. Due to a different development in history, we also find a complementary form of religious freedom as in Germany, Austria and other European countries, called 'positive freedom of religion', which in favour of the public relevance of religion opens up free space to the diversity of religions for equal development and self-representation in public life, including even in state-run schools. Rights for all are understood as the guarantee of the self-development of all, with regard to both individual and corporative spiritual life. In this understanding 'religious freedom' is not something that stifles religious activities, but stimulates them. It is not an expression of indifferent neutralism but one of sympathetic openness. Asian religions and Islam are invited to understand this aspect of legal provision that is otherwise often mistrusted or misunderstood. The positive form of religious freedom is particularly important for religious minorities. In providing opportunities for all religions in a society, minorities are treated with equal respect and given free space to display their own rich heritage and cultivate their own religious life in public life as well as private fields, within a legal framework of mutual tolerance.

There is one significant exception to all this, when unfortunately liberties as a constitutional framework are rejected, and that is when alleged divine law becomes authoritative constitutional law and the official governmental doctrine at that, as was the case in Taliban-ruled Afghanistan and still is in some other Islamic countries (for instance Saudi Arabia and Sudan).

It is dangerous if political 'universalist' concepts or theories go beyond the restricted function of merely providing a framework in a spirit of toleration and instead proceed to fill the frame ideologically, thereby, in the case of politically imposed religious influences, jeopardizing the free relationship between the respective spheres of the state and religion. This is not only the case in those countries where the shari'ah has become state law. In a milder form it also occurs when political administrations in democracies try to instrumentalize religion in accordance with the interests of the ruling political party.

In theological terms, our main concluding argument is to support and institutionalize free space in all cultures, which will allow spiritual traditions to flourish and radiate into the life of any given culture, and beyond it to others. Inherent to this argument is the conviction that, given such a platform of enabling free development, all spiritual traditions do actually possess rich resources on which to draw in a quest to contribute to global justice and peace.

In the spirit of religious freedom, both in its negative (protecting and defending) and positive (publicly encouraging and supporting) form, each faith tradition will hopefully lose its anxieties, for they will be respected by each other in their specificity and integrity. Interfaith encounters that deserve this name live by mutual respect. Clearly the real test is how the right of religious minorities is preserved and actively promoted to enable them to develop and present their own faiths. The corresponding 'hermeneutic of recognition and respect' (Nipkow 1998, vol. 2; 1999: 25) rests upon mutual recognition (hermeneutic of acknowledgement) of the 'Otherness' of the 'Other' (cf. E. Lévinas, Chapter 10 above).

Acknowledgement is more than toleration as an attitude of grudgingly letting the other live. It means taking the truth experiences of others seriously. Two attitudes would undermine this intention completely, confessionalist dogmatism and rational imperialism. The former incorporates a sense of religious superiority, the latter a sense of philosophical supremacy. An ecumenical hermeneutic is incompatible with churches that would regard others as spiritually incomplete and ontologically deficient (for instance to judge them as not being a 'true' church). An interfaith hermeneutic of recognition of the individuality of each religion, Christian and non-Christian, is equally incompatible with an allegedly 'pluralistic' approach which in reality is 'monistic' (see the preceding section). 'Others must be allowed to be "others" before we for our part can engage them in conversation again' (Werbick 1996: 115). Hence interfaith encounter must promote a common search in absolute honesty and sincerity (Talbi 1976: 155). It is the very dignity of each religion that believers share deep convictions they hold to be true. Any attempt to discard the issue of truth betrays a 'weak, passive' notion of tolerance instead of a 'strong, active idea of tolerance'.

Contributions to moral issues that in each of the spiritual traditions spring from faith provide for a much deeper foundation than a consensus on common values which leaves faith, the very heart of spiritual convictions, aside. The optimistic slogan coined at the 1925 Stockholm World Conference of the Practical Christianity Movement, 'Doctrine divides, service unites', is partly misleading. Despite all existing doctrinal differences that may separate the religions, shared actions toward peace will be rooted more firmly if faith and doctrine allow for universal brotherhood and sisterhood.

Hinduism – Internal Peace and International Peace

Sarvepalli Radhakrishnan (1888–1975), one of the greatest Hindu philosophers of our times, and President of the Republic of India from 1962 until 1967, once stated

> We should like our generation to go down to history not as the one which split the atom or made the hydrogen bomb but as the one which brought together the peoples of the world and transformed them into a world community. Now that the nations have come to each other's doorsteps, we have to develop new methods of human relationships. If civilization is to endure, understanding among our peoples is essential.
>
> (1995: 9)

Hindu scriptures cannot be easily summarized. In these concluding remarks I do not seek presumptuously to attempt any detailed description or comments that I have no right or authority to do as a Christian theologian and educationist. But a study on 'God, Human Nature and Education for Peace' having begun with the interpretation of biblical scriptures should also engage with a heritage which from its very origin and by its very nature has very much to say on our issue. The following remarks on Hinduism are paradigmatical reminders complementing what experts such as Robert Jackson and Eleanor Nesbitt in England have been researching and examining for many years.

For our present purposes it is not the field of methodology in religious education (for instance the 'ethnographical' or 'interpretive' approach; Jackson 1997; Jackson and Nesbitt 1990; Nesbitt 1998), but the contribution to global justice and peace of a universal worldview that draws attention to three important terms, among others, and can serve as 'a binding thread' for practically the entire literature, whether the revealed Vedic scriptures or other materials, old and new, as Ravindra Dave puts it (2001: 48): the three terms are unity, universality and eternality. It is this holistic and universalizing approach since ancient times that in Hinduism has created an integrative relationship between spiritual practice and ethics – our specific focus in this last chapter. Furthermore, when listening to Swami Vivekananda who stated this integrative relationship in just a few words, namely that 'the justification of all ethics is the sacrifice of the small self for the good of all' (Tapasyananda 1990: 46, as quoted in Dave 2001: 48), we note that this statement links directly to the hypotheses of evolutionary ethics presented and discussed in the preceding chapter on altruism. The term 'sacrifice' of 'self' also reminds us of the Christian view of Jesus' death and central aspects of Christian ethics (cf. Chapter 7). Yet this similarity in language must also prompt us to look more carefully. For according to the leading hermeneutical principles outlined above, fruitful learning from each other involves learning in the spirit of mutual recognition in honesty and sincerity, and this in turn implies awareness too of differences in faith. My spiritual and educational goal is not a reductionist revelling in superficially recognized similarities, but an acknowledgement of responsibly cultivated difference.

In summarizing the spiritual and ethical foundation enshrined in the holy Vedas, Vivekananda asserts that

> The God in Heaven becomes the God in Nature, and the God in Nature becomes the God who is Nature, and the God who is Nature becomes the God within the temple of the body, and the God dwelling in the temple of the body *at last becomes the temple itself* – becomes the soul and man.
>
> (Tapasyananda 1990: 169, as quoted in Dave 2001: 48)

The sequence of Vivekananda's identifications explains the Hindu notion of unity not as a fixed system but as a road with several stages. The relationship between the divine and humans is a development, directed towards a unifying experience integrating God, nature and the spiritual core (soul) of the individual. This is different from the notion of God in the Abrahamic religions; in particular in its strong dualistic form in Islam. Here nature is, indeed, full of 'signs' too, but of God's presence as creator and preserver. Nature is not seen as being permeated by the divine so that God and nature become identical; nor are Muslims allowed to discard the absolute difference between God and human beings as a matter of complete dependence (see pp. 204–7). Except for Islamic mysticism the Qur'an states the unbridgeable gap between God's majesty and superiority and all creatures, notwithstanding the fact of a relationship by revelation. I am referring to Islam, not to Judaism or Christianity, because in Asia it is this Hindu–Muslim juxtaposition that influences the political constellations that one has to keep in mind in order to see the field where Hindu spirituality ought to prove its peace-making power, as too ought Islamic spirituality.

The specific strength of Hindu spirituality becomes manifest over against materialism: 'if wealth leads one to self-centredness, excessive greed or unrighteousness, then one may end up with affluence, but without real happiness' (Dave 2001: 53). Spirituality aims at spiritualization in opposition to material dependence with the aim of balancing three things: private welfare (including material welfare), inner independence by not becoming a slave of materialism, and charity with selflessness to others. If you earn money, do not do it with one hand, not with two hands, but with one hundred hands (Shata hasta). If you show 'your generosity to fellow beings, please do not do it with one hand, not with two hands, and not even with one hundred hands. Do it with one thousand hands (Sahasra hasta)' (Dave 2001: 54).

Again, questions remain for both partners in an interfaith encounter. In Hindu–Christian dialogue the Hindu participants have 'to face the reality of the caste system and untouchability that for so long has had religious sanction'. Christians have to face 'the reality of religious wars and the numerous injustices perpetuated on people of other religious traditions in the course of the close alliance between colonization and evangelization of the world' (Ariarajah 1995: 114–15).

Mahatma Gandhi explicitly directed his selfless service and compassion to the downtrodden, coining the term 'Daridra Nārāyana', where the first word means the downtrodden and the second is the Hindu word for God. The world gratefully acknowledges Gandhi's contribution to peace, which rested upon social justice and open commitment against racism, social misery and political violence (see his principle of non-violence, 'Ahimsa') (Aram 1995). His success is, however, an exception. Unfortunately, while all religions profess love, peace, harmony and cooperation among all peoples, they mostly 'exhibit an oppressive side in their social manifestation' (Ariarajah 1995: 114) and they usually hesitate to engage in political protest in their own societies. Spiritual intentions are paralysed by national loyalties.

Hindu scholars have a clear consciousness of the crucial dilemma we have been discussing in the last chapters. They subordinate all spiritual practices, the multiple forms of Yoga (among them The Yoga of Knowledge: Inana Yoga; Action: Karma Yoga; Devotion: Bhakti Yoga, Meditation: Dhyana Yoga), to acquire internal peace by purifying the inner life, and 'it is this *internal peace* that alone can bring *international peace*'. But how, then, in light of the corrosive forces acting incessantly all around us, can 'the *"mechanisms of peace"* . . . be constructed in the *"minds of human beings"*?' (Dave 2001: 56). With this question we once more hit upon Kant's classical dilemma, the open question as to the effective implementation of a global ethic given the barriers to the vision of reconciliation worldwide or, in evolutionary terms, the fact of the stubborn and incorrigible sides of the very old legacy of human nature. How does Hindu spirituality take this problem into account on the thorny path to overcoming military, social and religious conflicts in Asia? The precious poetry of Hindu spirituality quoted below calls for concrete implementation.

Perennial Flame of Life

See unity in diversity.
Behold one divine form appearing in multiforms;
Immense is His vastness,
Unparalleled is His power.
All the countless creatures on earth and
Suns and planets which are seen,
And which are beyond our perceptions
Exist under His command.
Kindled in various forms,
The Perennial Flame is One.

(quoted in Dave 2001: 55)

The Buddhist Way – Participating, Distancing, Fading

Buddhism is a great response to human suffering embodied in ageing, sickness and death (the depressing trio of facts faced up to by Siddhartha Gautama). It is analytic in revealing the sources of suffering and the sequence of factors contributing to it, a fate that will exist as long as ignorance lasts. It is ascetic in disciplining the mind (not punishing and hurting the body as in Hindu ascetic practices) to free itself from illusions about reality as a whole. Unlike western curiosity about rebirth, Asians in general look at rebirth as a hard fact and a burden, and the way of the Buddha is a way of firm certainty ('incomparable security') as to how to obtain knowledge to be released from it. The round of rebirths will cease when the wheel of rebirth (samsara) is overcome by developing a consciousness that becomes liberated from the illusionary character of reality as such.

Maybe the Buddha Way of 'perceiving' world and self – a more correct form of language than speaking of 'faith', let alone of 'God', an idea which doesn't feature – is most prone to be misunderstood by people living in western countries, compared with other non-Christian religions. Our obsession with the individual as a subject in separation from and opposition to the world (see R. Descartes' famous split) will almost necessarily result in our failing to see that Buddhists view relations and functions only, not substance. Much as in postmodern 'constructivist' epistemology, they think that what we perceive to be substantial things and enduring realities are in fact mere 'appearances' and classifications of our consciousness (Dighanikaya XXII). Accordingly, an 'ego' as a continuing enduring entity and subject of perception is, strictly speaking, not discernible either (Mahavagga I, 6, 43). Thus, only transforming consciousness will lead to emancipation, in the Buddhist understanding of the word, which differs basically from the European Enlightenment concept.

In the exercise of our thinking faculty, let the past be dead. If we allow our thoughts, past, present, and future, to link up in a series, we put ourselves under restraint. On the other hand, if we never let our mind attach to anything, we shall gain emancipation.
(*The Diamond Sutra* and *The Sutra of Hui Neng*, 1969: 44, as quoted in Keightley 1986: 14)

One can easily see that the dialectical process of (a) perceiving suffering as the fate all beings are subjected to, and (b) step by step realizing the illusionary character of being has a double effect with regard to the issue of aggression, violence, war and, correspondingly, non-aggression, non-violence, peace. On the one hand, the interconnectedness of everything with everything, which Buddhism shares with Hinduism as their common traditional ontological heritage, makes the topics of the environment, animals, ecological destruction and any form of conflict become issues of salient concern, but with an optimistic prospect; on the other hand; all human suffering following from the restraints of being need not necessarily exist if one shares the same knowledge and receives the same liberating teaching about the illusive character of being (Dharma). In the Buddhist view, the world would be different if all people were to join the Buddha Way as a specific practice and means of becoming aware of the decisive truth. It is the truth that all distinctions in reality depend on the distinctions of our mind and will cease to exist when its illusionary nature is realized. This knowledge will bring about the end of all desires in life ('thirst or greed'), resulting in peaceful waning and fading, 'blowing away' (nirvana). The complete 'mass of suffering' is gone (Majjhimanikaya III, 26).

Again this approach focuses on inner peace, bodily and spiritually, as it is paradigmatically experienced in the ordained Sangha, the Buddhist monastic community. The central idea, however, is not this community, but getting rid of the 'self' and leaving behind everything else too. This mood implies selfless love, general kindness, compassion, tolerance, simplicity of life and striving for peace in the Buddha Way.

Judaism – Spirituality of Learning and Longing for Shalom

The way of Judaism is embedded in a completely different ontological context, like the ways of Christianity and Islam, all three of which are based on a belief in one God Almighty who created the world and has revealed his holy will. Thus the basic ontological structure is *encounter* between human creatures and God in His Otherness (cf. M. Buber, E. Lévinas), not unity of the divine, the cosmos and the human (Hinduism) or 'dissolution' (Nibbana, Nirvana) of what 'appears' to 'exist' (Buddhism).

The historical background differs, too, rendering Judaism a characteristic profile. Israel began in slavery, had to escape annihilation, was tested in the desert, had to conquer the land to live in. Wars became the order of the day, constantly threatening a militarily weak people that because of its unfortunate strategic position had to suffer in the crushing mill of superpowers. A rather short independent political existence in the form of two kingdoms was followed by the destruction of both. In the context of the Babylonian Exile the majority of the people were swallowed up; a minority only fervidly held fast, keeping, almost desperately, every custom and law that bound them to their past. Centuries of political subordination and suppression, occasionally provoking revolts, led to the final loss of the religious centre, capital and home, with the next 2000 years spent living in the Diaspora and carrying with them 'a portable fatherland' (Heinrich Heine). Then the incomprehensible was to happen, the Holocaust. Eventually a new state was built up, with unending new conflict and war.

The religion of a people is shaped by history and geography. Struggling with enemies and wrestling with God was to produce the strongest tensions, giving birth to divergent policies on warfare and peace making, and creating a long tradition of controversial attempts to interpret God's will. Unlike the Christian use of the Hebrew Bible as the Old Testament, for Jews the Bible and the Talmudic rabbinical interpretations belong to one and the same heritage. Down to our own day the Talmud is learned from childhood on. As soon as a Jewish boy is able to lisp the alphabet, he is set to pore over the pages of the bulky tomes. The study continues until the very day of death. Jews represent a community of learning, their religion being a 'pedagogical religion' (Leo Baeck). As Ernst A. Simon, a modern Jewish educationist and renowned expert in adult education once described it:

> We are sitting as fellows over the texts. 'Each is allowed to pose questions and to talk, and the most do so . . . Thus we learning Jews are participating in an unending conversation that originated with Moses and has never anywhere been completely interrupted since then. The melody of prayer is accompanied by the melody of learning.'
>
> (Simon 1989: 344)

This spirituality is anti-authoritarian and anti-totalitarian; the latter because there is no hierarchical institution, no doctrinal centralization, nor a spirituality focused around a personality (with the exception, of course, of the rebbe or the tsaddik in Hasidism), not even around the titanic Moses. This 'democratic' pattern didn't prevent controversies though – quite the contrary. Among Jews diversity of opinion has become commonplace; the sharpest conflicts characterize the religious wings and political camps. In this setting the traditions about war and peace could not look more different.

> Proclaim this among the nations:
> Prepare war,
> stir up the warriors
> . . .
> Beat your plowshares into swords,
> and your pruning hooks into spears.
> (Joel 3: 9–10)

> In days to come
> the mountain of the LORD's house
> shall be established as the highest of the mountains,
> and shall be raised above the hills;
> all the nations shall stream to it
> . . .
> For out of Zion shall go forth instruction,
> and the word of the LORD from Jerusalem.
> He shall judge between the nations,
> and shall arbitrate for many peoples;
> they shall beat their swords into plowshares,
> and their spears into pruning hooks;
> nation shall not lift up sword against nation,
> neither shall they learn war any more.
> (Isa. 2, 2–4)

The prophetic proclamations are divergent; the body of texts compiled across many centuries cannot but be incoherent. They are misunderstood if seen from an unhistorical perspective or from mistaken systematic doctrinal expectations. The paradox is the paradox of human reality and history itself and remains mostly unresolved. This was the main reason why our analysis of education for peace and the issue of justice – God's righteousness (justice) and man's injustice and propensity to aggression, violence and war – started with the paradoxical experiences and witnesses of the Hebrew Bible, this unique document in humankind's history.

Reconciliation is hard work; peace between the nations must be learned too. In the view of Judaism, the world is far from being naturally predestined to harmony and unity, such that breathing in a divine spirit of the universe would lead to internal and international peace (Hinduism). Nor will the human consciousness be able by new knowledge to make wars, dying and all suffering disappear (Buddhism). The sad facts remain facts, Jewish spirituality is a worrying, questioning, learning, fighting one, struggling with and against oneself, the LORD and others.

Where is the theological core of this realistic and pragmatic approach to spirituality? They are living in an unredeemed world, as Jews would say. Nevertheless, by their creator and partner in covenant they have been told to contribute to a world a little better than exists at present, in order at least 'still to bring a part of the divine truth into the world' 'for the sake of Heavens'. The Hebrew word for courage is 'oz', and the dialectic between peace and conflict is ingeniously expressed in the sentence 'May God give his people oz and God bless his people with shalom' (Goodman-Thau 1998: 60).

Israel would have never been able to survive without great inner strength and courage, including military resoluteness. But mostly in history the Jews possessed no political independence or military power at all. They had to suffer the role of defenceless victims, although, 'in several circumstances', as Eveline Goodman-Thau adds, 'they made others become victims' (1998: 59). In this tension the Bible proclaimed a vision of peace as God's final will and promise – within a highly remarkable context, that of striving for justice (cf. Chapter 4 above).

The rabbis regarded shalom as the cornerstone of God's creation; it would come to flow together with justice from the Lord's heart, burning to prove his care for his dispersed people and restoring them to Jerusalem. Several hundred years before, in experiencing this essential trait in God's nature, the prophets, in a remarkable change, had forcefully drawn attention away from rituals and sacrificial offerings and towards social commitment. Later, after the destruction of the rebuilt Herodian Temple by the Romans under Titus in AD 70, study of the Torah, together with continuing learning, praying and doing good in daily life, became the overall spiritual guidelines. Today the radical social prophetic message is regarded by many as the promising platform for the future, the gift of Judaism to the world. Jewish and Christian spirituality on this line (see pp. 207–8) can be described as a 'spirituality of social protest and mercy'; it is driven by God's own holy will to help the poor, oppressed and suffering as his creatures:

> Trample my courts no more;
> bringing offerings is futile;
> incense is an abomination to me
>
> . . .
>
> When you stretch out your hands,

> I will hide my eyes from you;
> even though you make many prayers,
> I will not listen;
> your hands are full of blood
> . . .
> cease to do evil,
> learn to do good;
> seek justice,
> rescue the oppressed,
> defend the orphan,
> plead for the widow.
>
> (Isa. 1: 12–13, 15–17)

The impressive biblical witnesses of the promise of future shalom are not exceptions; others read,

> I will abolish the bow, the sword and war from the land;
> and I will make you lie down in safety.
>
> (Hos. 2: 18)

> Not by might, nor by power,
> but by my spirit, says the LORD of hosts.
>
> (Zech. 4: 6)

Shalom as promise for the future requires a quest and struggle for the good in the present. Rab Bunim used to say that everybody has two pockets to put their hands into to pull out the slip of paper in either one or the other. Life is located between the two notes in the pockets, in the right pocket 'The world was created for me' to do what I am to do, in the left 'I am earth and ashes' (as quoted in Goodman-Thau 1998: 66, from Hasidim tradition).

Islam – Absolute Submission

In the view of the Qur'an, in the beginning 'mankind were but one community: then they differed' (Sura 10. 19). The historical background of Islam is a shared context of existing together with both Judaism and Christianity and believing in the same God. Thus Islam has much in common with the two older faith traditions. All three share God's revelation as witnessed in the Old Testament; in addition Islam positively acknowledges God's relevation in Jesus, son of Mary. However, Mohammed observed the split between Jews and Christians and knew about the disagreements in Christianity itself, in particular concerning how to interpret the nature of Jesus Christ. Against this plurality and diversity the Qur'an set unity, not indeed as something new, but as a warning reminder of something lost, a loss through which both Jews and Christians had become guilty. The 'People of the Scriptures' had been given everything they needed for the right way to go, but they left it, either by hiding what they knew, by reducing or changing it, therefore lying, or by not truly and faithfully enough believing in God's directives in their 'hearts' (Sura 5. 41). What is new in the Qur'an is the finality of God's relevation now become absolutely clear and hence eventually to be used and communicated to all for the benefit of all, for humankind as a whole.

In the view of Muslims, the separation just mentioned demonstrates that Christians are never to be allowed to claim the universality of their truth – a claim Muslims incline indeed to see as blasphemous in light of the purely preliminary status of God's revelation through Jesus. Instead of having finally overcome polytheism, Christians perpetuate it by a tritheism in speaking of Jesus as God, 'Allah is the Messiah, son of Mary' (Sura 5. 72), or by saying 'Allah is the third of three (Sura 5. 73); they are not true believers. Whoever adds someone or something to God will be awaiting the "paradise" in vain; "his abode is the Fire"' (Sura 5. 72).

The spiritual core of this response to the historical situation which was to become (and can explain) the beginning of the breathtaking expansion of Islam – within one century stretching from Spain to India – was the restoration of the lost spiritual and social unity of the world by proclaiming the unity of God. For the sake of the very order of the world as a whole, socially and politically, God had to be thought of and believed in as strictly 'one', 'unique', 'absolute'. The spiritual aspect concerns an existential need of human beings insofar as they are in search of the metaphysical security of knowing whether they are living in a world of continuing firm stability or not. And it is just this that Islam definitely offers in its conception of the unsurmountable dominance of God grounded in his unity.

In one of the earliest of Mohammed's prophetic proclamations, God is described and praised with an Arabic word (used only in this sura) that literally means something most compact, solid, of unsurpassable massiveness (Arabic: ṣamad):

> Say: He is Allah, the One!
> Allah, the eternally Besought of all! [literally translated: compact = ṣamad]
> He begetteth not nor was begotten.
> And there is none comparable unto Him.
>
> (Sura 112)

Through such a divine concentration the personal life of a true believer can be concentrated too, as the practice of Muslims illustrates, expressing what can be called a spirituality of absolute grateful submission and devotion. Its functions are not confined to the security of the individual, they extend also to securing the stability of collective human affairs as expressed in the Islamic community (umma). That means that in Islam one meets not simply a religion, but also an ideal of true human society. This is the reason why religious issues are immediately liable to generate political impact. If humankind wants an end to ideological controversies, political conflicts and wars, in Islamic eyes there is no other way than to join the same road of all human beings as potential Muslims, the way of 'Islam' as (literally taken) complete 'submission'. In long rows the male members bow their heads down to the ground in prayer – a symbol and expression of trusting dependence.

Any idea of pluralism in the sense of a plurality of divine powers at the highest level of authority, in Heaven and on earth, would bring with it competition, later uproar, eventually destruction. 'If there were therein gods beside Allah, then verily both (the heavens and the earth) had been disordered' (Sura 21. 22).

The restoration of peace as unity includes, too, as in Judaism, Islam's commitment to justice as God's own will and action. Nowhere does Islam pretend that God's rule has already been accomplished here on earth; what is constantly stressed instead in numerous Qur'anic utterances is the Last Judgement, when the righteous will receive their eternal reward and the unbelievers and evildoers will receive eternal punishment. Today militant Islamic groups and movements advance the issue of social justice as their characteristic programme in line with the teachings of the Qur'an. They condemn social injustice in capitalist Arabic countries and are given a warm welcome in the Palestinian refugee camps and in the homes of the poor.

Their militancy is criticized by many Muslims all over the world, but they cannot deny that from the very beginning the Qur'an itself encourages defending God's truth and advancing implementation of his divine rule over the world by force if necessary, otherwise, indeed, the Islamic history of the seventh and eighth centuries would be incomprehensible. This unrivalled expansion is unknown in the New Testament and early Christianity; nor is Judaism oriented to a religio-political world mission.

The Qur'an itself does not propose criteria on how to read its messages in every detail (on the hermeneutical problems of reading the Qur'an see Zirker 1999). Numerous interpretations remain possible, left open as the development of different schools of Islamic law shows, including interpretations relevant to the issue of violence and tolerance. On the one hand, there is the clear directive, 'There is no compulsion in religion' (Sura 2. 256). The reason why is not an anachronistic modern idea of tolerance, but a theological one; it is God's work, not Mohammed's (or anyone else's) to open or close the eyes of people to see the 'signs' and to understand His word. On the other hand, the numerous commands to wage war against those who resist the umma – the social and political equivalent to the religious proclamation – are clear as well. 'Fight in the way of Allah against those who fight against you, but begin not hostilities. Lo! Allah loveth not aggressors' (Sura 2. 190). 'And fight them until persecution is no more, and religion is for Allah' (Sura 2. 195).

It is necessary to keep in mind that there are several Arabic words used for 'struggle' and 'war' (for example, Qital, Harb, Fath), which are mostly used in profane language, besides Djihad which literally means 'commitment', 'effort'. Al-Djihad-fi Sabil Allah is the commitment for God's sake. Djihad doesn't mean the official wars of a state, but the religiously meritorious struggle of the individual (Tworuschka 2002: 138–9).

We also find statements indicating a sort of competition:

> For each We have appointed a divine law and a traced-out way. Had Allah willed He could have made you one community. But that He may try you by that which He hath given you (He hath made you as ye are). So vie one with another in good works. Unto Allah ye will all return.
> (Sura 5. 48)

The sentences seem to point to God's intention to allow for religious plurality; but one can hardly say that a basic religious affirmation of pluralism can be justified by the Qur'anic revelation. In the immediate context of the sentences concerning 'competition' we meet the warning not to join the Jews and Christians: 'follow not their desires, but beware of them lest they seduce thee from some part of that which Allah hath revealed unto thee' (Sura 5. 49). It seems to be a competition only in 'good works' and in striving to fulfil God's will, with no indication that the notion of a succession of revelations through which the Torah and the Gospel have been relegated as preliminary in the light of the Qur'an is in any way to be revised.

Today Muslim scholars read the famous statement on competition in a more liberal attitude as affirming global religious diversity (Kandil 1998). In their view 'diversity', a religious one included, is 'God's will' (Kandil 1998: 88). The interpretation of the Qur'an is, indeed, an ongoing process, as too, of course, is the case with the Bible. Although the Qur'an itself does not show (how could it?) any modern historical thinking which would permit readers to distinguish hermeneutically between the 'Word of God' and the 'Word of Man', some Muslim interpreters even apply 'constructivist' theses to the Qur'an, as we find with the Egyptian scholar Abû Zayd: 'The production of meaning happens in the interaction of the text and the reader. Hereby something new will spring into being, on the one hand, through the multitude of readers, on the other hand, through the difference in reading conditions' (Abû Zayd 1990: 201, as quoted in Zirker 1997: 184).

The issue of peace becomes a matter of a war between interpretations, with the risk of a deadly outcome for those who take novel standpoints. This problematic situation can be overcome if a 'framework' of constitutional law providing 'religious freedom' pacifies religious conflicts. In this sense human rights are the indispensable safeguard of public peace.

Christianity – a Spirituality of Praying, Protesting and Forgiving

Shortly before the end of the Second World War, the German theologian Dietrich Bonhoeffer was executed by the Nazi regime after many months in prison, having been found guilty of participation in the resistance movement. He became 'the father of a renewed Protestant spirituality'. Why? And how can other Christian voices of renewed or rediscovered spirituality throw light on the Christian contribution to justice, reconciliation and peace?

Essentially, our interpretation of the biblical heritage from Cain and Abel down to Jesus' death and resurrection and the apostle Paul (Chapters 3–8) was, of course, already meant as a voice from a Christian perspective. My interpretations in earlier chapters are to be regarded as a contextual reading of the Bible, reading it as literary 'experiment' as Abû Zayd labelled it (1990: 251), in the context of exploring present ways to peace. 'Re-lecturing' (in Spanish 'relectura') is a new way of rejuvenating biblical texts to let God's Holy Spirit enter our understanding, meet our needs and orient our actions. In a Christian context I use the term 'spirituality' in this precise way, becoming motivated and directed by His Spirit.

In reviewing and summing up all the preceding chapters, we can see that the biblical interpretations highlighted a central line of God-experience, God's paradoxical forgiving love. It is documented in the Book of Genesis (Chapter 3), the Psalms and prophets (Chapter 4). It is predominant in Jesus' parables (Chapters 5 and 6) and is concentrated in the records about his death on the cross as God's radicalized mystery of love (Chapter 7). The just (righteous) God justifies man, for humans cannot justify themselves in their guilt. Thus Paul's conversion by virtue of the experience of God's righteousness and grace against the background of sinful captivity under the law completed this line of analysis (Chapter 8).

Then, at the end of our study, we tested what we see almost all religions having in common, a vision of justice and peace for whose effectiveness for concrete implementation in education we as yet lack the necessary empirical assessment. Therefore, the educational and theological intentions were exposed to hypotheses and data from the field of the social sciences (Chapter 9), resulting in an integrated concept for practice (Chapter 10).

In this assessment Christian visions of global peace must be included in a self-critical way alongside secular universal ethical approaches such as that of human rights ethics, or the global ethic approach advocated by Küng, or again the theological attempt at a 'universal theology of religion' (Chapter 11). The result was a twofold insight: we should (a) provide a general political and legal framework of freedom within which (b) each religion in its specificity is to be summoned to strengthen those traditions and current movements that give justice, peace and active tolerance a chance.

With this concluding presentation we enter a field where, along with figures such as Dietrich Bonhoeffer and Martin Luther King, Christians come to the fore as courageous individuals together with groups and movements, daring the unusual, the non-conventional, the risky even, always being on the brink of meeting suspicions from both sides, the representatives of power structures outside and inside the church. Bonhoeffer, indeed, was denied a place on the list of those members of the churches who were persecuted by the Nazi regime and for whom Protestant congregations prayed on Sunday mornings.

The new spirituality concentrates on essentials and transcends confessional and religious limitations for it develops a new solidarity with others (cf. Chapter 10). Bonhoeffer's dictum, that to be a Christian today involves just two things, praying and doing good, focuses on essentials we share with Judaism, leaving aside, for present purposes, christological language and doctrine. Bonhoeffer's next demand links to the Jews in a much more explicit solidarity of guilt, when he remarked that only those who cry for the Jews are allowed to sing Gregorian chant.

New initiatives are spurred on by new religious discoveries which are mostly made under the pressure of suffering. I shall give two examples concerning experiences of women and the disabled. They will lead anew into the heart of Christian spirituality, a spirituality of acknowledging the strangeness of the 'Other', of overcoming in-group amity and out-group enmity as a main source of deficient peace and lacking full community.

Neither example can any longer be located within a specific Christian church or denomination; Christian spirituality has increasingly become ecumenical.

A final characteristic is the critical and self-critical openness between the church as an institution, on the one hand, and Christian 'grassroots' developments, both in the Protestant and Roman Catholic churches, on the other. The issues we are tackling unite us in confronting the churches' historical guilt.

Spiritual Experiences of Women

Bärbel von Wartenberg-Potter, since 2000 bishop of the Lutheran church in Lübeck in northern Germany, chose as a title for a volume of her essays a verse from Psalm 137 and transformed it in an informative, revealing way. The verses run,

By the rivers of Babylon –
there we sat down and there we wept
when we remembered Zion.
On the willows there
we hung our harps.

(Ps. 137: 1–2)

Wartenberg-Potter changed this, in English translation, to 'We shall *not* hang up our harps on the willows', with the subtitle 'commitment and spirituality' (1986). How can women succeed in standing on their own feet and finding a voice of their own? The women by the rivers of Babylon, displaced, alienated, had sadly given up, and since then nobody had ever learned about the 'language of their silence'. In the following centuries women continued sitting on church benches in pious devotion forgetting their own deeper desires, dignity, body and mind. Obediently they served the interests of males, of their fatherland or of whatever other sublime purposes, including God, even when he seemed to want or support war.

Christian spirituality has many faces, surely basically the face of prayer, hymns, meditation, liturgy; all of this remains valid, as we will see later, but a new trait is added as the new focus, forming a spirituality with the face of angry solidarity propelled by an 'inner fire'. Christian women remember Jesus who had women followers and who helped other women in need (Luke 13: 10–13). Feminist Christian movements also remember the early history of female workers who resisted humiliating labour conditions in the USA, demanding 'Bread and Roses'.

From a theological perspective women learned to perceive the impact of Jesus as the suffering friend on the cross who had become the incarnation of the new paradoxical power of God's weakness through a love that was breaking down barriers of hostility, both inside and outside. They learned to apply instruments of non-violence. This trait links their kind of spirituality to our interpretation of the meaning of crucifixion (Chapter 7): Jesus who died for others as the embodiment of God's love and grace. Correspondingly, women act in faith, hope and love for victimized fellow sisters.

The re-reading of the Bible in the new context of harm done to women in the light of acceptance by Jesus has led also to a new appreciation of the church. Why 'love' the church? Bärbel von Wartenberg-Potter's 'Love-letter to the Church' draws its confidence and commitment from the 'inner fire' just mentioned,

> This church, a community of human beings, carries in her lap the irresistible power of the unarmed truth of Jesus concerning God's immigration into the world. It is a God who stopped sitting on a heavenly throne watching the helpless hectic running of his creatures from afar. He intervened to let us know how to become truly human by our relationship to the God of love who intends nothing other than our temporal and eternal happiness.
>
> (1986: 30)

Spiritual Experiences of the Disabled

It was in 1978 that I met John Hull for the first time; together with Michael Grimmitt he was waiting for me at Birmingham airport, still able to see me with his eyes. Soon his disability rapidly proceeded to complete blindness (Hull 1990). In recent years John was to discover something that for 2000 years nobody had clearly seen before, until he as a blind person was able to 'see through'. His spirituality is a protesting, suffering and forgiving one too, concerning the Bible, the image of God and the role of Jesus Christ.

'The Bible is almost unequivocal in expressing the point of view of the able world. God is portrayed as an able-bodied God' (Hull 2001b: 80). Its measure is perfection. Blind people like all other disabled persons, do not belong to the normal, let alone the perfect. They will be healed; what is at the edges will be recalled to the centre.

> 'Then will the lame leap like the deer, and the mute tongue shout for joy', (Is 35: 6). This convergent humanisation is modelled upon the perfection of the creation, in which everything reproduces according to its kind (Gen 1: 24f.) so assuring the stability and the continuation of the characterized normality. The convergence is rooted in the domination of the normal and returns in eschatological visions toward the singularity of the average.
>
> (Hull 2001b: 80)

'Jesus is the archetype of this normality, without spot and blemish (1 Pet 1,11)', as John continues wondering why there were no disabled persons among his disciples. It would have been impossible for the simple reason 'that Jesus would have restored such people to normality' (ibid.). But then something was to occur,

> he himself becomes blinded (Mk 14: 65, Lk 22: 64), immobilised (Mk 15: 24), and marginalised (Gal. 3: 13, Heb. 13: 12). At first he accepts the infirmities of humanity by healing them, but finally he accepts the infirmities of humanity by participating in them, by becoming one of them. 'He was despised, shunned by all, pain-racked and afflicted by disease' (Is. 53: 3).
>
> (Hull 2001b: 80)

In John Hull's view, Jesus the miracle worker has lived on most powerfully in the church. 'Since blindness was a symbol of sin and unbelief, it has continued to represent stubbornness, ignorance and insensitivity' (Hull 2001b: 81). I add: not only a symbol, blindness meant to be a special sinner (John 9: 2). Surely, that blind people should receive the same compassion and care as other disabled people is better than leaving them unattended; the churches' mandate to serve (diakonia) is not questioned by John Hull. Yet we have to make a distinction of a far greater impact. To understand it requires two aspects of how our catagories of the world are structured: (1) from a moral level we have to switch to an ontological one which includes the moral as something secondary; and (2) this ontological level concerns bodily being and the being of our world as depending on the 'views' of different bodies.

'Christian faith confesses a biological spirituality, and believes in the resurrection of the body as the fulfilment of human potential (Ro 8: 23, 1 Cor 15: 42, Phil 3:21). Nevertheless, the body is transcended as well as transfigured' (Hull 2001b: 76). 'The body is not the antithesis of the spiritual but its organ' (p. 75), and thus the body can be transfigured and transcended by the spiritual (Mark 9: 2–8: the story of the transfiguration of Jesus).

> The body which is not transcended remains encircled within the membrane of the skin. Egocentricity is the enclosed body. The senses, although they appear to open the body out upon the world, do not do so unless they are met by the answering sense of the other. In the

reciprocity of eye contact, or skin contact, or conversational contact, we transcend the biological nature which is transfigured in the process.

(Hull 2001b: 76)

We remember the appreciation of face-to face contact in our discussion of ways to mutual understanding at a paramount place in Chapter 10; the very core of those reflections was 'bodily' exchange in 'reciprocity'. Now we can put this approach into an enlarged context of how different 'worlds' are generated, utilizing recent work in the philosophy of phenomenology which illuminates the body as the origin and main determinate of our knowledge (Hull 2001b: 76, in drawing on Merleau-Ponty 1968; Johnson 1987). A disabled person becomes extremely conscious of having an impaired body. Depending on the kind of disability, feeling for and consciousness of one's own world is shaped very specifically. 'In the case of a blind person, this is the world of touch, smell and hearing . . . The body regroups, consciousness reforms itself, and a new world appears' (Hull 2001b: 77). In following this line, Hull's main thesis is that a 'spirituality of disability' and a 'theology of disability', as he had pointed out in another essay (Hull 2001a), with the insight in the generation of 'many bodies, many worlds' (Hull 2001b: 78), can lead people to a view 'beyond self-centredness into solidarity with others', however different their world may be, suggesting '*a spirituality of various human worlds*' (p. 83; my emphasis).

Humanity is deadly endangered if individuals and groups remain imprisoned in the cages of their different worlds as 'laws' which close them up against others (cf. Chapter 8 on Paul). Therefore I speak of the ontological relevance of converting one's eyes. For Paul becoming blind was to become in a new way sighted; he got new eyes that were opened to a new structure of the world in which a former ontological 'law' was gone, now being ineffective, and a new ontological stance and moral maturity won – the ontological structure grounding the moral one, not the other way round. In terms of perspective taking, Paul's perspective on Jesus' crucifixion was exchanged with Jesus' perspective on him, releasing him from his former knowledge as a sighted person, a knowledge which in fact had made him blind. Jesus, who had said in concern for his killers, 'Father, forgive them, for they do not know what they are doing' (Luke 23: 34), overwhelmed also Paul, the ardent assistant of killers, by the liberating perspective of forgiveness, after which Paul could confess 'a new creation' (2 Cor. 5: 17), an ontological 'transfiguration'.

Intercultural and interfaith dialogue will fail its true great opportunities if it adopts only the first of the two following possible approaches, that of mere mutual enrichment alone. This approach is dominant in current practice both in school and in the churches, and certainly we should be all the poorer if the idea of mutual enrichment did not exist. But along the lines of the radical change of perspective just highlighted, the Christian experience of unconditional forgiveness and 'love of enemy', a second approach becomes apparent: accepting the other, whoever he or she may be and wherever he or she may live, regardless of my enrichment. This means acceptance of what cannot easily be assimilated to one's own predilections; it includes accepting the other *against one's own nature.* According to Martin Buber the true teacher does not have favourites among her class, but accepts everyone as a person, regardless of race, religion, personality, beauty or ugliness. Her look 'accepts all and includes all' (Buber 1926: 29), like He who, Buber adds, said 'I form light and create darkness'

(Isa. 45: 7). In this attitude of accepting everyone equally a teacher acts as 'the image of the true God' (Buber 1926: 29).

In January 2001 representatives of about four billion believers from 12 religions met in Assisi at the invitation of Pope John Paul II to participate in 'a pilgrimage for peace'. The response to the invitation was enthusiastic, commentators spoke of a historical event. The message embraced the obligation to support peace and justice, both together, for 'we must not forget that it is oftentimes a situation of oppression and exclusion that becomes a source of violence and terrorism', as the Pope soberly stated. The participants were addressed 'In the name of the Lord, each religion may strive for justice and peace, forgiveness, life and love'; and Rabbi Israel Singer (USA) reminded participants 'We must not leave peace to the generals!'

There was one simple thing that everybody shared: *prayer*. In separate groups in the identifiable tradition of each, but in a shared common quest in the same building, prayer was the foundation of the spiritual power looked for in a world torn apart. Through this kind of *differentiation* and *integration*, as a double and interrelated move, the meeting in Assisi stands as a quintessential symbol of reconciled diversity.

Prayer also indicates the knowledge of being in need of more than any given individual can contribute by herself or himself alone; in biblical language, humanity is in need of 'God'.

Prayer also testifies to the consciousness of imperfection and guilt, a knowledge about 'human nature' which should not be forgotten and replaced by the false, unrealistic, and ultimately oppressing idea of perfection. However, interpretations differ, to some extent widely, as this chapter has indicated. Nevertheless, we are about to enter a global community of new learning about ourselves with 'new approaches to moral and religious maturity'.

Bibliography

Scripture quotations are taken from the *New Revised Standard Version* of the Bible, New York and Oxford: Oxford University Press, 1989.

Qur'an quotations are taken from *The Meaning of the Glorious Qur'an, Text and Explanatory Translation* by Marmaduke Pickthall, Beirut: Dar Al-Kitab Allubnani, 1971.

All other translations are mine unless specified otherwise.

Abû Zayd, Nâsr Hamid (1990), *Mafhûm an-nass: Dirâsa fi-'ulûm al-qur'ân* (The Concept of the Text: A Study in the Religious Studies of the Qur'an), Cairo.

Alcock, N.Z. (1972), *The War Disease*, Oakville, Ont.: Canadian Peace Research Institute.

Alexander, Richard D. (1987), *The Biology of Moral Systems*, New York: Aldine de Gruyter.

Allman, William F. (1994), *The Stone Age Present*, New York: Simon and Schuster.

An-Na'im, Abdullahi, A. (1990), *Toward an Islamic Reformation: Civil Liberties, Human Rights, and International Law*, Syracuse, NY: Syracuse University Press.

Aram, Muthukumaraswamy (1995), 'The Principles of Mahatma Gandhi: A Global Inspiration and Challenge to Solve Inter-religious Conflicts', in Johannes Lähnemann (ed.), *'Das Projekt Weltethos' in der Erziehung*, Hamburg: EB-Verlag, pp. 145–53.

Ariarajah, S. Wesley (1995), 'The World Council of Churches and the Religions: Cooperation in the Field of Justice, Peace and the Integrity of Creation', in Johannes Lähnemann (ed.), *'Das Projekt Weltethos' in der Erziehung*, Hamburg: EB-Verlag, pp. 106–16.

Ariès, Philippe (1960), *L'enfant et la vie familiale sous l'ancien régime*, Paris: Plon.

Armstrong, Karen (1996), *In the Beginning*, New York: Ballantine.

Assmann, Jan (1990), *Ma'at: Gerechtigkeit und Unsterblichkeit im Alten Ägypten*, München: Beck.

Astley, Jeff and Francis, Leslie J. (eds) (1994), *Critical Perspectives on Christian Education: A Reader on the Aims, Principles and Philosophy of Christian Education*, Leominster: Gracewing.

Axelrod, Robert (1984), *The Evolution of Cooperation*, New York: Basic Books.

Baier, Annette C. (1991), 'Violent Demonstrations', in R. G. Frey and Christopher W. Morris (eds), *Violence, Terrorism and Justice*, Cambridge, Mass.: Harvard University Press, pp. 33–58.

Bailey, K. (1987), *Human Paleopsychology: Applications to Aggression and Pathological Processes*, London: Lawrence Erlbaum.

Baldermann, Ingo (1996), *Einführung in die Biblische Didaktik*, Darmstadt: Primus Verlag.

Barash, David (1979), *The Whisperings Within*, New York: Harper & Row (German edn: *Das Flüstern in uns. Menschliches Verhalten im Lichte der Soziologie*, Frankfurt/M.: S. Fischer, 1981).

Barkow, Jerome, Cosmides, Leda and Tooby, John (eds) (1992), *The Adapted Mind*, Oxford and New York: Oxford University Press.

Barrett, Charles K. (1994), *A Critical and Exegetical Commentary on the Acts of the Apostles: In Two Volumes*, vol. 1, Edinburgh: Clark.

Baumann, Ulrike and Wermke, Michael (eds) (2001), *Religionsbuch 7/8*, vol. 2, Berlin: Cornelsen.

Beier, Peter (1997), *Jenseits der Glut: Gedichte und Lesungen*, ed. Christian Bartsch, Düsseldorf: Presseverband der Evangelischen Kirche im Rheinland.

Berryman, Jerome W. (1991), *Godly Play: A Way of Religious Education*, San Francisco: HarperCollins.

Biehl, Peter, Bizer, Christoph, Degen, Roland, Mette, Norbert, Rickers, Folkert and Schweitzer, Friedrich (eds) (2001), *Gott und Geld* (Jahrbuch der Religionspädagogik, vol. 17), Neukirchen-Vluyn: Neukirchener Verlag.

Bienen, Derk, Rittberger, Volker and Wagner, Wolfgang (1998), 'Democracy in the United Nations System: Cosmopolitan and Communitarian Principles', in D. Archibugi, D. Held and M. Köhler (eds), *Re-imaging Political Community: Studies in Cosmopolitan Democracy*, Oxford: Polity Press, pp. 286–308.

Bierhoff, Hans-Werner and Montada, Leo (eds) (1988), *Altruismus: Bedingungen der Hilfsbereitschaft*, Göttingen-Toronto-Zürich: Hogrefe (Eng. edn: *Altruism in Social Systems*, Lewiston: Hogrefe and Huber, 1991).

Bock, M. and Klinger, E. (1986), 'Interaction of Emotion and Cognition in Word Recall', *Psychological Research*, **48**, pp. 99–106.

Böttger, Andreas (1998), *Gewalt und Biographie: eine qualitative Analyse rekonstruierter Lebensgeschichten von 100 Jugendlichen*, Baden-Baden: Nomos.

Boyd, Robert and Richerson, Peter J. (1985), *Culture and the Evolutionary Process*, Chicago: University of Chicago Press.

Brecht, Bertolt (1963), 'The Caucasian Chalk Circle' (1946/1960), in *Plays*, London: Methuen.

Brumlik, Micha (1991), 'Auf dem Weg zu einer Theorie des Antisemitismus?', *Kölner Zeitschrift für Soziologie und Sozialpsychologie*, **2**, pp. 357–63.

Brumlik, Micha (1999), 'Zur Begründung der Menschenrechte im Buch Amos', in Hauke Brunkhorst, Wolfgang R. Köhler, and Matthias Lutz-Bachmann (eds), *Recht auf Menschenrechte: Menschenrechte, Demokratie und internationale Politik*, Frankfurt/M.: Suhrkamp, pp. 11–19.

Brusselmans, Christiane and O'Donohoe, James A. (eds) (1980), *Toward Moral and Religious Maturity: The First International Conference on Moral and Religious Development*, Morristown, NJ: Silver Burdett.

Buber, Martin (1926), *Rede über das Erzieherische*, Berlin: Lambert Schneider.

Buber, Martin (1937), *I and Thou*, Edinburgh: Clark.

Burke, Charles (1975), *Aggression in Man*, Secausus, NY: Lyle Stuart.

Buss, David M. (1989), 'Sex Differences in Human Mate Preferences: Evolutionary Hypotheses tested in 37 Cultures', *Behavioral and Brain Sciences*, **12**, pp. 1–49.

Buss, David M. (1999), *Evolutionary Psychology: The New Science of the Mind*, Boston: Allyn and Bacon.

Büttner, Gerhard and Jörg Thierfelder (eds) (2001), *Trug Jesus Sandalen? Kinder und Jugendliche sehen Jesus Christus*, Göttingen: Vandenhoeck & Ruprecht.

Campbell, Bernard (1985), *Human Evolution*, New York: Aldine de Gruyter.

Coles, Robert (1990), *The Spiritual Life of Children*, Boston: Houghton Mifflin.

Comenius, Johann Amos (1668), *Unum necessarium* (German edn: *Das einzig Notwendige*, trans. Johannes Seeger, ed. Ludwig Keller, Hamburg: Agentur des Rauhen Hauses, 1964).

Comenius, John Amos (1964), *Selections from his Works*, Prague: Státní Pedagogické Nakladatelství.

Comenius, Johann Amos (1966), *De rerum humanarum emendatione consultatio catholica*, 2 vols, ed. O. Chlup, Prague: Academia Scientiarum Bohemoslavaca.

Commons, Michael L., Richards, Francis A. and Armon, Cheryl (eds) (1984), *Beyond Formal Operations: Late Adolescent and Adult Cognitive Development*, New York: Praeger.

Cosmides, Leda (1989), 'The Logic of Social Exchange: Has Natural Selection Shaped Human Reason? Studies with the Wason Selection Task', *Cognition*, **31**, 187–276.

Council of Europe (1993), Recommendation on Religious Tolerance in a Democratic Society (No 1202), in Peter Schreiner, Hans Spinder and Frans Vos (eds), *Education and Europe – Bildung und Europa: Common Statement and Information*, A publication of ICCS, ECCE, EFTRE, Münster: Comenius Institut.

Crane, John (2001), 'Truth in Conflict', paper presented at the European Forum for Teachers of Religious Education (EFTRE), Edinburgh, 30 August–2 September 2001.

Crüsemann, Frank (1992), *Die Tora: Theologie und Sozialgeschichte des alttestamentlichen Gesetzes*, München: Kaiser.

Daly, Martin and Wilson, Margo (1988), *Homicide*, New York: Aldine de Gruyter.

Dave, Ravindra (2001), 'Some Spiritual and Ethical Dimensions of Hinduism', in Johannes Lähnemann (ed.), *Spiritualität und ethische Erziehung: Erbe und Herausforderung der Religionen*, Hamburg: EB-Verlag, pp. 46–61.

Dawkins, Richard (1976), *The Selfish Gene*, New York and Oxford: Oxford University Press.

Dennen, Johan M. G. van der (1995), *The Origin of War: The Evolution of a Male-Coalitional Reproductive Strategy*, 2 vols, Groningen: Origin Press.

Derrett, John Duncan M. (1977), 'Workers in the Vineyard: a Parable of Jesus', in J. D. M. Derrett, *Studies in the New Testament*, vol. 1, Leiden: Brill.

Dershowitz, Alan M. (2000), *The Genesis of Justice: Ten Stories of Biblical Injustice that Led to the Ten Commandments and Moral Law*, New York: Warner Books.

Deutsch, Robert D. (1998), 'Probing Images of Politicians and International Affairs: Creating Pictures and Stories of Mind', in I. Eibl-Eibesfeldt and F. K. Salter (eds), *Indoctrinability, Ideology, and Warfare: Evolutionary Perspectives*, New York-Oxford: Berghahn Books, pp. 301–21.

Deutsche Shell (ed.) (2000), *Jugend 2000*, 2 vols, Opladen: Leske and Budrich.

Dewey, John (1987), *The Later Works, 1925–1953*, vol. 11: *1935–1937*, Carbondale and Edwardsville: Southern Illinois University Press.

Döbert, Rainer (1991), 'Oser and Gmünder's Stage 3 of Religious Development and Its Social Content: A Vicious Circle', in James W. Fowler, Karl Ernst Nipkow and

Friedrich Schweitzer (eds), *Stages of Faith and Religious Development: Implications for Church, Education, and Society*, New York: Crossroad, pp. 162–79.

Döbert, Rainer (1997), 'Welche Wertsystem überleben den diskursiven Test', in Wilhelm Lütterfelds and Thomas Mohrs (eds), *Eine Welt – Eine Moral? Eine kontroverse Debatte,* Darmstadt: Wissenschaftliche Buchgesellschaft, pp. 77–103.

Donnelly, Jack (1989), *Universal Human Rights in Theory and Practice*, Ithaca, NY and London: Cornell University Press.

Donner, Herbert (1984), *Geschichte des Volkes Israel und seiner Nachbarn in Grundzügen,* vol. 1: *Von den Anfängen bis zur Staatenbildungszeit,* Göttingen: Vandenhoeck & Ruprecht.

Ebeling, Gerhard (1979), *Dogmatik des christlichen Glaubens*, vol. 1, Tübingen: Mohr.

Eibl-Eibesfeldt, Irenäus (1971), *Love and Hate. The Natural History of Behavior Patterns*, New York: Holt, Rinehart & Winston.

Eibl-Eibesfeldt, Irenäus (1998), 'Us and the Others: The Familial Roots of Ethnonationalism', in I. Eibl-Eibesfeldt and F. K. Salter, *Indoctrinability, Ideology, and Warfare: Evolutionary Perspectives*, New York-Oxford: Berghahn Books, pp. 21–53.

Eibl-Eibesfeldt, Irenäus (1999), 'Universalien im menschlichen Sozialverhalten und ihre Bedeutung für die Normenfindung', in Dieter Neumann, Arno Schöppe and Alfred K. Treml (eds), *Die Natur der Moral*: *Evolutionäre Ethik und Erziehung*, Stuttgart-Leipzig: Verlag für Interkulturelle Kommunikation (IKO), pp. 99–116.

Eibl-Eibesfeldt, Irenäus and Salter, Frank Kemp (eds) (1998), *Indoctrinability, Ideology, and Warfare: Evolutionary Perspectives*, New York-Oxford: Berghahn Books.

Elias, Norbert and Scotson, John L. (1965), *The Established and the Outsiders: A Sociological Enquiry into Community Problems*, London: Sage.

Engels, Eve-Marie (1989), *Erkenntnis als Anpassung? Eine Studie zur Evolutionären Erkenntnistheorie*, Frankfurt/M.: Suhrkamp.

Erikson, Erik H. (1966), *Ontogeny of Ritualization in Man*, Philosophical Transactions of the Royal Society of London, B 251, pp. 337–49.

Euler, Harald A. (1997), 'Geschlechtsspezifische Unterschiede und die nicht erzählte Geschichte in der Gewaltforschung', in Heinz-Günter Holtappels, Wilhelm Heitmeyer, Wolfgang Melzer and Klaus-Jürgen Tillmann (eds), *Forschung über Gewalt an Schulen: Erscheinungsformen und Ursachen, Konzepte und Prävention*, Weinheim und München: Juventa Verlag, pp. 191–206.

Evangelische Kirche in Deutschland (1997), *Orientierung in zunehmender Orientierungslosigkeit: Evangelische Erwachsenenbildung in kirchlicher Trägerschaft*, Gütersloh: Gütersloher Verlagshaus.

Faust-Siehl, Gabriele, Bauer, Eva-Maria, Baur, Werner and Wallaschek, Uta (1990), *Mit Kindern Stille entdecken: Bausteine zur Veränderung der Schule*, Frankfurt/M: Diesterweg.

Faust-Siehl, Gabriele, Krupka, Bernd, Schweitzer, Friedrich and Nipkow, Karl Ernst (eds) (1995), *24 Stunden Religionsunterricht: Eine Tübinger Dokumentation für Forschung und Praxis*, Münster: Comenius-Institut.

Fiensy, D. A. (1991), *The Social History of Palestine in the Herodian Period*, Lewiston: Mellen.

Fowler, James W. (1981), *Stages of Faith: The Psychology of Human Development and the Quest for Meaning*, San Francisco: Harper & Row.

Fowler, James W. (1987), *Faith Development and Pastoral Care*, Philadelphia: Fortress Press.

Fowler, James W. (1991), *Weaving the New Creation: Stages of Faith and the Public Church*, San Francisco: HarperCollins.

Fowler, James W., Jarvis, David and Moseley, Romney M. (1986), *Manual for Faith Development Research*, Atlanta, Ga.: Center for Faith Development, Candler School of Theology, Emory University.

Frey, Siegfried (1998), 'Prejudice and Inferential Communication: New Look at an Old Problem', in I. Eibl-Eibesfeldt and F. K. Salter, *Indoctrinability, Ideology, and Warfare: Evolutionary Perspectives*, New York-Oxford: Berghahn Books, pp. 189–217.

Fuchs, Ernst (1958), *Hermeneutik*, 2nd edn, Bad-Cannstatt: R. Müllerschön Verlag.

Gay, Peter (1993), *The Cultivation of Hatred*, New York-London: W. W. Norton.

Geiger, Gebhard (1998), 'Ideology, Indoctrination, and Noncognitive Foundations of Belief in Legitimacy: A Biobehavioral Analysis of Legitimate Violent Social Action', in I. Eibl-Eibesfeldt and F. K. Salter, *Indoctrinability, Ideology, and Warfare: Evolutionary Perspectives*, New York-Oxford: Berghahn Books, pp. 409–20.

Girard, René (1986), *The Scapegoat*, London: Athlone (French edn: *Le bouc émissaire*, Paris: ed. Grasset & Fasquelle, 1982).

Glaser, Barney G. and Strauss, Anselm L. (1968), *A Discovery of Grounded Theory: Strategies for Qualitative Research*, London: Weidenfeld and Nicolson.

Goodman-Thau, Eveline (1998), 'Schwerter zu Pflugscharen: Jüdisch-prophetische Visionen als Basis des Friedensengagements der Religionen?', in Johannes Lähnemann (ed.), *Interreligiöse Erziehung, 2000: Die Zukunft der Religions- und Kulturbegegnung*, Hamburg: EB-Verlag, pp. 58–69.

Gurr, Ted Robert and Harff, Barbara (1994), *Ethnic Conflict in World Politics*, Boulder, Col.: Westview Press.

Gutman, Amy (1995), 'Das Problem des Multikulturalismus in der politischen Ethik', *Deutsche Zeitschrift für Philosophie*, Berlin, **43** (2): 273–305.

Halisch, Frank (1988), 'Empathie, Attribution und die Entwicklung des Hilfehandelns', in H.-W. Bierhoff and L. Montada (eds), *Altruismus: Bedingungen der Hilfsbereitschaft*, Göttingen-Toronto-Zürich: Hogrefe, pp. 79–103.

Hamilton, William D. (1964), 'The Genetic Evolution of Social Behaviour', I/II, *Journal of Theoretical Biology*, **7**, 1–16 and 17–52.

Hamilton, William D. (1971), 'Geometry of the Selfish Herd', *Journal of Theoretical Biology*, **31**, 295–311.

Hanisch, Helmut and Pollack, Detlev (1997), *Religion – ein neues Unterrichtsfach: Eine empirische Untersuchung zum religiösen Umfeld und zur Akzeptanz des Religionsunterrichts aus der Sicht von Schülerinnen und Schülern in den neuen Bundesländern*, Stuttgart: Calwer Verlag; Leipzig: Evangelische Verlagsanstalt.

Heimbrock, Hans-Günter (ed.) (1998), *Religionspädagogik und Phänomenologie: Von der empirischen Wendung zur Lebenswelt*, Weinheim: Deutscher Studien Verlag.

Heller, David (1986), *The Children's God*, Chicago-London: University of Chicago Press.

Hengel, Martin and Schwemer, Anna Maria (1997), *Paul Between Damascus and Antioch: The Unknown Years*, London: SCM Press (German edn: *Paulus zwischen Damaskus und Antiochien: Die unbekannten Jahre*, Tübingen: Mohr-Siebeck 1999).

Herms, Eilert (1982), 'Erfahrung, II: Philosophisch', in Gerhard Krause and Gerhard Müller (eds), *Theologische Realenzyklopädie*, vol. 10, Berlin-New York: de Gruyter, pp. 89–109.

Herms, Eilert (1992), *Offenbarung und Glaube: Zur Bildung des christlichen Lebens*, Tübingen: Mohr.

Herrmann, Siegfried (1973), *Geschichte Israels in alttestamentlicher Zeit*, München: Kaiser.

Hick, John (1989), *An Interpretation of Religion: Human Responses to the Transcendent*, New Haven: Yale University Press; London: Macmillan.

Hinnecke, Anke (2000), *Faszination Religion: Thema: Krieg und Frieden*, Stuttgart: Aha-Verlag.

Howard, Michael (1984), *The Causes of Wars and Other Essays*, London: Temple Smith.

Hull, John M. (1990), *Touching the Rock: An Experience of Blindness*, London: SPCK.

Hull, John M. (1991), *God-Talk with Young Children: Notes for Parents and Teachers*, London: Trinity Press International (German edn: *Wie Kinder über Gott reden*, Gütersloh: Gütersloher Verlagshaus, 1997).

Hull, John M. (2000), 'Money, Modernity, and Morality: Some Issues in the Christian Education of Adults', *Religious Education*, **95** (1), 4–22.

Hull, John M. (2001a), 'Blindness and the Face of God: Toward a Theology of Disability', in Ziebertz *et al.*, *The Human Image of God*, Leiden-Boston-Köln: Brill, pp. 215–29.

Hull, John M. (2001b), 'The Spirituality of Disability: The Christian Heritage as both Problem and Potential', in Johannes Lähnemann (ed.), *Spiritualität und Erziehung: Erbe und Herausforderung der Religionen*, Hamburg: EB-Verlag, pp. 73–84.

Humboldt, Wilhelm von (1793), 'Theorie der Bildung des Menschen', in Andreas Flitner and Klaus Giel (eds), *Werke*, vol. 1, Darmstadt: Wissenschaftliche Buchgesellschaft, pp. 234–40.

Huntington, Samuel P. (1993), 'The Clash of Civilizations?', *Foreign Affairs*, **72** (3), 22–49.

International Catholic Child Bureau (1984), *The Child and the Spiritual Void of Today*, Geneva: General Secretariat, 65 Rue de Lausanne, CH 1202, Geneva.

Jackson, Robert (1997), *Religious Education: An Interpretive Approach*, London: Hodder & Stoughton.

Jackson, Robert and Nesbitt, Eleanor (1990), *Listening to Hindus*, London: Unwin Hyman.

Jacob, E. (1966), 'Art. Versöhnung', in Bo Reicke and Leonhard Rost (eds), *Biblisch-historisches Handwörterbuch*, Göttingen: Vandenhoeck & Ruprecht, vol. 3, pp. 2096-7.

James, P. D. (1998), *A Certain Justice*, Harmondsworth: Penguin.

Janowski, Bernd (1999), *Die rettende Gerechtigkeit: Beiträge zur Theologie des Alten Testaments*, 2, Neukirchen-Vluyn: Neukirchener Verlag.

Janowski, Bernd (2000), '"Hingabe" oder Opfer? Zur gegenwärtigen Kontroverse um die Deutung des Todes Jesu', in Erhard Blum (ed.), *Mincha* (Festgabe für Rolf Rendtorff), Neukirchen-Vluyn: Neukirchener Verlag, pp. 93–119.

Janowski, Bernd and Welker, Michael (2001), *Opfer: theologische und kulturelle Kontexte*, Frankfurt/M.: Suhrkamp.

Johnson, Mark (1987), *The Body in the Mind: The Bodily Basis of Meaning, Imagination and Reason*, London: University of Chicago Press.

Jolly, Richard (1978), *Disarmament and World Development*, Oxford: Pergamon Press.

Jonas, Hans (1997), *Das Prinzip Verantwortung: Versuch einer Ethik für die technologische Zivilisation*, Frankfurt/M.: Suhrkamp.

Jörns, Klaus-Peter (1997), *Die neuen Gesichter Gottes: Was die Menschen heute wirklich glauben*, München: Beck.

Jüngel, Eberhard (1972), *Unterwegs zur Sache: Theologische Bemerkungen*, München: Kaiser.

Jüngel, Eberhard (1977), *Gott als Geheimnis der Welt: Zur Begründung der Theologie des Gekreuzigten im Streit zwischen Theismus und Atheismus*, Tübingen: Mohr (Siebeck).

Jüngel, Eberhard (1986), *Paulus und Jesus: Eine Untersuchung zur Präzisierung der Frage nach dem Ursprung der Christologie*, 6th edn, Tübingen: Mohr (Siebeck).

Jüngel, Eberhard (1998), *Das Evangelium der Rechtfertigung des Gottlosen als Zentrum des christlichen Glaubens*, Tübingen: Mohr (Siebeck).

Jüngel, Eberhard (2001), *God's Being is in Becoming*, Edinburgh: T & T Clark (1st edn in German: *Gottes Sein ist im Werden*, Tübingen 1966).

Kandil, Fuad (1998), 'Religiöser Pluralismus als Problem für die "Selbstgewissheit": Zwei Ansätze zur subjektiven Verabeitung des Problems im Koran', in Johannes Lähnemann (ed.), *Interreligiöse Erziehung 2000: Die Zukunft der Religions- und Kulturbegegnung*, Hamburg: EB-Verlag, pp. 79–90.

Kant, Immanuel (1785), *Foundations of the Metaphysics of Morals*, Riga: J. F. Hartknoch (2nd edn 1786) (Eng. version in: *Lectures on Metaphysics*, trans. and ed. Karl Ameriks, The Cambridge Edition of the Works, Cambridge: Cambridge University Press, 1979).

Kant, Immanuel (1793), *Religion Within the Limits of Reason Alone*, Königsberg: F. Nicolovius (2nd edn 1794) (Eng. version in: *Religion and Rational Theology*, trans. and ed. Allen Wood, The Cambridge Edition of the Works, Cambridge: Cambridge University Press, 1996).

Kant, Immanuel (1795), *Perpetual Peace*, Königsberg: F. Nicolovius (2nd edn, 1796).

Keightley, Alan (1986), 'Teaching Buddhism in the Upper Secondary School', Part I and Part II, *British Journal of Religious Education*, **9** (1), 4–16.

Kennedy, Paul, Messner, Dirk and Nuscheler, Franz (2002), *Global Trends and Global Governance*, London: Pluto Press.

Kirchenamt der Evangelischen Kirche in Deutschland (1991), *Der Dienst der Evangelischen Kirche an der Hochschule*, Gütersloh: Gütersloher Verlagshaus.

Kohlberg, Lawrence (1977), 'Eine Neuinterpretation der Zusammenhänge zwischen der Moralentwicklung in der Kindheit und im Erwachsenenalter', in Rainer Döbert, Jürgen Habermas and Gertrud Nunner-Winker (eds), *Entwicklung des Ichs*, Köln: Kiepenhauer und Witsch, pp. 225–52 (US edn: 'Continuities in Childhood and Adult Moral Development Revisited', in Paul B. Baltes and K. W. Schaie (eds), *Life-Span Developmental Psychology: Personality and Socialization*, New York: Academic Press, 1973, pp. 179–204).

Kohlberg, Lawrence (1981), *Essays on Moral Development*, vol. I: *The Philosophy of Moral Development*, San Francisco: Harper & Row.

Krellmann, Hanspeter (ed.) (1989), *Babel ist überall*, München: Deutscher Taschenbuch Verlag.
Krüger, Lorenz (1988), 'Biologische Evolution und menschliche Erkenntnis', in H. H. Holz, N. I. Lapin and H. J. Sandkühler (eds), *Die Dialektik und die Wissenschaften: Philosophische Fragen moderner Entwicklungskonzeptionen*, Köln: Pahl-Rugenstein, pp. 69–88.
Krupka, Bernd (2002), *... die rechte Hand muss wissen, was die linke tut. Interkulturelles Lernen: Handeln im Zusammenspiel von Kulturdifferenz, Macht, Diskrimierung und Fremdenwahrnehmung*, Münster – New York: Waxmann.
Kuld, Lothar and Gönnheimer, Stefan (2000), *Compassion: Sozialverpflichtetes Lernen und Handeln*, Stuttgart: Kohlhammer Verlag.
Kümmel, Friedrich (1964), 'Zum Problem des Gewissens', *Der Evangelische Erzieher*, **16** (9), 264–75.
Küng, Hans (1990), *Projekt Weltethos*, München-Zürich: Piper (English edn: *Global Responsibility: In Search of a New World Ethic*, London: SCM Press, 1991).
Küng, Hans (1991), *Global Responsibility: In Search of a New World Ethic*, London: SCM Press (German edn: *Projekt Weltethos*, München: Piper, 1990).
Küng, Hans (1997), *Weltethos für Weltpolitik und Weltwirtschaft*, München: Piper.
Küng, Hans and Kuschel, Karl-Josef (eds) (1993), *A Global Ethic: The Declaration of the Parliament of the World's Religions*, London: SCM Press.
Küng, Hans and Kuschel, Karl-Josef (eds) (1998), *Wissenschaft und Weltethos*, München: Piper (2nd edn, München: Piper, 2001).
Küng, Hans and Schmidt, Helmut (eds) (1998), *A Global Ethic and Global Responsibilities: Two Declarations*, London: SCM Press.
Kuschel, Karl-Josef (1995), *Abraham: A Symbol of Hope for Jews, Christians and Muslims*, London: SCM Press. (German edn: *Was Juden, Christen und Muslime trennt – und was sie eint*, München: Piper 1994).
Kuschel, Karl-Josef (1998), *The Poet as Mirror: Human Being, God and Jesus in Twentieth Century Literature*, London: SCM Press (German edn: *Im Spiegel der Dichter: Mensch, Gott und Jesus in der Literatur des 20 Jahrhunderts*, Düsseldorf: Patmos Verlag, 1977).
Lacey, Michael (1992), *A Culture of Rights: The Bill of Rights in Philosophy, Politics and Law 1791–1991*, Cambridge: Cambridge University Press.
Lähnemann, Johannes (ed.) (1998), *Interreligiöse Erziehung 2000: Die Zukunft der Religions- und Kulturbegegnung*, Hamburg: EB-Verlag.
Lähnemann, Johannes (ed.) (2001), *Spiritualität und ethische Erziehung: Erbe und Herausforderung der Religionen*, Hamburg: EB-Verlag.
Langeveld, Martinus J. (1956), *Kind en religie: Enige vragen voorafgaande aan een Godsdienst-Paedagogiek*, Utrecht: Erven J. Bijleveld.
Latané, Bibb, and Darley, John M. (1970), *The Unresponsive Bystander. Why doesn't he help?*, New York: Appleton-Century-Crofts.
Laura, Ronald S., and Leahy, Michael (1994), 'Religious Upbringing and Rational Autonomy', in Jeff Astley and Leslie J. Francis (eds), *Critical Perspectives on Christian Education*, Leominster: Gracewing, pp. 408–25.
Lévinas, Emmanuel (1987), *Totalität und Unendlichkeit. Versuch über die Exteriorität*, Freiburg-München: Alber (French edn: *Totalité et Infini. Essai sur l'Extériorité*, La-Haye: Nijhoff, 1961).

Lévinas, Emmanuel (1991), *Außer sich: Meditationen über Religion und Philosophie*, München: Hanser.

Lévinas, Emmanuel (1992), *Jenseits des Seins oder anders als Sein geschieht*, Freiburg-München: Alber (French edn: *Autrement qu'être ou au-delà de l'essence*, La-Haye: Nijhoff 1974).

Leyhausen, Paul (1968), 'Einführung in die Eindruckskunde', in Konrad Lorenz and Paul Leyhausen (eds), *Antriebe tierischen und menschlichen Verhaltens*, München: Piper, pp. 48–53.

Lippmann, Walter (1950 [1922]), *Public Opinion*, New York: Macmillan (1st edn 1922; 13th printing, 1950).

Lorenz, Konrad (1954), 'Moral-analoges Verhalten geselliger Tiere', *Forschung und Wirtschaft*, **4**, pp. 1–23.

Lorenz, Konrad (1963), *Das sogenannte Böse: Zur Naturgeschichte der Aggression*, Wien: Borotha-Schoeler.

Lotz, Thomas A. (2001), 'Life-World: A Philosophical Concept and its Relevance for Religious Education', in Hans-Günter Heimbrock, Christoph Th. Scheilke and Peter Schreiner (eds), *Towards Religious Competence: Diversity as a Challenge for Education in Europe*, Münster-Hamburg-Berlin-London: LIT, pp. 74–84.

Luard, Evan (1987), *War in International Society: A Study in International Sociology*, London: Yale University Press.

Lumsden, Charles J. and Wilson, Edward O. (1981), *Genes, Mind, and Culture: The Coevolutionary Process*, Cambridge, Mass.: Harvard University Press.

Luz, Ulrich (1997), *Das Evangelium nach Matthäus*, Zürich-Düsseldorf: Benziger; Neukirchen-Vluyn: Neukirchener Verlag.

MacIntyre, Alasdair (1981), *After Virtue: A Study in Moral Theory*, Notre Dame, Ind.: University of Notre Dame Press.

Mackie, John L. (1982), 'Cooperation, Competition and Moral Philosophy', in Andrew M. Colman (ed.), *Cooperation and Competition in Humans and Animals*, Wokingham: Van Nostrand Reinhold.

Merleau-Ponty, Maurice (1968), *The Visible and the Invisible*, Claude le Fort (ed.), Chicago: Northwestern University Press.

Metz, Johann Baptist (2000), 'Compassion – Zu einem Weltprogramm des Christentums im Zeitalter des Pluralismus der Religionen und Kulturen', in Johann B. Metz, Lothar Kuld and Adolf Weisbrod (eds), *Compassion: Weltprogramm des Christentums. Soziale Verantwortung lernen*, Freiburg/Br.: Herder Verlag, pp. 9–18.

Mohr, Hans (1997), 'Alternative Verhaltensstrategien und kultureller Kontext', in Alfred K. Treml (ed.), *Natur der Moral? Ethische Bildung im Horizont der modernen Evolutionsforschung*, Frankfurt/M.: Diesterweg Verlag, pp. 18–21.

Mokrosch, Reinhold (2002), 'Scheitern – Schuld – Vergebung', in Gottfried Bitter, Rudolf Englert, Gabriele Miller and Karl Ernst Nipkow (eds), *Neues Handbuch Religionspädagogischer Grundbegriffe*, München: Kösel, pp. 114–17.

Moltmann, Jürgen (1981), *The Trinity and the Kingdom of God: The Doctrine of God*, London: SCM.

Montada, Leo, Schneider, A. and Reichle, B. (1988), 'Emotionen und Hilfsbereitschaft', in H.-W. Bierhoff and L. Montada, *Altruismus: Bedingungen der Hilfsbereitschaft*, Göttingen-Toronto-Zürich: Hogrefe, pp. 130–53.

Moser, Tilmann (1976), *Gottesvergiftung*, Frankfurt/M.: Suhrkamp.

Moskowitz, Ruben (2001), 'Widersprechen sich beim Konflikt im Nahen Osten Gerechtigkeit und Frieden?', *Neve Shalom/Wahat Al-Salam Rundbrief (Newsletter)*, December 2001, pp. 5–6 (Doar-Na-Shimshon, 99761, Israel).

Müller, Harald (1998), *Das Zusammenleben der Kulturen: ein Gegenentwurf zu Huntington*, Frankfurt/M.: Fischer Taschenbuch Verlag.

Mummendey, Amélie (1984), *Social Psychology of Aggression: From Individual Behavior towards Social Interaction*, Berlin: Springer.

Nesbitt, Eleanor (1998), 'Bridging the Gap Between Young People's Experience of their Religious Tradition at Home and School: The Contribution of Ethnographic Research', in Johannes Lähnemann (ed.), *Interreligiöse Erziehung 2000: Die Zukunft der Religions- und Kulturbegegnung*, Hamburg: EB-Verlag, pp. 471–85.

Neuhaus, Richard J. (1984), *The Naked Public Square: Religion and Democracy in America*, Grand Rapids, Mich.: Eerdmans.

Newman, Paul (1992), *Paul's Glory-Christology*, New Testament Tools and Studies 69, Leiden: Brill.

Nipkow, Karl Ernst (1982), *Grundfragen der Religionspädagogik*, vol. 3: *Gemeinsam leben und glauben lernen*, Gütersloh: Gütersloher Verlagshaus (3rd edn, 1992).

Nipkow, Karl Ernst (1985), 'Can Theology have an Educational Role?', in M. C. Felderhof (ed.), *Religious Education in a Pluralistic Society*, London: Hodder & Stoughton, pp. 23–38.

Nipkow, Karl Ernst (1987), *Erwachsenwerden ohne Gott? Gotteserfahrung im Lebenslauf*, München: Kaiser (5th edn, Gütersloh: Gütersloher Verlagshaus, 1997).

Nipkow, Karl Ernst (1988), 'The Issue of God in Adolescence Under Growing Post-Christian Conditions: A Württembergian Survey', *Journal of Empirical Theology*, **1** (1), 43–53.

Nipkow, Karl Ernst (1990), *Bildung als Lebensbegleitung und Erneuerung: Kirchliche Bildungsverantwortung in Gemeinde, Schule und Gesellschaft*, Gütersloh: Gütersloher Verlagshaus (2nd edn, 1992).

Nipkow, Karl Ernst (1994), 'Ziele interreligiösen Lernens als mehrdimensionales Problem', in Johannes A. van der Ven and Hans-Georg Ziebertz (eds), *Religiöser Pluralismus und Interreligiöses Lernen*, Kampen: Kok, Weinheim: Deutscher Studien Verlag, pp. 197–232.

Nipkow, Karl Ernst (1996), 'Pluralism, Theology and Education: a German perspective', in Jeff Astley and Leslie J. Francis (eds), *Christian Theology and Religious Education: Connections and Contradictions*, London: SPCK, pp. 38–59.

Nipkow, Karl Ernst (1997), 'Konfirmanden – Kirche – Jesus Christus', in Christof Landmesser, Hans-Joachim Eckstein and Hermann Lichtenberger (eds), *Jesus Christus als die Mitte der Schrift: Studien zur Hermeneutik des Evangeliums*, Berlin-New York: Walter de Gruyter, pp. 907–30.

Nipkow, Karl Ernst (1998), *Bildung in einer pluralen Welt*, vol.1: *Moralpädagogik im Pluralismus*, vol. 2: *Religionspädagogik im Pluralismus*, Gütersloh: Gütersloher Verlagshaus.

Nipkow, Karl Ernst (2002), 'Möglichkeiten und Grenzen eines evolutionären Paradigmas in der Erziehungswissenschaft', *Zeitschrift für Pädagogik*, **48** (5), 670–89.

Nipkow, Karl Ernst (2003), 'Public Church and Public School Systems in Pluralistic Contexts: a European Perspective', in Richard R. Osmer and Friedrich Schweitzer (eds), *Faith Development Theory and the Future of Public Life*, St Louis, Mo.: Chalice Press.

Oberthür, Rainer (2000), *Die Seele ist eine Sonne: Was Kinder über Gott und die Welt wissen*, München: Kösel.

Olweus, Dan (1993), *Bullying at School: What We Know and What We Can Do*, Oxford: Blackwell.

Oser, Fritz and Gmünder, Paul (1984), *Der Mensch – Stufen seiner Entwicklung: ein strukturgenetischer Ansatz*, Zürich-Köln: Benziger.

Ouaknin, Marc-Alain (1995), *Symbole des Judentums, Wien 1995*, (French edn: *Symbole du Judaisme*, Paris: ed. Assouline, 1995).

Palmer, Parker J. (1986), *The Company of Strangers: Christians and the Renewal of America's Public Life*, New York: Crossroad.

Panikkar, Raimundo (1987), 'The Invisible Harmony: A Universal Theory of Religion or a Cosmic Confidence in Reality?', in Leonard Swidler (ed.), *Toward a Universal Theology of Religion*, Maryknoll, NY: Orbis Books, pp. 118–53.

Pestalozzi, Johann Heinrich (1991 [1799]), 'Wie Gertrud ihre Kinder lehrt', in Karl Ernst Nipkow and Friedrich Schweitzer (eds), *Religionspädagogik: Texte*, vol. 1: *Von Luther bis Schleiermacher*, München: Kaiser, pp. 226–39 (extracts) (Eng.: 'How Gertrude teaches her children', Worthing: Allen & Unwin, 1915/1924).

Peterson, M. J. (1992), 'Transnational Activity, International Society, and World Politics', *Millenium*, **21** (3), pp. 371–88.

Picco, Giandomenico *et al.* (2001), *Crossing the Divide: Dialogue among Civilizations*, South Orange, NJ: School of Diplomacy and International Relations, Seton Hall University.

Pieper, Joseph Z. T., and van der Ven, Johannes A. (1998), 'The Inexpressible God: God Images among Students of Dutch Catholic Secondary Schools', *Journal of Empirical Theology*, **11** (2), 64–80.

Placher, William C. (1989), *Unapologetic Theology: A Christian Voice in a Pluralistic Conversation*, Louisville, Ky.: Westminster-John Knox Press.

Powers, T. (1984), 'What is it about?' *The Atlantic Monthly*, January, pp. 35–55.

Radhakrishnan, Sarvapalli (1995), *The Spirit of Religion*, Delhi: Hind Pocket Books.

Reich, K. Helmut (1989), 'Between Religion and Science: Complementarity in the Religious Thinking of Young People', *British Journal of Religious Education*, **6** (11), 62–9.

Reich, K. Helmut (2002), *Developing the Horizons of the Mind: Relational and Contextual Reasoning and the Resolution of Cognitive Conflict*, Cambridge: Cambridge University Press.

Richerson, Peter J. and Boyd, Robert (1998), 'The Evolution of Human Ultrasociality', in I. Eibl-Eibesfeldt and F. K. Salter (eds), *Indoctrinability, Ideology and Warfare: Evolutionary Perspectives*, New York-Oxford: Berghahn Books, pp. 71–95.

Rittberger, Volker, Schrade, Christina and Schwarzer, Daniela (1999), 'Transnational Civil Society Actors and the Quest for Security' in Muthiah Alagappa and Takashi Inoguchi (eds), *International Security Management and the United Nations*, New York: United Nations University Press, pp. 107–38.

Ritter, Werner H. (1989), *Glaube und Erfahrung im religionspädagogischen Kontext*, Göttingen: Vandenhoeck & Ruprecht.

Ritter, Werner H. (ed.) (2000), *Religion und Phantasie: Von der Imaginationskraft des Glaubens*, Göttingen: Vandenhoeck & Ruprecht.

Robinson, Edward (1977), *The Original Vision: A Study of the Religious Experience of Childhood*, Oxford: The Religious Experience Research Unit, Manchester College.

Robinson, Mary (2002), 'Ethics, Human Rights and Globalization', paper presented at the Second Global Ethic Lecture of the Global Ethic Foundation, University of Tübingen, 21 January, 2002.

Rössler, Dietrich (1976), *Die Vernunft der Religion*, München: Piper.

Salter, Frank Kemp (1998), 'Indoctrination as Institutionalized Persuasion: Its Limited Variability and Cross-Cultural Evolution', in I. Eibl-Eibesfeldt and F. K. Salter (eds), *Indoctrinability, Ideology, and Warfare: Evolutionary Perspectives*, New York-Oxford: Berghahn Books, pp. 421–52.

Schaarschmidt, Ilse (1965), 'Der Bedeutungswandel der Begriffe "Bildung" und "bilden" in der Literaturepoche von Gottsched bis Herder', in Wolfgang Klafki (ed.), *Beiträge zur Geschichte des Bildungsbegriffs*, Weinheim: Beltz, pp. 25–87.

Scheunpflug, Annette (2001), *Biologische Grundlagen des Lernens*, Berlin: Cornelsen Scriptor.

Schiller, Friedrich (1795/1982), *On the Aesthetic Education of Man: In a Series of Letters*, Oxford: Clarendon Press.

Schleiermacher, Friedrich (1799), *On Religion: Speeches to its Cultured Despisers*, trans. and ed. Richard Crouter, Cambridge: Cambridge University Press.

Schmid, Hans (1989), *Religiösität der Schüler und Religionsunterricht: Empirischer Zusammenhang und religionspädagogische Konsequenzen für die Berufsschule*, Bad Heilbrunn: Klinkhardt.

Scholem, Gershom (1962/1973), *Von der mystischen Gestalt der Gottheit: Studien zu Grundbegriffen der Kabbala*, Zürich: Rhein-Verlag, 1962; Frankfurt/M.: Suhrkamp, 1973.

Schoneveld, Jakobus (2001), 'Living in the Holy Land: Respecting Differences', ed. World Conference on Religion and Peace (WCRP): Peace Education Standing Commission, *Peace Education from Faith Traditions*, Nürnberg: Verlag Peter Athmann, pp. 24–5.

Schröder, Heinz (1979), *Jesus und das Geld, Wirtschaftskommentar zum Neuen Testament*, 2nd edn, Karlsruhe: Badenia-Verlag.

Schubert, James N. (1998), 'The Role of Sex and Emotional Response in Indoctrinability: Experimental Evidence on the "Rally Round the Flag" Effect', in I. Eibl-Eibesfeldt and F. K. Salter (eds), *Indoctrinability, Ideology, and Warfare: Evolutionary Perspectives*, New York-Oxford: Berghahn Books, pp. 241–62.

Schulte-Markwort, Michael J. (1994), *Gewalt ist geil: mit aggressiven Kindern und Jugendlichen umgehen*, Stuttgart: Trias.

Schuster, Robert (1984), *Was sie glauben: Texte von Jugendlichen*, Stuttgart: Steinkopff.

Schweitzer, Eduard (1982), *Das Evangelium nach Lukas* (Neues Testament Deutsch, vol. 3), Göttingen: Vandenhoeck & Ruprecht.

Schweitzer, Friedrich (1992), *Die Religion des Kindes: Zur Problemgeschichte einer religionspädagogischen Grundfrage*, Gütersloh: Gütersloher Verlagshaus.

Schweitzer, Friedrich (1994), 'Elternbilder – Gottesbilder: Wandel der Elternrolle und Entwicklung des Gottesbildes im Kindesalter', *Katechetische Blätter*, **119**, 91–5.

Schweitzer, Friedrich (2000), *Das Recht des Kindes auf Religion: Ermutigungen für Eltern und Erzieher*, Gütersloh: Gütersloher Verlagshaus (English edn in preparation).

Schweitzer, Friedrich, Nipkow, Karl Ernst, Faust-Siehl, Gabriele and Krupka, Bernd (1995), *Religionsunterricht und Entwicklungspsychologie: Elementarisierung in der Praxis*, Gütersloh: Gütersloher Verlagshaus (2nd edn, 1997).

Sennett, Richard (1998), *The Corrosion of Character*, New York: W. W. Norton.

Shaftesbury, Anthony A. C. (1773), *The Moralists: A Philosophical Rhapsody*, in Complete Works, London, vol. 3; 1737; cf. Complete Works. Standard Edition, Wolfram Benda, Gerd Hemmerich and Ulrich Schödlbauer (eds) (with a German trans.), vol. II, 1: Moral and Political Philosophy, Stuttgart-Bad Cannstadt: Frommann-Holzboog, 1987.

Shaw, R. Paul and Wong, Yuwa (1989), *Genetic Seeds of Warfare: Evolution, Nationalism, and Patriotism*, Boston: Unwin Hyman.

Sheehy, Gail (1974), *Passages: Predictable Crises of Adult Life*, New York: Dutton.

Sieben, Hermann (1998), 'Neve Shalom/Wahat al Salam: Ein Interview über das Friedensdorf in Israel', in Johannes Lähnemann (ed.), *Interreligiöse Erziehung 2000: Die Zukunft der Religions- und Kulturbegegnung*, Hamburg: EB-Verlag, pp. 394–400.

Simon, Ernst A. (1989), 'Totalität und Antitotalitarismus als Wesenszüge des überlieferten Judentums', in Schalom Ben-Chorim and Verena Lenzen (eds), *Lust an der Erkenntnis: Jüdische Theologie im 20. Jahrhundert*, München-Zürich: Piper, pp. 319–51.

Simon, Werner (ed.) (2002), *Meditatio: Beiträge zur Theologie und Religionspädagogik der Spiritualität*, Münster: LIT Verlag.

Singer, Peter (1981), *The Expanding Circle: Ethics and Sociobiology*, Melbourne and Oxford: Oxford University Press.

Slee, Nicola (1990), *Easter Garden: A Sequence of Readings on the Resurrection Hope*, London: Collins-Fountain Paperbacks.

Sloterdijk, Peter (1995), *Im selben Boot*, Frankfurt/M.: Suhrkamp.

Soosten, J. von (1994), 'Die "Erfindung" der Sünde: Soziologisch-semantische Aspekte zu der Rede von der *Sünde im alttestamentlichen Sprachgebrauch*', in *Jahrbuch für Biblische Theologie* 9, Neukirchen-Vluyn: Neukirchener Verlag, pp. 87–110.

Spaemann, Robert (2001), 'Die Taube auf dem Dach: Gott ist nicht der Veranstalter des Bösen', in Robert Leicht (ed.), *Geburtsfehler? Vom Fluch und Segen des Christentums: Streitbare Beiträge*, Berlin: Wichern-Verlag, pp. 53–71.

Stachel, Günter (1974), *Dokumentation von Religionsunterricht – 94 Unterrichtsprotokolle*, vol. A/1, Mainz: Seminar für Katholische Religionspädagogik.

Stuhlmacher, Peter (1979), *Vom Verstehen des Neuen Testaments: Eine Hermeneutik*, Göttingen: Vandenhoeck & Ruprecht.

Stuhlmacher, Peter, (2000), 'Eschatology and Hope in Paul', *Evangelical Quarterly*, **72** (4), 315–33.

Stuhlmacher, Peter (2001), *Revisiting Paul's Doctrine of Justification*, with an essay by Donald A. Hagner, Downers Grove, Ill.: Intervarsity Press.

Swidler, Leonard (ed.) (1987), *Toward a Universal Theology of Religion*, Maryknoll, NY: Orbis Books.
Talbi, Mohamed (1976), 'Islam und Dialog', in M. Fitzgerald, A. Th. Khoury, and W. Wanzura (eds), *Moslems und Christen – Partner?* Graz: Styria Verlag, pp. 144–77.
Tapasyananda, Swami (1990), *The Four Yogas of Swami Vivekananda*, Calcutta: Advaita Ashram.
Thatcher, Adrian (1996), '"Policing the Sublime": A Wholly (Holy?) Ironic Approach to the Spiritual Development of Children', in Jeff Astley and Leslie J. Francis (eds), *Christian Theology and Religious Education*, London: SPCK, pp. 117–39.
Tellus Institute (2001), *Halfway to the Future: Reflections on the Global Condition*, Boston, MA: Tellus Institute.
Tibi, Bassam (1993), 'Islamic Shari'a and Human Rights – International Law and International Relations', in Tore Lindholm and Kari Vogt (eds), *Islamic Law Reform and Human Rights*, Oslo and Copenhagen: Nordic Human Rights Publications, pp. 75–96.
Tiefensee, Eberhard (2000), 'Religiös unmusikalisch: Folgerungen aus einer weithin krisenfesten Areligiösität', *Katechetische Blätter*, **125**, 88–95.
Tiger, Lionel (1998), 'Notions of Nature, Culture, and the Sources of Indoctrinability', in I. Eibl-Eibesfeldt and F. K. Salter (eds), *Indoctrinability, Ideology, and Warfare: Evolutionary Perspectives*, New York-Oxford: Berghahn Books, pp. 97–106.
Treml, Alfred K. (2000), *Allgemeine Pädagogik: Grundlagen, Handlungsfelder und Perspektiven der Erziehung*, Stuttgart: Kohlhammer.
Trivers, R. L. (1971), 'The Evolution of Reciprocal Altruism', *Quarterly Review of Biology*, **46**, 35–57.
Tworuschka, Monika (2002), *Grundwissen Islam: Religion, Politik, Gesellschaft*, Münster: Aschendorff.
Ven, Johannes van der (1989), 'Theodicy or Cosmodicy: A False Dilemma?', *Journal of Empirical Theology*, **2** (2), 5–27.
Ven, Johannes van der (1990), *Entwurf einer empirischen Theologie*, Kampen: Kok; Weinheim: Deutscher Studien Verlag.
Vogel, Christian (1989), *Vom Töten zum Mord: Das wirkliche Böse in der Evolutionsgeschichte*, München: Carl Hanser Verlag.
Vogel, Christian (2000), *Anthropologische Spuren: Zur Natur des Menschen*, ed. Volker Sommer, Stuttgart-Leipzig: Hirzel.
Voland, Eckart (2000), *Grundriss der Soziobiologie*, 2nd enlarged edn, Heidelberg-Berlin: Spektrum Akademischer Verlag.
Voland, Eckart and Dunbar, R. I. M. (1995), 'Resource Competition and Reproduction: The Relationship Between Economic and Parental Strategies in the Krummhörn Population (1720–1874)', *Human Nature*, **6**, 33–49.
Voland, Eckhart and Stephan, P. (2000), ' "The Hate that Love Generated" – Sexually Selected Neglect of One's Own Offspring in Humans', in C. Van Schaik and C. H. Janson (eds), *Infanticide by Males and its Implications*, Cambridge: Cambridge University Press, pp. 447–65.
Vollmer, Gerhard (2001), 'Können wir den sozialen Mesokosmos verlassen?', in Sigrid Görgens, Annette Scheunpflug and Krassimir Stochanov (eds), *Universalistische Moral und weltbürgerliche Erziehung: Die Herausforderung der Globalisierung*

im Horizont der modernen Evolutionsforschung, Frankfurt/M.: IKO-Verlag.

Walzer, Michael (1995), 'The Concept of Civil Society', in Michael Walzer (ed.), *Toward a Global Civil Society*, Providence, RI: Berghahn Books, pp. 7–27.

Walzer, Michael (1999), 'Zur Erfahrung von Universalität', in Karl-Josef Kuschel, Alessandro Pinzani and Martin Zillinger (eds), *Ein Ethos für eine Welt? Globalisierung als ethische Herausforderung*, Frankfurt/M.-New York: Campus Verlag, pp. 38–47.

Wartenberg-Potter, Bärbel von (1986), *Wir werden unsere Harfen nicht an die Weiden hängen*, Stuttgart: Kreuz-Verlag.

Weber, Hans-Ruedi (1979), *Jesus and the Children: Biblical Resources for Study and Preaching*, Geneva: World Council of Churches.

Wendt, Irmela and Boratyński, Antoni (1991), *Der Krieg und sein Bruder*, Düsseldorf: Patmos (Eng. edn: *The End of War*, New York and Jerusalem: Pitspopany Press, 1995).

Werbick, Jürgen (1996), Toleranz und Pluralismus: Reflexionen zu einem problematischen Wechselverhältnis, in Ingo Broer and Richard Schlüter (eds), *Christentum und Toleranz*, Darmstadt: Wissenschaftliche Buchgesellschaft, pp. 107–21.

Wickler, Wolfgang (1991), *Die Biologie der Zehn Gebote: Warum die Natur für uns kein Vorbild ist*, München-Zürich: Piper.

Wiefel, Wolfgang (1987), *Das Evangelium nach Lukas* (Theologischer Handkommentar zum Neuen Testament, vol. 3), Berlin: Evangelische Verlagsanstalt.

Wilson, Edward O. (1975), *Sociobiology: The New Synthesis*, Cambridge, Mass.: The Belknap Press of Harvard University.

Wilson, Edward O. (1993), 'Altruismus', in Kurt Bayertz (ed.), *Evolution und Ethik*, Stuttgart: Reclam, pp. 133–52.

Wuketits, Franz M. (1995). 'Entwurzelte Seelen: Biologische und anthropologische Aspekte des Heimatgedankens', *Universitas*, **1**, 11–24.

Ziebertz, Hans-Georg, Schweitzer, Friedrich, Häring, Hermann and Browning, Don (eds) (2001), *The Human Image of God*, Leiden-Boston-Köln: Brill.

Ziebertz, Hans-Georg (1994), 'Gottesbilder in der Adoleszenz', *Katechetische Blätter*, **119**, 606–15.

Zirker, Hans (1999), *Der Koran: Zugänge und Lesarten*, Darmstadt: Wissenschaftliche Buchgesellschaft.

Zulehner, Paul M. and Volz, Rainer (1998), *Männer im Aufbruch. Wie Deutschlands Männer sich selbst sehen und die Frauen sehen: ein Forschungsbericht*, Ostfildern: Schwabenverlag.

Name Index

Subject Index